Best Snowshoe Trails of
CALIFORNIA

100 OF THE FINEST ROUTES
IN THE CASCADES & THE SIERRA

MIKE WHITE

 **WILDERNESS PRESS** · BERKELEY, CA

Best Snowshoe Trails of California: 100 of the Finest Routes in the Cascades & the Sierra

1st EDITION 2001
2nd EDITION January 2005

Copyright © 2001, 2005 by Mike White

Front cover photo copyright © 2005 by Ed Cooper
Interior photos, except where noted, by Mike White
Maps: Mike White
Cover design and locator maps: Larry B. Van Dyke
Book design: Emily Douglas
Book editor: Jessica Benner

ISBN 0-89997-364-7
UPC 7-19609-97364-5

Manufactured in the United States of America

Published by: **Wilderness Press**
                1200 5th Street
                Berkeley, CA 94710
                (800) 443-7227; FAX (510) 558-1696
                info@wildernesspress.com
                www.wildernesspress.com

Visit our website for a complete listing of our books and for ordering information.

Cover photo: Merced River in winter, Yosemite National Park

DEDICATION

Many years ago, a young adult took a ragtag bunch of screwball teenagers, on what was to be my first overnight backpack, up the Eagle Creek Trail in the Columbia River Gorge, east of Portland, Oregon. Characteristic of Northwest weather, our sunny day turned into a frigid night when a cold rain became an even colder snow as our group desperately tried to fend off the miserable chill by huddling together in our flannel sleeping bags beneath a makeshift plastic tarp. Experiences that fail to kill or permanently maim may be unpleasant but tend to produce great memories, and that trip created enough for a much longer tale. This book is dedicated to Jim Rawlings, who not only led me on this excursion, which has led to countless others over the years, but through his concern for me and his example of love started me on the greatest journey of my life. Thanks Jim for introducing me to the Savior.

ACKNOWLEDGMENTS

First, many thanks are extended to Caroline Winnett, who originally conceived the idea for the *Snowshoe Trails* series. The second edition became a reality through the diligent efforts of Roslyn Bullas, Jessica Benner, Larry Van Dyke, Emily Douglas and the talented staff at Wilderness Press.

My utmost appreciation goes to all of those fellow snowshoers who traveled with me during the course of the field work: Chris Taylor, Dan and Michelle Palmer, Dwight Smith, Darrin Munson, Carmel Bang, Dave Miller, Cathy Anderson-Meyers, Bob Redding, Mike Wilhelm, and Keith Catlin. The solo trips I took out of necessity were vivid reminders of the value and importance of these friendships.

Once again the greatest contributor to this project is my wife, Robin, whose loyalty and support are never failing. Simply stated, without her contribution this book would not exist. Her sacrificial examples of love are a tremendous source of encouragement.

Finally, I am compelled to thank God for the opportunity to experience some of the awesome places in His creation, and for the gifts and abilities by which I am able to recount these visits to others. I am truly blessed—how many others can say their occupation is to tell others where to go?

— Mike White
October 2004

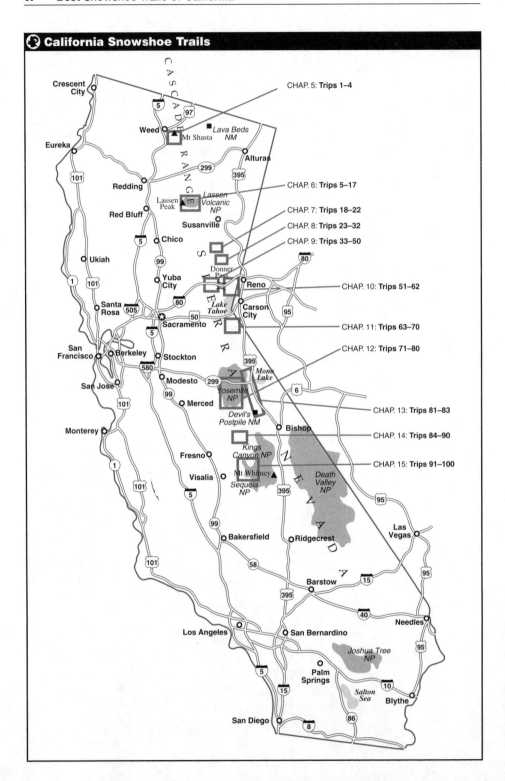

California Snowshoe Trails

CHAP. 5: **Trips 1–4**

CHAP. 6: **Trips 5–17**

CHAP. 7: **Trips 18–22**

CHAP. 8: **Trips 23–32**

CHAP. 9: **Trips 33–50**

CHAP. 10: **Trips 51–62**

CHAP. 11: **Trips 63–70**

CHAP. 12: **Trips 71–80**

CHAP. 13: **Trips 81–83**

CHAP. 14: **Trips 84–90**

CHAP. 15: **Trips 91–100**

Table of Contents

I. General Information

II. Trips

The winter view from atop Andesite Peak

CHAPTER 1

Introduction

The name "California" conjures up a number of images in the minds of Americans, but few of them include the winter majesty that comes to the mountains of the state's two most significant ranges, the Cascades and the Sierra. While some people may dream of idyllic days of skiing the perfect powder beneath sunny skies at one of the state's premier downhill resorts, a few others will recall with equal clarity days of splendor amid the winter beauty of the premier backcountry areas of California's mountains, and of those, the majority will have experienced such times on cross-country or backcountry skis. But finally, a small but growing number of outdoor recreationists are discovering the joys of California's winter backcountry while they are strapped into a pair of snowshoes.

The third largest state in the union has much to offer the winter recreationist. A nearly continuous spine of mountains roughly paralleling the entire length of coastline captures a significant amount of moisture from an eastward procession of Pacific storms, giving both the Sierra and the Cascades a blanket of snow that provides a bounty of possibilities for exploring the winter backcountry. Whatever type of mountain terrain you seek, California offers virtually every conceivable landscape: from the majestic cleft of Yosemite Valley to the towering, isolated presence of Mt. Shasta's volcano, all kinds of mountain scenery can be found somewhere in the state.

Not only is California a large geographical area, but it also has over thirty million souls within its borders. Fortunately, at least for mountain-lovers, 93% of those live in urban areas. Although many of California's mountain areas receive high use in summer, winter sees little penetration of the backcountry. Aside from concentrated use at ski resorts, most out-of-staters and Californians alike avoid most of the mountain areas once the thermometer plunges and a dusting of white carpets the hills. Serenity and solitude are still obtainable rewards during the winter in both the Sierra and the Cascades.

Although the Golden State is seen by many as the perfect environment in which to reside, the major population centers have considerable impact on the nearby mountains. Most of the winter recreation in California is concentrated around the Interstate 80 corridor, which provides access for millions of Bay Area and Sacramento Valley residents to the lands of the Tahoe National Forest, including the Lake Tahoe Basin. Although this region is by far the most popular winter destination in California's mountains, winter backcountry use is still being adequately dispersed and overcrowding avoided in most of the areas.

THE CASCADE RANGE

The Cascade Range extends from British Columbia through Washington and Oregon and then into far northern California. The Cascades are primarily volcanic in origin, and the California part is noted for its two largest volcanoes, Mt. Shasta, which at 14,162 feet towers over the surrounding landscape, and Lassen Peak, which at 10,457 feet is the centerpiece of Lassen Volcanic National Park. Until surpassed by Washington's Mt. St. Helens in 1980, Lassen Peak was the most recent volcano to erupt in the continental United States, when a series of eruptions occurred from 1914 to 1921. Both Shasta and Lassen are extremely picturesque mountains whose stunning scenery can be experienced on a number of trips described in this guide.

Rising up out of the northern California landscape and dwarfing the countryside for miles in every direction, Mt. Shasta so dominates this region that it has been a landmark for travelers throughout the ages. Even modern-day motorists screaming down nearby Interstate 5 crane their necks in order to take in the full profile of the mountain. So prominent is this mountain that all sorts of spiritual sects revere the peak as some sort of mystical entity. For snowshoers, Mt. Shasta affords the opportunity to travel upon its flanks from a nearly 7000-foot trailhead. This elevation combined with the northern latitude makes the area an excellent base of winter activity throughout a lengthy season. Far from major metropolitan centers, Shasta affords plenty of peace and quiet along with the incredible scenery.

Lassen Volcanic National Park is a nearly forgotten winter paradise secluded in the northern California countryside. The Lassen Park Road, which transects the park, closes for the year as soon as the first significant snowfall makes driving hazardous. Once the road is closed a whole host of opportunities springs up for snowshoers and skiers alike. Lassen Peak and the high country surrounding it is a sublime setting for a number of backcountry tours. The scenery is breathtaking, running the mountain spectrum from alpine peaks to dense forests. Weeks could be spent exploring the nooks and crannies of the park during winter. Although 13 trips are described in this guide, many more worthwhile adventures await the eager snowshoer blessed with the time to experience the majesty of the Lassen backcountry.

THE SIERRA NEVADA

Geologists generally set the boundary between the Cascades to the north and the Sierra Nevada to the south at the Middle Fork of the Feather River. Rock types in the Cascades are generally volcanic in origin, while those in the Sierra are principally plutonic and the river seems to separate these two types as well as any arbitrary boundary possible. By whatever designation, the mountains of both ranges are filled with exquisite scenery.

Near the northern extremity of the Sierra lie the lands of Plumas Eureka State Park. Centered around the discovery of gold on Eureka Peak, the park has kept alive the history of the old mining days. The mountains within Plumas Eureka are strikingly beautiful peaks with steep faces and craggy summits, in contrast to the gentle forested hills typical of the surrounding area. With a handful of scenic lakes, canyons and even a waterfall, Plumas Eureka State Park offers other opportunities for snowshoers to enjoy a secluded, picturesque mountain environment that receives light use in winter.

Just south of Plumas Eureka State Park is the gold country of the Sierra City district. The dominant geographical feature of this area is the majestic Sierra Buttes, a series of towering rock pinnacles at the apex of a span of vertical cliffs overlooking the Sardine Lakes. At 8591 feet, the Buttes stand alone on the skyline, visible from high points all across northern California. Throughout the territory below, a bustling resort community thrives in the summer, but much of the region becomes dormant in the winter. Along with the Sierra Buttes, a bountiful array of lakes provide potential destinations for winter recreationists. Unfortunately, the majority of those recreationists are snowmobilers, providing an additional challenge for those seeking peace and quiet during a backcountry adventure. However, there are areas where encounters with snowmobiles are avoided altogether or kept to a minimum.

Unlike the previous four areas, the thoroughfare of Interstate 80, the network of state highways, and the close proximity to the Bay Area and Sacramento, produce a busy area of activity, even during winter. Thirty-one trips grouped into two chapters (9 and 10) provide plenty of options for distributing recreationists across the region. A wide range of trips is offered with a variety of destinations including summits, lakes, cabins, vista points and canyons. Scenic beauty has not been compromised for ease of access; the region is both accessible and beautiful. For additional trips around Lake Tahoe, consult *Snowshoe Trails of Tahoe* by the author.

South of Lake Tahoe, the Carson Pass region offers snowshoers high alpine scenery. The pass itself is at a lofty elevation of almost 8600 feet, providing a high enough altitude for a long snowpack. Jagged peaks and cirque lakes beckon the winter traveler in search of dramatic mountain scenery. Much of the terrain is open, providing for incomparable vistas.

Yosemite National Park is the most famous of California's national parks and monuments. This popularity is easily understood by those who have witnessed the thundering cascade of Yosemite Falls, the 3500-foot granite face of El Capitan, or the stunning profile of Half Dome, all features of Yosemite Valley. However, the park includes much more territory than just the famous valley, and much of that is accessible to recreationists during the months of winter. The main difference between summer and winter in Yosemite is the absence of crowds from November through March, which in some ways makes winter the perfect season to visit Yosemite. While 10 trips are included in this guide, additional Yosemite routes can be found in *Snowshoe Trails of Yosemite* by the author.

The Sierra south of Yosemite harbors more stunning mountain scenery. The lower latitude, limited access, and presence of snowmobiles all affect use by snowshoers. Highway 168 provides access to one Sno-Park that is closed to mechanized vehicles and suitable for human-powered recreationists.

Some of the most dramatic mountain scenery is found along the east side of the Sierra, where the mountains rise almost straight up out of the Great Basin in stark relief. Impressive peaks and deeply cut canyons are here in abundance. The east side of the Sierra is accessible only from U.S. Highway 395 and in winter no open roads cross the Sierra to intersect this highway for hundreds of miles between Highway 88 in the north and Highway 178 in the south. For those who don't mind the long approach or the sometimes less than ideal access, the eastern Sierra offers great rewards.

Despite Yosemite's claim to fame as the most popular national park in California, the stunning terrain found in Kings Canyon and Sequoia national parks is unparalleled. Visitation to these parks in winter is extremely light, providing recreationists with the opportunity to stand beneath a giant sequoia, gaze across a picturesque meadow, or enjoy a far ranging vista from a snow-covered granite dome in relative seclusion. The diverse topography within the parks allows for a wide variety of snowshoe trips, from easy and short strolls to multi-day backcountry excursions.

The mountains of California, whether within the Cascades or the Sierra, will not disappoint those who venture into the backcountry after a fresh winter snowfall. Stunning scenery coupled with the generally pleasant California weather often produce idyllic conditions that rival the dreams of any avid outdoor recreationist.

WHY SNOWSHOE?

Throughout the course of my various snowshoe projects of the last few years, many people have queried me as to why anyone would choose to snowshoe. Generally, these inquiries come from two groups of people—skiers who can't imagine any other way to travel across the snow, and those who have absolutely no experience traveling over the snow by any method. Having politely responded to all those who ask, I will now attempt to articulate the reasonably lucid reasons why people snowshoe and the advantages that snowshoes actually possess over Nordic skis.

"If you can walk you can snowshoe," is my favorite retort to those who want to know the degree of difficulty snowshoeing may present. Snowshoeing requires very little skill, at least for slopes that aren't particularly steep. Mastery of what little technique is necessary is quickly obtained by anyone who can walk upright. A few laps around a snow-covered parking lot is all most people need to feel reasonably comfortable on low-angle slopes. Actually, getting strapped into the shoes is usually harder for most neophytes to figure out than walking in them. In contrast to skis, which require repeated practice of a whole host of techniques in order to obtain proficiency, walking in snowshoes is exceedingly simple. Snowshoeing is well-suited to the occasional user who doesn't have the luxury of hitting the slopes three times a week to hone their technique. Just like riding a bicycle, once you master the process you never have to figure it out again.

One disclaimer needs to be noted: as easy as snowshoeing can be technically, it is still an aerobic exercise and everyone who is interested in the sport should be in reasonable physical condition. You can't expect to have remained on a couch in front of the TV for the past decade and then suddenly arise, strap on a pair of snowshoes and conquer the wilderness without some level of aerobic conditioning.

Another advantage of snowshoes is control. Becoming out of control on snowshoes is fairly unusual. Becoming out of control on skis is very easy. The lure of speed is an attraction to many humans. This aspect of skiing is one of the main fascinations of the sport, which when practiced outside the bounds of control can lead to serious problems, such as testing the tensile strength of human bone, being accidentally propelled over precipitous slopes, or meeting a tree with your head. Although being injured while snowshoeing is still a possibility, the chances of this happening while out of control are extremely minimal.

Snowshoeing is simple, at least on level-to-moderate slopes. One of the other major advantages that snowshoes have over skis is the ability of skilled snow-shoers to climb up steep slopes and maneuver through difficult terrain. While many accomplished ski-mountaineers can negotiate fairly steep hillsides, snowshoes are much better choices for high-angle slopes and in areas that provide maneuvering challenges.

All in all, snowshoeing has much to offer. The simplicity, ease of use, and control are very appealing to those who don't have the time or the inclination to master the techniques of skiing necessary for the complete enjoyment of the sport. If you've never snowshoed, there is no better time to don a pair and head into the fantastic backcountry of California's mountains.

CHAPTER 2

Winter Travel

WEATHER

Having lived at the eastern base of the Sierra since 1976, I have seen a number of winters come and go. The one conclusion I have reached regarding the weather is that "normal" is a statistical average that rarely coincides with the real world. During the past twenty-plus years, the weather has run the climatic spectrum, from El Niños to multi-year droughts, with everything in between. During drought periods, walking the John Muir Trail on bare ground was possible in some winter months, while in other years just reaching the mountains was impossible due to the extreme weather.

Despite the scientific advances in weather forecasting, from year to year one does not know what the Sierra winter will be like until the season progresses. However, reliable, short-term weather forecasts are easily available to virtually anyone with a computer, phone or television. A list of appropriate weather forecast sources for the mountains of California is in Appendix II. The wise recreationist uses available weather information in planning trips.

Wild variations aside, the climate of the Sierra and, to a lesser extent, the southern Cascades can be classified on the whole as dry. The sun shines a great deal of the time. Many an ideal trip occurs during days of bright sunshine following a storm that has blanketed the mountains with a layer of fresh powder.

Most winter storms bringing moisture to the southern Cascades and Sierra plow into the range from the west, dropping snow on the higher elevations before moving east across the Great Basin. Typically, storms last no more than a day or two, separated by periods of dry, sunny or partly sunny weather. However, severe storms lasting for days and dropping incredible amounts of snow are not uncommon, particularly as the El Niño winter of '97-'98 has shown. Some days the weather in the backcountry is idyllic, some days life-threatening.

Average yearly snowfall ranges from 105 inches at the town of Mt. Shasta, 190 inches at Manzanita Lake, 101 inches at Sierra City, 252 inches at Blue Canyon, 108 inches at the South Entrance of Yosemite, 195 inches at Huntington Lake, and 58 inches at Lee Vining. Snowfall is substantially greater at higher elevations. Typically, snow falls between the months of November and April, although the heaviest snow usually comes from late December through early March. Snowfall has occurred in every month of the year at the upper elevations. Winter temperatures for the sites mentioned above are relatively mild, the average winter daytime highs ranging from the teens to the forties, with average nighttime lows rarely in single digits. Temperatures can be quite a bit colder at the higher elevations in the mountains. Snowfall is substantially greater in the high country, and temperatures may be as much as 30 degrees colder. This potential for more extreme weather at the upper elevations demands that winter recreationists in this realm should be prepared for the elements.

AVERAGE TEMPERATURE & SNOWFALL CHARTS

Mount Shasta City 3520'

	Dec.	Jan.	Feb.	March	April
AVG. HIGH TEMP.	43.7°	42.5°	47.4°	51.4°	58.9°
AVG. LOW TEMP.	26.4°	25.6°	28.2°	29.8°	33.5°
AVG. SNOW DEPTH	3"	6"	3"	1"	0"
AVG. SNOWFALL	23.2"	28.8"	18.7"	16.1"	7.3"

Manzanita Lake 5885'

	Dec.	Jan.	Feb.	March	April
AVG. HIGH TEMP.	42.1°	41.0°	42.7°	44.7°	51.2°
AVG. LOW TEMP.	22.1°	20.1°	20.9°	22.9°	27.6°
AVG. SNOW DEPTH	10"	19"	24"	12"	2"
AVG. SNOWFALL	18.4"	37.1"	33.4"	35.5"	21.1"

Sierra City 4185'

	Dec.	Jan.	Feb.	March	April
AVG. HIGH TEMP.	47.6°	47.2°	50.5°	53.7°	60.8°
AVG. LOW TEMP.	28.9°	28.0°	29.0°	30.8°	34.5°
AVG. SNOW DEPTH	3"	9"	7"	4"	1"
AVG. SNOWFALL	15.7"	25.5"	21.3"	22.9"	7.8"

Blue Canyon 4690'

	Dec.	Jan.	Feb.	March	April
AVG. HIGH TEMP.	45.8°	43.6°	45.1°	45.4°	52.2°
AVG. LOW TEMP.	32.7°	30.7°	31.5°	31.5°	36.2°
AVG. SNOW DEPTH	10"	20"	26"	26"	15"
AVG. SNOWFALL	41.1"	50.9"	44.6"	52.5"	26.6"

Donner Memorial State Park 5925'

	Dec.	Jan.	Feb.	March	April
AVG. HIGH TEMP.	40.8°	40.3°	43.4°	46.6°	53.3°
AVG. LOW TEMP.	15.0°	13.6°	15.3°	20.1°	24.7°
AVG. SNOW DEPTH	11"	22"	31"	27"	14"
AVG. SNOWFALL	30.4"	39.8"	39.3"	35.6"	17.3"

Twin Lakes 7800'

	Dec.	Jan.	Feb.	March	April
AVG. HIGH TEMP.	39.4°	37.8°	39.6°	41.3°	46.6°
AVG. LOW TEMP.	17.7°	16.3°	16.4°	17.9°	22.2°
AVG. SNOW DEPTH	25"	51"	68"	78"	58"
AVG. SNOWFALL	66.4"	78.6"	71.9"	77.0"	37.2"

Yosemite Valley (Park Headquarters) 3970'

	Dec.	Jan.	Feb.	March	April
AVG. HIGH TEMP.	47.4°	47.5°	54.0°	58.3°	65.5°
AVG. LOW TEMP.	27.0°	26.6°	29.2°	31.7°	36.4°
AVG. SNOW DEPTH	2"	4"	4"	2"	0"
AVG. SNOWFALL	10.0"	18.1"	12.2"	12.0"	5.8"

South Entrance Yosemite National Park 5150'

	Dec.	Jan.	Feb.	March	April
AVG. HIGH TEMP.	48.7°	46.4°	48.5°	50.1°	56.4°
AVG. LOW TEMP.	26.5°	25.7°	26.5°	27.8°	31.3°
AVG. SNOW DEPTH	3"	8"	8"	8"	2"
AVG. SNOWFALL	17.5"	22.7"	20.2"	26.3"	12.3"

Huntington Lake 6950'

	Dec.	Jan.	Feb.	March	April
AVG. HIGH TEMP.	44.6°	43.8°	44.7°	45.3°	50.1°
AVG. LOW TEMP.	25.2°	23.4°	23.2°	24.0°	28.0°
AVG. SNOW DEPTH	14"	26"	41"	39"	21"
AVG. SNOWFALL	31.7"	38.8"	38.9"	39.6"	24.8"

Dana Meadows 9800'

	Dec.	Jan.	Feb.	March	April
AVG. SNOW DEPTH	20"	60"	76"	81"	64"

High & low temperatures & snowfall data not available for this site

Lee Vining 6780'

	Dec.	Jan.	Feb.	March	April
AVG. HIGH TEMP.	41.2°	40.3°	43.1°	52.0°	59.4°
AVG. LOW TEMP.	20.1°	19.5°	22.0°	28.5°	32.9°
AVG. SNOW DEPTH	0"	3"	4"	1"	0"
AVG. SNOWFALL	9.2"	20.1"	19.1"	6.7"	0.8"

Although guarantees are nonexistent, sunshine and mild temperatures are a reasonable expectation for a day of snowshoeing in the mountains of California. For instance, an average January day in Yosemite Valley has a 39% chance of being sunny and a 74% chance of no precipitation. However, you must be prepared for any condition—sunshine, snow, sleet, rain, wind and cold all can be extreme at one time or another. Wild variations may even occur during the same day, or even the same hour.

Be sure to have the appropriate clothing and equipment to successfully endure whatever conditions might possibly be encountered.

SEASON

The winter snowpack varies greatly from year to year throughout California, making accurate predictions of the optimum time for snowshoeing difficult. Compounding this dilemma is the effect of the wide range of elevations found across the mountains. For instance, snowfall is highly variable at an elevation of 3970 feet in Yosemite Valley, while at 8600 feet in Tuolumne Meadows good snow conditions may be present all the way through June in some years. Typically, however, there is enough snow above 5000 feet on the west slope of the mountains for decent snowshoeing from December to April. During years of abundant snowfall, the snowshoeing season can be extended considerably, depending on spring temperatures. Since the east side of the range lies in the rain shadow of the crest, more elevation than on the west is usually required for an adequate snowpack, and fluctuations are typically even greater than on the west side.

Conditions are also determined by exposure. South-facing slopes are the first to lose their snow, followed by west-, east-, and finally north-facing slopes. Forested areas, protected from the direct rays of the sun, will keep their snow longer than open meadows or exposed hillsides. Obtaining accurate information on current conditions in the southern Cascades and the Sierra is fairly easy via the phone or over the Internet.

When determining the best time for a particular trip, consider all these factors seriously. Consult the weather, avalanche and ski reports for current conditions before the trip. Most Forest Service and Park Service ranger stations have useful information as well.

ROUTEFINDING

No backcountry skill is more important in winter than the ability to find your way over snow-covered terrain. There are no trails to follow, at least none built into the soil and maintained by the government, as in the summer. Unless you have the luxury of following a marked trail or the tracks of a previous party, for most of the trips in this book you must be able to interpret major and minor features of the terrain, read a map, and navigate through the backcountry. Space does not allow for a dissertation on the necessary elements of navigation, orientation and routefinding, so you must gather a good understanding of

Blue diamonds may aid recreationists in staying on route along marked trails

this subject from other sources. The following principles should serve as an outline of a more detailed comprehension of this art.

- Always study your route carefully before you leave home.
- Always leave a detailed description of your proposed route with a reliable person.
- Always carry a topographic map of the area.
- Always carry a compass.
- Constantly observe the terrain as you progress.
- If necessary, mark your trail (and remove your markers on your return).
- Always keep your party together as you travel.

A GPS receiver is helpful for determining your position in the backcountry. However, no piece of equipment is an adequate replacement for the skills of navigation, orientation, and routefinding.

OBJECTIVE HAZARDS

SUN

For most people, the best days to be snowshoeing in the mountains are days when the snow is fresh and the skies are blue. Unfortunately, these conditions produce their own set of problems: sun, snow, and altitude combine to create the perfect reflective oven for baking exposed skin. However, winter usually finds snowshoers fully covered by some sort of apparel, with the exception of the face. Remember to apply an effective sunblock to all exposed areas of skin before venturing out onto snow-covered terrain in the intense winter sun. Reapply the sunblock as it wears off throughout the trip.

Snow blindness is a very real problem in winter, caused by prolonged exposure of the eyes to ultraviolet rays. Wear a pair of goggles or sunglasses that filter out at least 90% of UVA and UVB rays, particularly on sunny days. In addition, side shields on glasses help to reduce reflective rays.

DEHYDRATION

Becoming dehydrated in the midst of so much frozen liquid may seem ludicrous, but without enough water to replenish reserves, a vigorous activity like snowshoeing can put anyone in danger of just such a problem. Lots of moisture can be lost during strenuous exercise in cold, dry weather simply through respiration. Always carry plenty of water—most streams and lakes are frozen, and eating snow is an inadequate long-term solution.

If you find open water, bear in mind that many water sources in the mountains are contaminated with pathogens. All water should be treated, even the clearest-looking.

ALTITUDE

Most elevations accessible to the casual winter recreationist in the southern Cascades and the Sierra are not extreme. However, some people, particularly those who live near sea level, may suffer the effects of altitude sickness and its more serious counterpart, acute mountain sickness. Symptoms of altitude sickness include headache, fatigue, loss of appetite, shortness of breath, nausea, vomiting, drowsiness, dizziness, memory loss, and loss of mental acuity. Although rare at these elevations, acute mountain sickness is possible. It requires immediate descent and medical attention.

To avoid these maladies, drink plenty of fluids, eat a diet high in carbohydrates prior to and during a trip, and acclimatize slowly. A rapid descent will usually resolve any of the aforementioned symptoms. A severe case of altitude sickness is unlikely at these elevations during one-day trips, although not impossible.

COLD

Hypothermia is a condition in which the body's core temperature drops below normal in response to prolonged exposure to cold. Air temperature is not always the determining factor, as many cases of hypothermia occur when the thermometer registers above freezing. Wind chill, fatigue, and wetness (from rain, melting snow, submersion, or even excessive perspiration) can cause hypothermia.

The best solution for avoiding hypothermia is prevention. Do not get too cold, too tired, or too wet. Dress in layers and take time to adjust clothing as conditions change, preventing yourself from becoming too cold as well as preventing excessive wetness, from either precipitation or perspiration. Refrain from pushing on toward exhaustion when tired. Drink plenty of fluids and eat enough energy-producing food. Carry extra clothes in your vehicle to change into after a trip. If you suspect one of your party is experiencing the symptoms of hypothermia, handle the situation immediately. And remember that due to loss of mental acuity, you will not be able to detect symptoms in yourself.

Frostbite, a condition where tissue actually freezes after prolonged exposure to cold, is a potential concern during cold weather. Most susceptible to frostbite are the feet, hands, face, and ears. Adequate equipment, including properly fitting footwear, warm socks, gloves, and hat, should counteract the prolonged cold that can cause this malady.

AVALANCHES

Certainly, the most impressive winter hazard in the backcountry is the avalanche. Space does not allow for a complete discussion of avalanches here, and you should read as much as you can about them (see Suggested Reading in Appendix II: *Mountaineering: The Freedom of the Hills, ABC of Avalanche Safety, Allen & Mike's Really Cool Backcountry Ski Book,* and *Snowshoeing*). Avalanches usually occur due to lack of cohesion between the surface layer and the underlying snow, which can exist for a variety of reasons. They most commonly occur during and soon after storms, and during periods of rising temperatures, but are not limited to these times.

The most avalanche-prone areas include gullies, slopes between 30 and 45 degrees, north-facing slopes in winter, south-facing slopes in spring, lee slopes, treeless slopes, and slopes where younger trees are bordered by more mature forest. In addition, hillsides with a convex slope are more prone to avalanche than ones with a concave slope. As much as possible, avoid these areas, particularly during periods of instability.

Avalanches pose real dangers on moderate slopes

Even small avalanches pack a considerable wallop. Many years ago after a successful spring climb in the Sawtooth Ridge above Twin Lakes, we decided to glissade down a snow-filled gully for our return route. After a prolonged period of questioning the wisdom of the descent, I dropped to my butt and pushed off down the gully. About halfway down the slope I felt some pressure on my back and instantly started to somersault down the gully. I came to rest at the base of the slope, stripped of my hat, gloves and pack, which were now scattered haphazardly across the snow. My outer parka was halfway over my head, and snow filled every available passageway through my remaining clothing. Once I gathered my wits and surveyed the situation, I realized that this tremendous force, which tossed me and my equipment all over the mountain, was created by an avalanche a mere 12 inches high and 6 feet across.

Many people have put forth theories about what to do if caught in an avalanche. My own experience, along with reports from others caught in similar circumstances, has led me to believe that most avalanches occur far too quickly and with too much force for a victim to do much of anything. However, conventional wisdom says you should try to get on your back with your head uphill and make a swimming motion with your arms in an attempt to stay on top of the avalanche, and also—if possible— work your way toward the edge. Good luck.

Although there is no substitute for a wide range of winter experience in determining avalanche risk, there are some guidelines which you would be wise to follow when traveling in the backcountry.

Minimizing Avalanche Danger
- Obtain the current avalanche report for the area.
- Select the safest route—follow ridges wherever possible.
- Test slopes for stability. (See Suggested Reading mentioned above for resources on appropriate procedures.)
- Travel through suspect terrain quickly, one at a time, from safety zone to safety zone.
- Carry the proper equipment & know how to use it. (Necessary equipment may include shovels, probes, beacons, avalanche cord, cellular phone, first-aid kit.)

CORNICES

Another impressive feature of the winter landscape is the cornice, an overhanging mass of snow formed at the crest of a ridge where prevailing winds drift snowfall leeward over the edge. Cornices pose two problems: eventually and without warning a cornice will break off and plunge to the slope below, and falling cornices can trigger avalanches on unstable slopes. Obviously, the larger the cornice, the greater the potential for this damage. A less obvious danger arises when you're traveling along a ridge: if you snowshoe on the corniced edge of a ridge, you may go for a sudden ride.

A cornice may collapse suddenly and without warning

TRAIL ETIQUETTE

In general, trail etiquette is much the same in winter as in summer.

- Avoid snowshoeing on existing cross-country ski tracks. This allows skiers to reuse their tracks for return trips and leaves an existing track for future users.

- Yield the right of way to snowmobiles and cross-country skiers. Granting the lane to snowmobiles is purely common sense. A person on snowshoes will never win a standoff with a snowmobile. As for skiers, a snowshoer usually has more control over his or her movements than does a skier.

- Pack out all litter. Winter, summer, spring or fall, all garbage should be removed from the backcountry.

- Keep pets and their products under control. If you choose to share the backcountry with your dog, make sure it is a reasonably sociable animal. Chances are you will meet other dogs and people on the trail; nothing is more undesirable than having to break up a fight between animals or personally fend off unfriendly canines. Please scatter their droppings as well. Popular trails can become quite unkempt between snowfalls.

SANITATION

Winter presents a whole new situation for dealing with the proper disposal of waste materials. Urinating is fairly straightforward—as long as you don't pee into the snow above a frozen lake or stream. Find a spot well off the trail or a good distance away from your campsite to avoid the resulting visual pollution.

Defecating in the winter backcountry is not nearly as benign. Short of removing the waste altogether, which remains to most of us an undesirable alternative, there is no adequate way that doesn't adversely affect the environment. Burying stools in warmer times of the year allows the waste to gradually decompose and, when a suitable site is chosen, provides minimal risk of groundwater contamination. The danger in winter is that you will select a site where spring thaws cause an excessive amount of poop to find its way into the groundwater or a stream. Some experts speculate that the spread of giardia in the backcountry is due primarily to poor sanitation practices of winter users.

So what should we do? Taking care of your business at home before or after a trip avoids the problem altogether. However, if nature calls at a less convenient time, the best solution is to pack it out. For those who are not blessed with the ability to regulate their stools and have no desire to pack around their own poop, there are a few guidelines to follow. First of all, visual pollution is certainly a concern with site selection—pick a site well away from potential discovery by others. Nothing ruins the winter landscape more quickly than the unfortunate discovery of a previous traveler's waste products staining the snow. Secondly, choose a location that obviously won't contaminate a water source. Third, find a southern exposure and try to place your results just below the surface. This allows the freeze-thaw cycle to begin

Cross-country ski tracks along the Yuba Pass Trail

breaking down the stool the best way possible, as well as helping to dilute the waste products over the course of the spring melt.

What about used toilet paper? Once again, the best solution is to pack it out. Burning your toilet paper is sometimes recommended for backcountry users in other seasons becomes fairly impractical during winter. Carrying out your used paper seems somewhat less obnoxious than packing out the stool, and the minor inconvenience is outweighed by the greater good.

Although this guide is primarily concerned with day trips, overnight users should take care to avoid water sources and drainages when disposing of waste water and any leftover food.

CHAPTER 3

Equipment

SNOWSHOES

The early Seventies saw a significant change in the design and composition of snowshoes. Before this era, the typical snowshoe was constructed of wood and leather. With names like "bearpaw" and "beavertail" describing the classic shapes, outdoorsmen plodded through the snow with altered strides and rangy motions. Most of these predecessors of the modern snowshoe were large and cumbersome. They provided adequate flotation by utilizing a large surface area, which forced users to compensate for their wide and long dimensions by adopting a gait reminiscent of a cowboy walking away from his horse after a long day's ride. In this present era, these old classics are more likely found nailed to the rough-wood paneled walls of a mountain cabin or café than on backcountry snow. Traditionalists may find a diminishing number of suppliers who still provide old wooden snowshoes for sale.

Taking advantage of modern materials, new designs have revolutionized the manufacture of snowshoes (find a list of suppliers in Appendix I). Lightweight metals, space-age-plastics, and other materials have enabled designers to create lighter, smaller and more efficient snowshoes that are far easier to use. As compared to the cumbersome, oversized snowshoes of old, trim shoes with modern traction devices allow recreationists to pursue their sport with ease over a greater variety of terrain. High-angled slopes that would have been next to impossible for traditional shoes are commonly ascended and descended successfully with the newer equipment. The advanced design of snowshoes has definitely made the winter landscape more accessible by users of all skill levels.

Most modern snowshoes fall into the category known as western, named for their origin in the mountain west. Although some molded models have had recent success, most western snowshoes have a tubular metal frame and some type of synthetic decking. Advanced bindings with traction devices are attached to the snowshoe at a single flex point, making them well-suited for icy or hard-packed snow conditions.

Snowshoers in the southern Cascades and the Sierra may meet a wide variety of snow types. Soft, fluffy powder is most often encountered after a storm, with snowfalls of up to 4 feet not uncommon. During these periods, enthusiasts are likely to crave the largest snowshoes they can strap to their feet. Once the snow becomes consolidated, some users switch to smaller shoes with greater maneuverability. During hard-pack conditions users want the smallest shoe available, with the best traction devices. The spring season presents possibly the greatest challenge, when snow is firm early in the day but turns to wet mush in the afternoon sun.

Manufacturers offer different snowshoes for different types of snow, but most snowshoers will try to get by with a single pair. With prices averaging $200 per pair, owning different sets for a variety of snow conditions may be a luxury. One manufacturer has overcome the cost barrier to owning several pair by making interchangeable tails that can be added to or taken off the main shoe to adapt the length to different snow conditions.

Selecting the best snowshoes for all the possibilities can be daunting. In general, try to get by with the smallest shoe that will reasonably handle the many types of snow encountered in the backcountry. If planning to backpack with snowshoes, you will need a larger size than ones used simply for day trips. For those users who want to climb on steep terrain, a lightweight, smaller shoe with a good traction device is the best choice. If money is no object, buy as many shoes as needed for the variety of situations you will encounter. If it is, make a careful assessment of your needs and buy one or two pairs that will handle most of the situations you expect to find.

POLES

Some people don't use ski poles, but for most snowshoers they provide a nice extra measure of stability. In addition, they provide the upper body with a certain degree of exercise and bear some portion of the load that your legs would otherwise carry alone. Some poles can be threaded together when their baskets are removed, thereby doubling as avalanche probes.

CLOTHING

The backcountry rule for clothing is summed up in one word—layering. Many layers of lightweight clothing allow greater flexibility to adapt to the changing conditions of strenuous exercise in winter. Adding or subtracting a layer or two allows the backcountry user to regulate his or her body temperature more easily than a few thick layers of clothing would.

UNDERWEAR

Many synthetic materials have been developed for use in the backcountry. Select ones that will conduct perspiration to your outer layers of clothing quickly while maintaining warmth. As nice as cotton feels against your skin, once it gets wet, you get cold.

PANTS

Choose pants made from synthetic material or wool that are lightweight, loose-fitting, water-resistant and durable. A pair of nylon shell pants over your regular pants will help to shed snow and protect your legs from wind. Gore-Tex or an equivalent material will help keep you dry in wet conditions.

TORSO

Modern fabrics have greatly aided recreationists in staying warm and dry. As stated, multiple layers allow you to adjust to changing conditions whether they be external or internal fluctuations in temperature. With the advent of pile, fleece and other synthetic products, the snowshoer has a wide range of choices for what to wear around the upper body next to the primary layer of underwear. Shirts, vests, pullovers and jackets can all be used alone or in combination to achieve comfort. Down-filled vests and jackets are still popular choices for warmth, weight, and compressibility—just make sure they don't get wet. Your outer layer should be a waterproof or water-resistant parka with a hood that will protect you from wind and weather.

HATS

In the mountains of California a hat with a brim should help protect you from the intense rays of the sun on those idyllic, clear days. When it's cold you will need one to keep your head warm. A "stocking hat" can be adjusted to protect your face during extreme conditions and is an excellent choice.

GLOVES/MITTS

Cold hands can make you nearly as miserable in the backcountry as having cold feet. Mitts will keep your hands warmer than gloves. Usually the best combination for handwear is an inner liner of synthetic material or wool and an outer shell of waterproof nylon reinforced in critical areas.

BOOTS

Protecting your feet from the cold temperatures and wet conditions of winter is of the utmost importance. Many snowshoe trips, starting out as pleasant excursions into winter wonderlands, have turned into living nightmares due to agonizingly wet and bitterly cold feet. Not too long ago there weren't many options for footwear in the snowshoeing world. Whatever hiking boots you used during summer were the same ones you would strap into your snowshoes in winter, properly coated with multiple applications of some waxy sealant in a less-than-totally-effective attempt to keep your feet dry. Nowadays, a number of companies are producing winter-type boots suitable for many outdoor pursuits, some more appropriate for snowshoeing than others.

Winterizing one's summer boots is still an option that many continue to pursue, and one that is quite effective in spring. If choosing this option, make sure the footwear is substantial enough to provide adequate support and comfort when attached to a pair of snowshoes. In addition, sufficiently protecting boots from wetness is a must, particularly in spring, when warm days begin to turn the snowpack into a wet mush. Consult your local backcountry retailer for the best water-protection product for your particular type of boot.

If you decide to use winter boots, select a pair that will provide the necessary rigidity required for successful operation of your snowshoes. Many winter boots are designed for walking around in the snow, but are not necessarily made for snowshoeing. Some models come with felt liners for extra protection from the cold. Make sure if you purchase a pair that these boots fit with and without the liners. Talk to an informed clerk at a reliable outdoor store for their recommendations.

GAITERS

A good pair of gaiters is a winter essential for keeping snow out of your boots. Select gaiters that are made from durable fabrics and are easy to put on and remove.

SOCKS

Socks are probably the most important piece of clothing when it comes to keeping you warm. There seem to be as many sock combinations as there are backcountry users, so pick a mix that works best for you. Select liners of synthetic fabrics that will pass moisture easily to the outer socks. Outer socks should be thicker wool or synthetic blends which can keep your feet warm even when wet.

SAFETY DEVICES

AVALANCHE BEACONS

If you expect to travel extensively through potential avalanche terrain, a set of avalanche beacons is a wise choice. To be effective, everyone in your party must carry a device and be trained in its use. Batteries should always be checked prior to your departure.

AVALANCHE CORD

A less expensive alternative to beacons, avalanche cord is a thin strand of rope, 100 feet or so in length, that snowshoers tie to their bodies, much like mountaineers would tie into a climbing rope. In the event of an avalanche, rescuers can follow an exposed section of cord to the buried victim.

AVALANCHE PROBES

Probes aid in finding a buried victim. The most efficient way to carry avalanche probes is to have ski poles that will connect into a single probe. Teammates can pierce the snowpack with the probes in search of victims.

SNOW SHOVELS

Everyone in your party should carry a lightweight snow shovel. Not only essential in an avalanche rescue, snow shovels are of immense help if a temporary shelter has to be constructed.

CELLULAR PHONES

Technology has produced many wonderful gadgets designed to make our lives easier, although I am not sure if that statement applies to cellular phones. Personal pet peeves aside, cellular phones provide an instant link with the outside world in case of an emergency. As long as they are not abused, cellular phones can be a tremendous resource in times of real trouble. However, coverage in the mountains is spotty at best and you may not be able to achieve a connection. Technology is no replacement for the requisite knowledge and skill to handle an emergency situation.

NAVIGATIONAL AIDS

While hikers and backpackers, without much thought, typically follow a well-defined trail to their favorite destination during summer, winter travelers are governed by a much different set of rules. In the absence of the established trails of summer, a modicum of navigational skill is necessary to safely negotiate the snow-covered backcountry. Most trail signs and blazes on trees are lost, and even dominant physical features, such as streams and lakes, can disappear or be significantly altered by a normal snowpack. In order to successfully negotiate the winter landscape, you must have certain equipment and sufficient knowledge of its use.

GPS SYSTEMS

With the advent of access to the GPS system by the general public, many outdoor lovers have come to depend upon hand-held monitors for accurately locating their position in the backcountry. Particularly in winter, when trails and landmarks become obscured by the deepening snows, GPS devices can be a great asset, although certainly not an absolute necessity. In densely forested terrain or during inclement weather, the GPS can save you from confused wandering, which could lead to much more severe consequences. However, a GPS device is no substitute for backcountry savvy and the knowledge of how to read the landscape coupled with the ability to use a map and compass.

MAP & COMPASS

When traveling through mountain snows, a USGS 7.5-minute topographic map is an essential element for your pack, especially when journeying along unmarked routes. Typically, these maps provide detailed topographic information, including contours, elevations of important landmarks, and the location of physical features such as streams, lakes, peaks, and canyons. As with many tools, these maps are next to useless without an understanding of them. If you presently lack the ability to use these maps, you may be able to gain it through programs of local outdoor groups, adult education courses, or by consulting an appropriate publication.

In addition to these USGS maps, a number of other maps cover the mountainous regions of California. The Forest Service publishes topographic maps on plastic film for many of the federally designated wilderness areas that are at an adequate scale for navigation in the backcountry. The Forest Service also provides maps of its districts, but they lack contour lines and are at too small a scale to be useful for backcountry travel. Numerous recreation maps are published by private companies for the more popular areas, but also oftentimes lack the necessary scale for finding your way in the wild. There is no good substitute for the USGS maps.

A map covering the area of your travel is a necessary item, but is incomplete without a properly working compass. Poor visibility due to weather or terrain can disorient backcountry users, and a compass is the best way to regain one's bearings. Avoid cheap models—a flawed compass is worse than none at all.

MAPS

A map is provided for each trip in this book, produced from reduced copies of 7.5-minute USGS quadrangles. The first number following the "Map" heading in a trip description refers to the book's map for that trip.

TOPOGRAPHIC MAPS

Most major outdoor retailers no longer carry USGS maps per se, opting for kiosks that print custom made topographic maps instead. Below is a listing of the USGS 7.5-minute topographic maps with corresponding snowshoe trip numbers.

USGS Map Name	Trip Number	USGS Map Name	Trip Number
1. McCloud	1-4	27. Caples Lake	67-70
2. Mt. Shasta	4	28. Carson Pass	66-69
3. Manzanita Lake	5-7, 15	29. Pickel Meadow	84
4. West Prospect Peak	8-9, 15	30. Twin Lakes	85
5. Lassen Peak	6, 8-17	31. Dunderberg Peak	86, 87
6. Reading Peak	8-9	32. Lundy	86, 87
7. Johnsville	18-22	33. Falls Ridge	73
8. Gold Lake	18-21	34. Tioga Pass	73
9. Clio	28-29	35. Mt. Dana	88
10. Calpine	29-32	36. Ackerson Mountain	71-73
11. Sierra City	23-27	37. Tamarack Flat	73
12. Haypress Valley	24-27, 29	38. Yosemite Falls	73-76
13. Sattley	29-32	39. Tenaya Lake	73
14. Sierraville	56, 57	40. Vogelsang Peak	73
15. Sardine Peak	56, 57	41. Koip Peak	89
16. Independence Lake	54, 55, 57	42. El Capitan	76-78
17. Hobart Mills	54, 55, 57	43. Half Dome	74-76, 78
18. Cisco Grove	33-40	44. Merced Peak	73
19. Soda Springs	40-42	45. Mariposa Grove	79, 80
20. Norden	43-52	46. Mt. Abbot	90
21. Truckee	51, 52	47. Mt. Morgan	90
22. Martis Peak	60, 61	48. Huntington Lake	81-83
23. Mt. Rose	62	49. General Grant Grove	91-94
24. Granite Chief	58, 59	50. Lodgepole	95-97
25. Tahoe City	57-59	51. Giant Forest	98-100
26. Freel Peak	63-65		

The United States Geological Survey produces the 7.5-minute quadrangles, generally regarded as the finest maps available to the general public. State indexes can be ordered from the government at (800) USA-MAPS or (800) HELP-MAP, or by writing to:

USGS Information Services
Box 25286
Denver, CO 80225

Using the appropriate state and map names, you can order directly from the Customer Service Department of the USGS at 1 (888) ASK-USGS (or online at **www.usgs.gov**). In 2004, maps were selling for $6 apiece, plus a small shipping and handling charge per order. The USGS accepts VISA or MasterCard.

COMPUTER SOFTWARE

Software companies have developed computer programs utilizing the USGS maps as a base. Some of these programs are better than others, having a variety of options you can use to customize maps for personal use. With a decent desktop color printer, you can produce maps at home that rival the quality of the USGS ones, albeit not on the same-size sheet of paper. The cost of a typical program is around the cost of 10 to 15 maps, which makes the price of the software reasonable if you plan on purchasing many maps. Your local backpacking store is usually the best source for these programs. Sometime in the future we may be able to buy computer disks directly from the USGS containing a specified number and selection of topo maps.

FOREST SERVICE MAPS

The US Forest Service produces a number of good maps that are well-suited for general purposes but, as a rule, should not be substituted for the more accurate USGS maps. These small-scale maps are often helpful in determining highway routes to trailheads and for gaining a wider perspective of the territory. They can be purchased at the appropriate Forest Service Ranger Station (see Forest Service listings in the Trip chapters).

PARK SERVICE MAPS

The Park Service provides a fine array of maps for a variety of recreational purposes that may be purchased at the Visitor Centers in Lassen Volcanic, Yosemite, Kings Canyon, and Sequoia national parks. The Winter Trails maps for Yosemite, Kings Canyon, and Sequoia are of particular interest for snowshoers and are relatively inexpensive. In Yosemite, they can be obtained at the Visitor Center and the Village Store in Yosemite Valley, the service stations at Crane Flat and Wawona, and frequently at the trailheads. In Kings Canyon and Sequoia, they can be obtained at the Grant Grove, Lodgepole, and Foothills visitor centers, or from the Giant Forest Museum.

ADDITIONAL MAPS

Private-sector maps of the more popular recreation areas of California have been produced by a handful of concerns. In particular, a plethora of independent maps have been created for Yosemite National Park—you could go broke trying to accumulate them all. However, the maps listed in each Trip chapter should be more than adequate to provide the information you need.

EQUIPMENT CHECKLIST

GEAR:

Snowshoes
Ski Poles/Avalanche Probes
Pack

10 Essentials:

1. Maps
2. Compass
3. Flashlight or Headlamp
   (extra batteries & bulb)
4. Knife
5. Extra food

6. Extra clothing
7. Sunglasses & sunscreen
8. Matches
   (in waterproof container)
9. Candles (or firestarter)
10. First Aid/Emergency Kit

Toilet paper
Repair Kit: cord, tape, safety pins, etc.
Water bottles or hydration system (or thermos for hot drinks)
Signalling Devices: whistle & mirror

SAFETY EQUIPMENT:

Avalanche cord
Avalanche beacons
Snow shovel
Cellular phone

OPTIONAL GEAR:

Camera
Binoculars
GPS Receiver

CLOTHING:

Winter boots
Gaiters
Socks (liners & outer socks)
Shell Parka
(Gore-Tex or equivalent)
Shell Pants
(Gore-Tex or equivalent)
Jacket
Vest
Shirt
Gloves or Mitts
Hats (for sun & cold)
Underwear
Pants

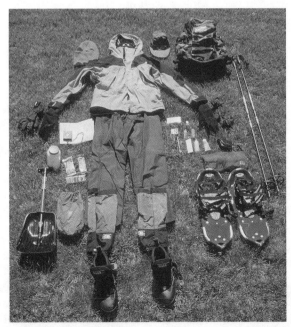

Typical snowshoeing gear

CHAPTER 4

How to Use This Guide

This guidebook is designed primarily for snowshoers who want to go on one-day trips in the southern Cascades or the Sierra Nevada. There are a few trips that are described as overnight or multi-day trips. I have tried to not simply tailor existing cross-country ski routes for snowshoe trips, but to identify areas that are specifically well-suited for snowshoeing, although some trips will indeed correspond to known cross-country ski routes.

More than half of the trips in this guide are classified as suited for snowshoers of moderate abilities, 25% for beginners, 17% for the more experienced, and three trips received an extreme rating. These ratings are both subjective and liable to the vagaries of nature. A trip rated difficult may easily be accomplished on a day when the weather is clear and the snow conditions perfect, while a half-mile trip rated as easy can turn into a desperate struggle for snowshoers wading through five feet of fresh powder while a driving wind knocks them to and fro.

My intention was to provide enough information to direct readers to the trailhead, to a destination, and back again—but not so much as to require much reading time on the trail.

Duration: This information is my subjective evaluation of how much of a typical winter's day should be required for the complete enjoyment of a particular trip. Surely, there will be those who can complete trips in less time than is listed, just as others may feel hurried. Hopefully, the average snowshoer will find these estimates reasonable.

Distance: Distances have been accurately determined in the field using the 7.5' USGS quadrangles. Since exact routes are difficult to duplicate on the ever-changing winter landscape, there may be some slight variations in distance covered, but certainly nothing dramatic. When the total distance depends on how much of a road is plowed, that is noted.

Difficulty: For the purpose of this guide, difficulty ratings have been grouped into four categories: easy, moderate, difficult and extreme. Easy trips should be well-suited to beginning snowshoers as the terrain is gentle, the trips are relatively short, and the routefinding is minimal. Moderate trips pass over more complex terrain, are typically longer, and require some routefinding skills to successfully negotiate. Trips that receive a difficult rating move the snowshoer across steeper terrain, cover greater distances and may necessitate considerable routefinding skill. These journeys may present more objective dangers as well, such as avalanche potential or a greater possibility of exposure to inclement weather. The last rating, extreme, is for those trips that push the limits of technical skill, endurance and vulnerability to the forces of nature. These journeys are for experienced snowshoers who are technically proficient, in good condition, and well qualified to evaluate potential hazards.

Elevation: The first four-digit entry under this heading is for the trailhead elevation at the start of a trip. The second number is the elevation at the high point of a round trip, except in cases where the destination is substantially lower than the highest point en route. For these trips, three elevations are listed, the third being the destination. For the few one-way trips that require a shuttle, three elevations are listed: the beginning trailhead, the high point, and the ending trailhead.

Maps: Here you will find the names of the USGS 7.5' quadrangles that cover the trip.

Introduction: The introduction provides a brief overview of the highlights of the journey.

How to get there: Clear instructions are given for getting to the trailhead.

Description: The trip description gives complete directions for the route. Still, the intent is to avoid an overly detailed discourse so that you can enjoy the backcountry experience without continual dependence on a book.

FYI: Under the "For Your Information" heading, are additional matters of importance.

Warm-ups: Many winter enthusiasts find a trip to the winter backcountry incomplete unless they sit by the fire sipping their favorite brew after an exhilarating romp through the snow. Those who enjoy a hot drink or a warm meal following a snowshoe trip will find some suggestions here. A completely subjective and random formula was used in evaluating these establishments. They had to in some way capture certain undefinable elements related to an outdoor ambiance, as well as provide decent food or drink at a reasonable cost. Other intangibles were considered, not the least of which was whether the staff was reasonably friendly to poorly dressed, unshaven, perspiration-soaked, snow-sodden customers.

CHAPTER 5

Mount Shasta

Mt. Shasta reigns over northern California with undeniable grandeur. The 14,162-foot peak majestically towers 10,000 feet over the surrounding terrain, overwhelmingly the most dominant landmark for many miles around in any direction. This huge snow-draped mountain is actually a stratovolcano within the Cascade Range, second in height only to Mt. Rainier in Washington state, which is only 248 feet higher. Although the last eruption of Mt. Shasta is believed to have occurred around 1786, the mountain is still considered to be active geologically. Shastina, the 12,330-foot symmetrical sister cone 1.5 miles directly west of the summit, gives further indication of the region's volcanic origin. Many other geologic examples of volcanism are spread around the immediate vicinity of the mountain.

Mt. Shasta harbors seven named glaciers, many of them graced with romantic-sounding Native American names like Konwakiton and Wintun. These seven represent the single greatest concentration of glaciers within California. The Whitney Glacier is the state's largest both in length (2 miles) and volume. Most of these rivers of ice are found on the north and east slopes of the mountain, where the sun's rays are less direct than on the west and south. Having been in retreat for much of the 20th century, Shasta's glaciers are now thought to have stabilized or even to be advancing slightly. Whatever their true condition, these tongues of ice provide a rare opportunity for recreationists to view glaciers within the state of California.

The alpine zone above 8000 feet around the mountain was set aside in 1984 as a 32,000-acre wilderness area as part of the California Wilderness Bill. Covering the area from near timberline to the summit, the Mt. Shasta Wilderness provides protected status for the open slopes of the mountain. Although groves of white-bark pine occur on the north and east sides and pockets of mountain hemlock are here and there, most of the peak below timberline is covered by a light forest of Shasta red fir. This trademark tree, with deeply furrowed red bark and curved combs of blue-green needles, extends from timberline down to an elevation of about 6500 feet. Thanks to the sandy, porous volcanic soils found on the flanks of the peak, the trees are generally widely spaced, granting recreationists plenty of open scenery. All of the following snowshoe trips on Mt. Shasta pass through this red fir zone.

The origin of the name "Shasta" is hard to pinpoint, although most historians suspect a Native American derivation. The first recorded sighting of the peak by a non-Native American occurred in 1841 by a Spanish explorer named Fray Narcisco

Duran. Notable explorers Peter Skene Odgen and John C. Fremont both sighted the peak during expeditions across the West.

Snowshoers wishing to experience Mt. Shasta have the luxury of beginning their trips at an elevation of nearly 7000 feet from the Bunny Flat trailhead, assuring a reasonably good chance of decent snow throughout a long season. The four routes described in this chapter vary in difficulty from an easy stroll along a snow-covered road to Panther Meadow to a full-blown assault on the peak itself. The two intermediate choices offer a moderate climb to the historic Sierra Club lodge at Horse Camp and a somewhat difficult ascent of 8108-foot Gray Butte. Whichever route is selected, all of them offer the fantastic scenery of a true winter wonderland.

While snowmobiles are banned from the Wilderness Area, they are permitted to travel on the slopes below the Everitt Memorial Highway.

Location: Mt. Shasta is 40 miles south of the Oregon border and 10 miles east of the town of Weed.

Access: The major thoroughfare of Interstate 5 passes just west of Mt. Shasta, providing auto-bound-travelers relatively direct access to the mountain. From an I-5 interchange at the community of Mt. Shasta (225 miles north of Sacramento) the Everitt Memorial Highway climbs 3500 feet in 11 miles to the Bunny Flat trailhead (see Trip 1 for description). Siskiyou County does a good job of keeping the road open during winter except when extremely adverse weather conditions are present.

Amenities: Along with such necessities as groceries, gasoline and auto repairs, the city of Mt. Shasta offers plenty of affordable lodging and dining choices, even in winter when most mountain communities pull down their shades and roll up their sidewalks. The Fifth Season at 300 N. Mt. Shasta Blvd. offers a great selection of outdoor gear for purchase or for rent: (530) 926-3606. Check out their website at www.thefifthseason.com.

Season & Weather: Due to the great access provided by the Everitt Memorial Highway to a nearly 7000-foot trailhead, recreationists can enjoy a lengthy season for their snow-related activities. An adequate snowpack usually appears by late autumn and lasts well into April or May. Good snow conditions for climbing the peak often persist all the way into July.

That they create their own weather is often said of gigantic mountains such as Shasta. Regardless of whether such a statement is scientifically accurate, its truth for those suddenly caught in an unsuspected whiteout seems real enough. Mt. Shasta is not the place to be when the weather is foul. Winter storms can produce exceedingly high winds, extremely frigid temperatures and gigantic snowfalls; the last place to be is on the open, exposed slopes of this mountain under those conditions.

Since Shasta is in the extreme northern part of California, the mountain is exposed to oncoming Pacific storms that may avoid areas of the state farther south. Always check the weather forecast before venturing out into the backcountry. The Forest Service usually posts a printed weather forecast near the registration area at Bunny Flat. The mountain itself may provide some of the best clues to an approaching storm: an increase of southwest winds will usually be an indicator of an oncoming front, as will the formation of a cloud cap over the summit that begins to drop down the mountain with the passage of time. Sometimes this cloudiness moves slowly or even stabilizes, while at other times it may seem to engulf the whole mountain almost instantaneously. Whenever signs of an advancing storm is observed, a quick retreat from the mountain is always wisest. Also, make sure your party is properly equipped to endure the harshest of conditions.

PERMITS

Day Use: Recreationists are encouraged to sign in and out at the registration area at Bunny Flat.

Overnight Use: Backcountry permits are required for overnight stays within the Mt. Shasta Wilderness. Permits can be obtained during business hours at the ranger stations in McCloud and Mt. Shasta, or by self-registration at Bunny Flat.

Parties wishing to establish a base camp at Horse Camp will be charged $5 per tent or $3 for an individual. Fees should be left at the Sierra Club hut.

All persons climbing above 10,000 feet will be assessed a $15 fee for a three-day pass. Recently an Annual Summit Pass has become available for $25. In winter, passes are available at the registration area at Bunny Flat (correct change only) or at the local ranger stations during normal office hours.

MAPS

Mt. Shasta Map	*A Guide to the Mt. Shasta Wilderness*	*Shasta-Trinity*
1:24,000, 2001, plastic	*& Castle Crags Wilderness*	*National Forest*
Wilderness Press	1:31,680, 1990, plastic	1:126,720, 1997, paper
(800) 443-7227	Shasta-Trinity National Forest	Shasta-Trinity
		National Forest

FOREST SERVICE

Mt. Shasta Ranger District	McCloud Ranger District	Forest Supervisor
204 West Alma	P.O. Box 1620	Shasta-Trinity National Forest
Mt. Shasta, CA 96067	2019 Forest Road	3644 Avtech Parkway
(530) 926-4511	McCloud, CA 96057	Redding, CA 96002
	(530) 964-2184	(530) 226-2500

IMPORTANT PHONE NUMBERS

Avalanche Hotline	(530) 926-9613
Climbing Rangers	(530) 926-9614
5th Season-- Mt. Shasta current conditions	(530) 926-5555

WEBSITES

Mt. Shasta Wilderness Avalanche & Climbing Advisory	**www.shastaavalanche.org**
Shasta-Trinity National Forest	**www.r5.fs.fed.us/shastatrinity**

TRIP 1

Bunny Flat to Panther Meadow

Duration: One-half day

see map on page 30

Distance: 3.75 miles round trip
Difficulty: Easy
Elevation: 6950/7485
Maps: *McCloud* 7.5′ quadrangle; *A Guide to the Mt. Shasta Wilderness & Castle Crags Wilderness*, Shasta-Trinity National Forest

Introduction: Siskiyou County routinely plows the Everitt Memorial Highway to Bunny Flat (6950 feet), providing northern California recreationists access to ample quantities of snow all through winter and well into spring. Snowshoers of all abilities can enjoy this easy route along the pleasantly graded and easily discernible extension of the highway to Panther Meadow. Wandering in and out of red fir forest, the route offers exceptional scenery along the way, culminating in a fine view from the meadows of Mt. Shasta and the broad vista of the surrounding terrain to the west. For those interested in longer trips a number of extensions are possible (see FYI).

How to get there: From Interstate 5, take the Cemtral Mt. Shasta exit and follow Lake Street northeast through the city of Mt. Shasta. About a mile from the freeway East Lake Street curves and becomes Everitt Memorial Highway. Follow the highway past the high school and out of town, climbing up the southwest slopes of Mt. Shasta to the end of the plowed road at Bunny Flat, 11 miles from I-5.

At Bunny Flat you will find a large parking area and a restroom building with 4 pit toilets and an information area. Avalanche and weather conditions are posted regularly along with other pertinent information.

Description: You head east from the parking area along the continuation of the unplowed road through widely dispersed Shasta red firs which allow nice views of the mountain near the vicinity of Bunny Flat. On a steady, gently uphill grade you quickly come to a curve in the road which leads into slightly thicker forest, temporarily obscuring your view of the peak. More minor curves await as you continue up the road all the while playing peek-a-boo with Mt. Shasta. Soon you reach the beginning of Panther Meadow, 1.75 miles from Bunny Flat.

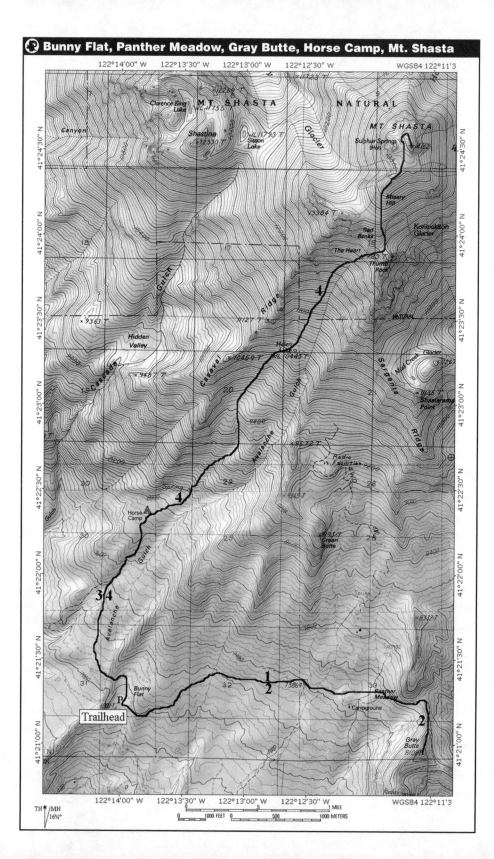

Panther Meadow is a large, sloping clearing which affords fine views of the mountain and the terrain to the west, including Castle Crags, the Eddys and the Trinity Alps in the distance. Up above are the striking face of Green Butte, the open cirque of Ski Bowl, Shastarama Point, and Sargents Ridge.

FYI: Many extensions to your trip are possible from Panther Meadow. You could continue around the south side of the mountain another 1.25 miles to The Gate, the pronounced notch north of Red Butte. From there you could travel through the hemlock forest of Squaw Creek or journey farther east to where you have fine views of Mud Creek and the Konwakiton Glacier. Another option is to continue up the unplowed Everitt Memorial Highway as it curves and climbs an additional 400 feet in little over a mile to the site of the old ski lodge. Providing the slopes are stable, snowboarders and skiers would enjoy cavorting down the slopes of either the Ski Bowl or Sun and Powder Bowl on the way back toward Bunny Flat.

Be aware that the territory south of Everitt Memorial Highway is open to snowmobiles.

Warm-ups: Mexican food is a sure-fire way to take the chill off after a day in the backcountry. Casa Ramos, at 1136 S. Mt. Shasta Blvd., will certainly spice up your day with their wide selection of entrees for lunch or dinner. If you heat up too much, you can cool down again with a round of their bountiful margaritas. For more information call (530) 926-0250.

Mt. Shasta as seen from Panther Meadow

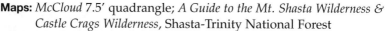

Gray Butte

Duration: Three-quarter day
Distance: 5.5 miles round trip
Difficulty: Difficult to extreme
Elevation: 6950/8108
Maps: *McCloud* 7.5′ quadrangle; *A Guide to the Mt. Shasta Wilderness &
Castle Crags Wilderness*, Shasta-Trinity National Forest

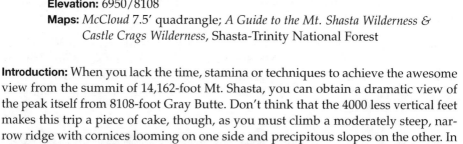

see map
on page
30

Introduction: When you lack the time, stamina or techniques to achieve the awesome view from the summit of 14,162-foot Mt. Shasta, you can obtain a dramatic view of the peak itself from 8108-foot Gray Butte. Don't think that the 4000 less vertical feet makes this trip a piece of cake, though, as you must climb a moderately steep, narrow ridge with cornices looming on one side and precipitous slopes on the other. In addition, you shouldn't even consider this outing when hard-pack snow, avalanche potential or high winds present added difficulties. When the conditions are right, the 2.75-mile climb from Bunny Flat can be quite a thrill, especially when you gaze at the immense form of the second highest peak in the Cascade Range from the airy summit of Gray Butte.

How to get there: From Interstate 5, take the Central Mt. Shasta exit and follow Lake Street northeast through the city of Mt. Shasta. About a mile from the freeway, East Lake Street curves and becomes Everitt Memorial Highway. Follow the highway past the high school and out of town, climbing up the southwest slopes of Mt. Shasta to the end of the plowed road at Bunny Flat, 11 miles from I-5.

At Bunny Flat you will find a large parking area and a restroom building with four pit toilets and an information area. Avalanche and weather conditions are posted regularly along with other pertinent information.

Description: You head east from the parking area along the continuation of the unplowed road through widely dispersed Shasta red firs, which allow nice views of the mountain near the vicinity of Bunny Flat. On a steady, gently uphill grade, you quickly come to a curve in the road, which leads into slightly thicker forest, temporarily obscuring your view of the peak. More minor curves await as you continue up the road, all the while playing peak-a-boo with Mt. Shasta. Soon you reach the beginning of Panther Meadow, 1.75 miles from Bunny Flat.

From Panther Meadow, leave the snow-covered highway where it bends up toward the old ski area. You head across the eastern extension of the meadow on a gentle grade until you must climb more steeply up the forested hillside beyond the meadow. Aiming for the saddle directly north of Gray Butte, you make a slightly rising traverse across the hillside. As you near the saddle the grade of ascent increases. From the saddle you have nice views of Red Butte and the pronounced gap immediately northwest of it, known as The Gate.

Now the climbing begins as you must follow the narrow ridge south to the summit. From the saddle you briefly climb and then just as quickly descend to a low spot in the ridge before making a sustained ascent up the peak. The trick to the climb lies in avoiding the cornices on the crest to your left and the steeper slopes of the west face just a few steps to your right. Carefully proceed up the ridge until you stand atop the airy summit of Gray Butte.

The narrow ridge you've just surmounted and the little summit you stand upon lend a decidedly alpine feeling to the surroundings. The view from the modest summit is certainly rewarding—as expected, the massive bulk of Mt. Shasta dominates the unobstructed vista, while Lassen Peak and its neighbors pierce the winter sky to the south. Across the valley below, Castle Crags, the Eddys and the Trinity Alps create a sweeping western panorama.

Remain alert as you depart from the summit of Gray Butte as the descent may require greater skill than the ascent. From the saddle you can follow the easier terrain back to Bunny Flat.

FYI: You should attempt to climb Gray Butte only when conditions are favorable. Avoid the peak during unstable avalanche conditions, foul weather, or high winds.

Warm-ups: If you can't get started in the morning without an obligatory cup of coffee, stop by Has Beans at 1011 S. Mt. Shasta Blvd. Open from 5:30 a.m. to 8:00 p.m. (9:00 p.m. Friday and Saturday), the friendly staff will satisfy your cravings with their wide-ranging selection of coffees, teas and pastries. Check out their website at **www.hasbeans.com** or phone either (530) 926-3602 or (800) 427-2326 for more information.

TRIP 3

Horse Camp

see map
on page
30

Duration: One-half day or overnight
Distance: 3 miles round trip
Difficulty: Moderate
Elevation: 6950/7880
Maps: *McCloud 7.5'* quadrangle; *A Guide to the Mt. Shasta Wilderness &
Castle Crags Wilderness*, Shasta-Trinity National Forest

Introduction: Summer or winter, the trip to Horse Camp is one of the most popular
routes on Mt. Shasta. The majority of climbers begin their summit attempt either by
following this route to a base camp at Horse Camp or by continuing farther up the
mountain to a flat near Lake Helen. The trailhead near 7000 feet ensures that those
snowshoers with lofty visions of bagging the Cascades' second highest peak will
have an adequate snowpack over the course of a lengthy season. Although the
climb to Horse Camp is steady, the elevation gain is less than 1000 feet in 1.5 miles,
a moderate climb over a relatively short distance.

Once at Horse Camp, snowshoers have a marvelous view of the southwest
side of Mt. Shasta and a western vista of Castle Crags, the Eddys and the Trinity
Alps. The impressive view is one reason the Sierra Club ended up owning over
700 acres around Horse Camp. Other reasons included a fresh-water spring and
nearby meadows providing feed for the horses that packed visitors up from the
valley below. The stone lodge was completed in the early 1920's, and J.M. "Mac"
Olberman became the first custodian. Over the years this unique figure made
countless improvements to the area, including construction of Olberman's Cause-
way, a flagstone-lined climbers' path extending from the hut to the base of the
steeper climbing above.

Today snowshoers and skiers can visit the lodge, which is still much the same as
when Mac was custodian. Although overnight use is not allowed, camping is permitted outside the lodge for a nominal fee. A double pit toilet is nearby.

How to get there: From Interstate 5, take the Central Mt. Shasta exit and follow Lake
Street northeast through the city of Mt. Shasta. About a mile from the freeway, East
Lake Street curves and becomes Everitt Memorial Highway. Follow the highway
past the high school and out of town, climbing up the southwest slopes of Mt. Shasta to the end of the plowed road at Bunny Flat, 11 miles from I-5.

At Bunny Flat you will find a large parking area and a restroom building with four pit toilets and an information area. Avalanche and weather conditions are posted regularly along with other pertinent information.

Description: From Bunny Flat, head up the open slope for a short distance until you find a convenient place to cross the lightly forested ridge to your left. Once on the opposite side of the ridge you have a couple of choices. A marked trail leads west across the drainage of Avalanche Gulch before turning north and then northeast up the mountain through light forest. However, most winter travelers seem content to follow the more open west bank of the drainage toward Horse Camp. Whichever route you choose, you climb moderately up the side of the mountain toward timberline and the open slopes of Avalanche Gulch. Before reaching actual timberline you should veer north for a short distance to reach the Sierra Club hut at Horse Camp.

The hut is a popular winter destination and the entrance will be shoveled unless you're the first party there after a storm. Inside you will find items of interest such as books, magazines and photos along with the furnishings. Although the hut is stocked with firewood, use it only in case of emergency. Likewise, the hut is not intended for overnight use. If you desire to camp in the area, find a suitable site nearby. The Sierra Club charges a $5 fee per tent ($3 for single) to camp on their property and gladly accepts donations for the upkeep of the hut. Dual pit toilets are located a short distance away.

FYI: Summer visitors have the added luxury of obtaining water from the nearby spring. Don't expect to have access to the spring during winter. Consequently, if you plan on camping, bring plenty of extra fuel for melting snow.

Warm-ups: Many locals consider Lily's to be the best restaurant in Mt. Shasta. Whether you desire breakfast, lunch, dinner or Sunday brunch, the tantalizing dishes and pleasant decor won't disappoint. Since the city of Mt. Shasta is just off Interstate 5, you don't have to worry about establishments closing up for the winter or operating for limited hours, as usually happens in more remote mountain communities. Lily's is located at 1013 S. Mt. Shasta Blvd. Call (530) 926-3372 for more information, or view their menus on the web at **www.LilysRestaurant.com**.

TRIP **4**

Mt. Shasta

Duration: Overnight trip
Distance: 11.25 miles round trip
Difficulty: Extreme
Elevation: 6950/14162
Maps: *Mt. Shasta & McCloud 7.5'* quadrangle; *A Guide to the Mt. Shasta Wilderness & Castle Crags Wilderness*, Shasta-Trinity National Forest

Introduction: Normally, even the climb of Mt. Shasta is considered to be quite a feat, but the idea of a winter ascent is met with raised eyebrows from those who clearly understand the difficulties posed by an off-season climb. Climbers must deal with the added challenges of potentially severe weather, avalanche possibilities, and a lack of running water, along with the normal obstacles such as higher altitudes and steep terrain. Winter weather at these elevations brings the possibility of high winds, frigid temperatures and white-out conditions, perhaps all at the same time. Unstable snow makes avalanches a real danger—Avalanche Gulch is so named for a reason. And, without access to running water, plenty of fuel is required so that stoves can complete the laborious task of melting snow. However, with a string of good weather, stable snow conditions and plenty of fuel, hearty recreationists may be able to overcome these adversities and attain one of the premier outdoor goals in the state—the summit of Mt. Shasta.

In summer an attempt on Mt. Shasta should be viewed circumspectly, but in winter even more attention must be given to the factors involved in climbing the mountain. This is certainly not a trip for the faint of heart or the inexperienced. Any winter attempt on Mt. Shasta is a major event requiring technical skill, stamina, advanced planning and proper equipment (including ice axes and crampons). Lives have been lost on this peak even in the seemingly more benign months of summer. Only experienced parties should consider the undertaking. Snow lingers on Mt. Shasta well into summer, making a spring snowshoe ascent a fine proposition when the days are longer and the weather more stable.

To say that Mt. Shasta is the dominant northern California landmark is an understatement, as the immense mountain bursts up into the sky 10,000 feet above the surrounding terrain. At 14,162 feet, Shasta is the second highest volcano in the Cascade chain, a mere 228 feet lower than Washington's Mt. Rainier. In addition, the peak is only 312 feet lower than California's Mt. Whitney, the highest piece of terra firma in the continental United States. Thanks to such a lofty status, Shasta offers a spectacular long-range vista from the summit, including many notable landmarks across northern California and southern Oregon.

Aside from the customary considerations of a winter climb, a few additional requirements are worth noting. First, each person must pay a $15 fee for the privilege of climbing above 10,000 feet on Mt. Shasta. Permits are available at the Mt. Shasta or McCloud ranger stations, although self-registering at Bunny Flat will be more convenient as long as climbers have the correct change or a personal check. The permit is valid for only three days from the date of registration. Second, group size in the Mt. Shasta Wilderness is limited to 10 people per party, and the length of stay is limited to 7 days. Third, for parties wishing to utilize an overnight campsite near Horse Camp, the Sierra Club charges $5 per tent or $3 for an individual (pay fees inside the hut). Finally, due to an increasing waste management problem in the alpine zone, the Forest Service has instituted a waste packout system. Climbers are required to pick up a zip-lock bag at Bunny Flat containing implements and instructions for the purpose of removing their feces from the upper slopes of the mountain. Upon return to Bunny Flat the bags can be deposited in a bin outside the restrooms.

How to get there: From Interstate 5, take the Central Mt. Shasta exit and follow Lake Street northeast through the city of Mt. Shasta. About a mile from the freeway, East Lake Street curves and becomes Everitt Memorial Highway. Follow the highway past the high school and out of town, climbing up the southwest slopes of Mt. Shasta to the end of the plowed road at Bunny Flat, 11 miles from I-5.

At Bunny Flat you will find a large parking area and a restroom building with four pit toilets and an information area. Avalanche and weather conditions are posted regularly along with other pertinent information.

Description: From Bunny Flat, head up the open slope for a short distance until you find a convenient place to cross the lightly forested ridge to your left. Once on the opposite side of the ridge, you have a couple of choices. A marked trail leads west across the drainage of Avalanche Gulch before turning north and then northeast up the mountain through light forest. However, most winter travelers seem content to follow the more open west bank of the drainage toward Horse Camp. Whichever route you choose, you climb moderately up the side of the mountain toward timberline and the open slopes of Avalanche Gulch. Before reaching actual timberline, you should veer north for a short distance if you want to stop at the Sierra Club Hut at Horse Camp.

From Horse Camp ascend the left-hand slope above the broad drainage of Avalanche Gulch to the bench at 10,400 feet containing Lake Helen. The lake will be impossible to locate in winter as even in most summers it remains buried beneath the snowpack. However, the flat does provide a decent basecamp for parties wishing to set up their tents at an elevation above Horse Camp. A pit toilet east of the lake serves the large number of spring and summer climbers who use this route, but in the absence of access to the toilet in winter you should follow the human waste packout system as mandated by the Mt. Shasta Ranger District (see Introduction).

Beyond the bench the climbing becomes steeper for the next 2500 vertical feet, culminating in a 35° pitch near the top. Climb up the right side of Avalanche Gulch, eventually passing to the right of The Heart at 12,000 feet and continuing to the saddle at 12,800 feet between Thumb Rock and Red Banks. The small saddle provides a fine spot for a rest stop before resuming the climb up the mountain.

From the saddle travel behind the Red Banks and proceed along the edge of the Konwakiton Glacier temporarily until you can regain the ridge up the Red Banks to the snowfield above. You continue up Misery Hill to the level summit snowfield and then head toward the col between the summit and a smaller pinnacle to the west. You make the final climb to the top up the northwest side of the summit rocks.

Standing on the summit of Mt. Shasta you realize the sheer enormity of this mountain rising nearly 11,000 feet above the surrounding terrain. Clear skies will reveal lesser Cascade volcanoes, such as Lassen Peak to the south and Mt. McLoughlin across the Oregon border. The top of Mt. Shasta provides successful climbers with the quintessential bird's-eye view.

Once you tear yourself away from this lofty perch follow your steps back to Bunny Flat.

FYI: Sargents Ridge, although slightly more technically difficult, provides a less avalanche-prone path to the summit than the standard Avalanche Gulch route. From Bunny Flat work your way eastward along the snow-covered extension of the Everitt Memorial Highway over to a basecamp at the old Ski Bowl cirque. Then climb northeast over easy terrain, connecting with Sargents Ridge near Shastarama Point. Follow the nearly level ridge 0.25 mile past Shastarama Point to where the angle increases. Climb the steeper terrain along Sargents Ridge for 1600 feet to the Red Banks-Thumb Rock saddle and then join the standard route from there.

For those who are interested in a guided attempt on Mt. Shasta, three guide services are licensed by the Forest Service:

Alpine Skills International	Shasta Mountain Guides	Sierra Wilderness
11040 Donner Pass Road	P.O. Box 1543	Seminars, Inc.
Truckee, CA 96161	1815 Eddy Drive	P.O. Box 988
(530) 582-9170	Mount Shasta, CA 96067	Mount Shasta, CA 96067
www.alpineskills.com	(530) 926-3117	(888) 797-6867
	www.shastaguides.com	**www.swsmtns.com**

Experienced skiers and snowboarders may want to pack along their gear for the thrilling descent down the slopes of the mountain after reaching the summit.

Warm-ups: See Trips 1-3.

CHAPTER 6

Lassen Volcanic National Park & Vicinity

From a variety of scenic vista points scattered across northern California, serene, snow-clad Lassen Peak presents a dramatic profile painted against the backdrop of an azure-blue winter sky, belying the region's recent past of turbulent volcanic activity. While Europe was perched on the brink of the disastrous struggle of World War I, Lassen Peak began to make profound rumblings of its own when on Memorial Day of 1914, the first of a series of significant eruptions took place which continued for the next three years. The catastrophic activity reached a climax nearly a year after the first eruption when in May of 1915, a substantial mudflow followed three days later by a major eruption left a vast area of devastation in their wake. More subdued volcanic activity continued over the years, but by 1921 the region went back into a period of dormancy—but who knows when the mountain may reawake? While evidence of Lassen's volcanic activity is spread all around the park, the 3-mile-long Devastated Area on the northeast flank of the peak is perhaps the most notable example of the volcanic zenith of 1915 readily visible to modern-day tourists.

Although Lassen Peak is by far and away the most dominant peak in the park today, geologists speculate that Lassen actually began as a volcanic vent on the northern slopes of a much larger ancestral Mount Tehama. Built up over the eons to a huge mountain with a base that may have been as much as 11 miles wide, Mount Tehama collapsed inward during an eruption, leaving behind a large caldera. Unlike Crater Lake's formation in the wake of a similar collapse of Mt. Mazama in southern Oregon, the caldera of Mount Tehama was breached and unable to hold water. The circle of peaks including Brokeoff Mountain, Mt. Diller, Pilot Pinnacle and Mt. Conard are remnants of this ancient basin that are still visible in our era. One can obtain an idea of just how large this caldera once was by visually connecting this ring of peaks. Once Mount Tehama became a mere shadow of its former greatness, Lassen Peak emerged as the preeminent landmark, and it is today considered to be the world's largest example of a plug dome volcano, rising 2000 feet above the surrounding terrain to an elevation of 10,457 feet above sea level.

Prior to all this relatively recent volcanic hubbub, Lassen Peak and nearby Cinder Cone were declared national monuments in 1907. This status was upgraded and expanded shortly after the renewed volcanic activity prompted legislators to set aside these uniquely volcanic lands as Lassen Volcanic National Park in 1916. Ever since, the park has been a living volcanic laboratory for tourists and scientists alike. Until the eruption of Mt. St. Helens in 1980, Lassen Peak held the distinction of experiencing the most recent volcanic eruption in the lower 48 states.

Prior to the arrival of Europeans, the area around Lassen Peak was a seasonal magnet for Native Americans from four distinct tribes: the Alsugewi, Maidu, Yahi and Yani. Due to the harsh climate, these tribes avoided the area during the colder months of the year, opting to follow game into the mountains during the more hospitable weather of summer and fall. In 1911 a member of the thought-to-be-extinct Yahi tribe named Ishi appeared near Oroville, and he subsequently lived out his remaining days at the University of California, Berkeley as an invaluable ethnological resource. Ishi was considered to be the last Stone Age survivor in the United States.

Jedediah Smith was perhaps the first European-American to observe Lassen Peak as he passed by on his trip to the California coast in 1828. Permanent habitations didn't begin to occur until settlers started to inhabit the area in conjunction with the California gold rush. In the 1800s a pair of overland trails were established to assist in this westward migration, the first by Peter Lassen in 1847, followed by William Nobles' route of 1852. The names of these two figures live on today, attached to a variety of park features.

Among the countless geologic attractions found within Lassen Volcanic National Park are lava flows, cinder cones, craters, hot springs, steaming sulphur vents, mud pots and jagged volcanic peaks. All of these are in addition to the normal features one associates with particularly scenic mountainous areas such as glaciated canyons, picturesque lakes, beautiful meadows and lush forests. Lassen Peak, although the highest, isn't the only high peak in the park, as nearby a number of other tall serrated mountains rise to heights of over 8000 feet. To the delight of backcountry users, most of the lands within the 106,000 acre park are managed as wilderness.

As expected, most of the visitation to Lassen occurs during the generally pleasant weather of summer. In winter, when snow closes all but 6 miles of the 29-mile Lassen Park Road, the backcountry expands significantly, much to the delight of snowshoers and skiers alike. Options for one-day outings and multi-day adventures are practically unlimited. Whether lakes, peaks, canyons or geothermal features are the goal, Lassen offers an abundance of options that will appeal to even the most critical outdoor enthusiast. Although 13 trips within the park are described in this chapter, they are only a representative sample of the best Lassen has to offer, by no means an exhaustive list. Since the number of visitors drops so dramatically in winter, recreationists have great potential for solitude amid the beautiful scenery. Fortunately, due to the national park status, snowmobiles are forbidden within the park boundaries.

Lassen Park has two main centers of winter activity, both located where the Lassen Park Road is closed by winter snows. Scenic Manzanita Lake is the northern hub for cross-country skiing and snowshoeing, offering easy tours around the lake and nearby campground or more moderate trips along the Nobles Emigrant Trail and the Manzanita Creek Trail. Due to an elevation below 6000 feet, the season at Manzanita Lake is shorter than on the opposite end of the park. Once winter is on the wane and snowplows have cleared the Lassen Park Road 10 miles past the lake, the focus on the north end of the park shifts to the Devastated Area trailhead and an extended spring season above 6500 feet.

On the south side of the park, most winter visitors begin their excursions from the trailhead near the Lassen Chalet. A number of trips, spanning the range from easy to extreme, begin from this staging area. With an elevation near 6750 feet, this end of the park offers plenty of snow during all but the driest of winters. The scenery on most of these routes is breathtaking. The Southwest Campground is open year-round for those parties interested in snowcamping at a charge of $8 per night (payable at the entrance station). Although the Lassen Chalet is closed for the winter, the restrooms on the ground floor remain open, providing campers and recreationists with running water.

Whether you plan on entering through the Manzanita Lake or the Southwest Entrance, visitors will have to pay a fee to enter Lassen Volcanic National Park. Typically the stations are manned on weekends when the weather is decent, but when rangers are not present each party is expected to self-register (be sure to have the exact change). A 7-day pass in 2000 was $10—Lassen or Golden Eagle passes are only available at park headquarters in Mineral during office hours, 8:00 to 4:30 Monday–Friday.

For those who prefer a guided excursion across the snows of Lassen Park, the Park Service offers ranger-led, 1 to 2 mile tours on Saturdays from early January to early April. These afternoon trips leave the Lassen Chalet and last approximately 1.5 to 2 hours. Call park headquarters for more information.

Location: Lassen Park is approximately 50 miles east of both Red Bluff and Redding, and 40 miles west of Susanville.

Access: State Highway 89 traverses Lassen Park from north to south, and within the park is referred to as the Lassen Park Road. In winter less than a mile of this road is plowed from the Highway 44 junction (46 miles east of Redding) south to the Manzanita Lake Entrance (Trips 5-9), and only 5 miles are plowed from the Highway 36 junction (48 miles east of Red Bluff) north to the Lassen Chalet (Trips 10-17).

Amenities: Choices are sporadic and prone to seasonal closures during the winter months. You may be able to find gas, a meal or a night's lodging in some of the small communities along Highways 36 and 44, but don't plan your survival around the possibility. The nearest full-service community to the park is Chester, 25 miles east on Highway 36.

Season & Weather: Lassen Park offers two seasons for winter sports. Once a significant snowpack closes the Lassen Park Road, both Manzanita Lake and the Lassen Chalet become winter trailheads for cross-country skiers and snowshoers. In addition, the old ski area near the Chalet sees quite a few snowboarders climbing up the slopes for the ride back down. Winter activities usually begin sometime around Thanksgiving and often extend through the first weeks of April.

At the first hint of spring when the snow begins to melt around Manzanita Lake (elev. 5850), park officials begin the arduous task of plowing the 10-mile section of the Lassen Park Road up to the Devastated Area parking lot at 6450 feet. Once this task is completed, the spring season begins as recreationists now have access to the heart of Lassen's backcountry. Depending on the snow conditions, another couple of months are added to the season by moving the trailhead up to the Devastated Area.

Once the road has been cleared up to the Devastated Area, snowplows turn their attention to the southern part of the Lassen Park Road. Initially, the road is opened only as far as the Sulfur Works (elev. 6995), 1 mile from the Chalet. As the snowplows continue to progress up the road, additional parking areas are opened at the Bumpass Hell and Lassen Peak trailheads. The season is correspondingly extended well into spring—Lassen Peak is still a snow climb through the month of June in a year of average snowfall.

Lassen Peak experiences much the same weather patterns as Mt. Shasta, although there can be a substantial difference between the conditions at their respective summits as Shasta is nearly 4000 vertical feet higher. Pacific storms generally move in to the area accompanied by southwest winds and increasing cloudiness. Snowfall can be quite dramatic, as evidenced by 20-foot snow banks near the summit of the Lassen Park Road. The high country of Lassen Park is best avoided when foul weather is imminent.

PERMITS

Day Use: Lassen requests that all day users sign in and out at the trail registers located at the Lassen Chalet, and near the Loomis Ranger Station at Manzanita Lake.

Overnight Use: Backcountry permits are required for any overnight stay in Lassen Park. Permits can be obtained in person at park headquarters in Mineral (open Monday–Friday, 8 a.m. to 4:30 p.m.), or by phone (530) 595-4444 ext. 5134. Leave vehicles in designated parking areas only.

MAPS

Lassen Volcanic National Park & Vicinity 1:62,500, 1986, paper Wilderness Press (800) 443-7227	Lassen Volcanic National Park, Hiking Map & Guide 1:48,000, 1997, paper or plastic Earthwalk Press	Plumas National Forest 1:126,720, 1992, paper Plumas National Forest

PARK SERVICE

Lassen Volcanic National Park
P.O. Box 100
Mineral, CA 96063-0110
(530) 595-4444

IMPORTANT PHONE NUMBERS

Loomis Ranger Station   (530) 595-4444 ext. 5187
Ranger-led Snowshoe Walks   (530) 595-4444 ext. 5133

WEBSITES

Lassen Volcanic National Park   www.nps.gov/lavo/

TRIP **5**

Manzanita Lake

see map
on page
44

Duration: One-half day
Distance: 1.75 miles loop trip
Difficulty: Easy
Elevation: 5855
Map: *Manzanita Lake* 7.5′ quadrangle

Introduction: A prettier sight than a winter view of Lassen Peak across Manzanita Lake after a fresh dusting of snow is hard to imagine. When the sky is clear and the snow is pristine, fortunate snowshoers can revel in the beautiful scenery as they travel the easy, short loop on the level terrain around Manzanita Lake. Although the scenery is pleasant and the route around the lake is easy, visitation at this end of the park is less than at the Southwest Entrance.

The season here is relatively short, confined to the true months of winter as the snow around the lake begins to quickly disappear at the first hint of spring. Park employees typically begin to plow the road from this side of the park sometime in March or early April. Once the snow is gone at Manzanita Lake, winter recreationists often use the nearby campground throughout spring as a basecamp for their sallies into the snowy high country beyond the Devastated Area.

How to get there: From Highway 44, approximately 13 miles southwest of Old Station and 44 miles northwest of Susanville, turn onto Highway 89. Travel down 89 to the parking area near the entrance station.

Description: From the parking area, head along the Lassen Park Road to Manzanita Lake and follow the shoreline for 0.2 mile. Leave the road and proceed along the route of the hiking trail east of the lake another 0.25 mile to the bridge crossing of Manzanita Creek. You continue around the east, south and west shorelines of the lake until you reach the outlet, which is also crossed by a bridge. From the crossing follow the marked trail back to your starting point.

FYI: You can extend your journey around the lake by following the trail through the nearby campground.

Warm-ups: Choices are limited around the north end of the park in winter, but you may find something open in the Hat Creek area: Indian John's Pizza & Cafe at the

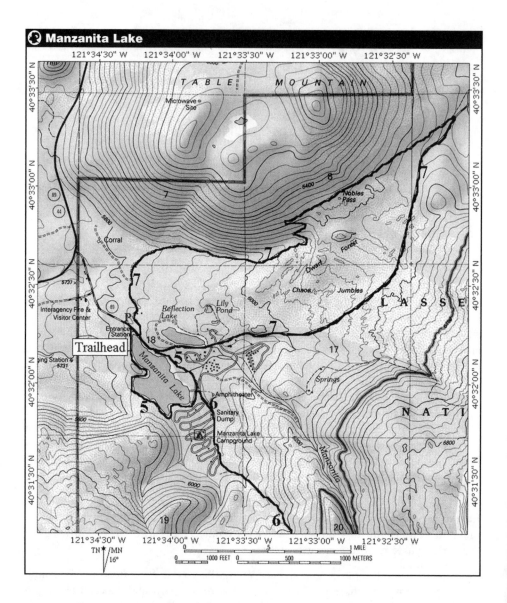

Hat Creek Resort is 10 miles northeast on Highway 44, and Uncle Runt's and the Old Station Cafe & Pub are 12 miles northeast near the 44/89 junction.

TRIP **6**

Manzanita Creek

Duration: Full day
Distance: 9.75 miles round trip
Difficulty: Moderate to difficult
Elevation: 5855/7200
Map: *Manzanita Lake* & *Lassen Peak* 7.5′ quadrangles

Introduction: Naming this route the Manzanita Creek Trail can be a tad deceptive as the path avoids the namesake creek for all but the final stretch of the nearly 5-mile journey to the head of the canyon below Crescent Cliff. Once past Manzanita Lake and the nearby campground, snowshoers enter into forested terrain away from the creek, forsaking the expansive panoramas so common to other more popular routes in Lassen Park. However, the trip isn't completely viewless as you have glimpses of Lassen Peak and Loomis Peak near the mid-point and the impressive profile of Crescent Cliff at the end.

What this trip does provide is the potential for solitude. If strolling through the backcountry with little or no company is a goal, then this route promises to deliver. The Manzanita Lake side of the park sees far fewer winter visitors than the Southwest Entrance, and of the limited number of recreationists who do visit this side only a small amount choose to take the journey up Manzanita Creek. Along with the peace and quiet, snowshoers will have the challenge of following the imperfectly marked touring route through the trees. A lack of landmarks along the way combined with the infrequently placed orange markers make this a trip for parties with good routefinding abilities only. Overnighters will find good campsites along the creek, provided the slopes below Loomis Peak are avoided.

How to get there: From Highway 44, approximately 13 miles southwest of Old Station and 44 miles northwest of Susanville, turn onto Highway 89. Travel down 89 to the parking area near the entrance station.

Description: Follow the Lassen Park Road past Manzanita Lake and Reflection Lake to the entrance into Manzanita Lake Campground.

Leave the Lassen Park Road and follow the access road on a winding course across Manzanita Creek, past the southern tip of Manzanita Lake and toward the campground. You continue on the main road past the turnoffs for the various campground loops until you reach the last of the loops (Loop F). Bear left at this junction

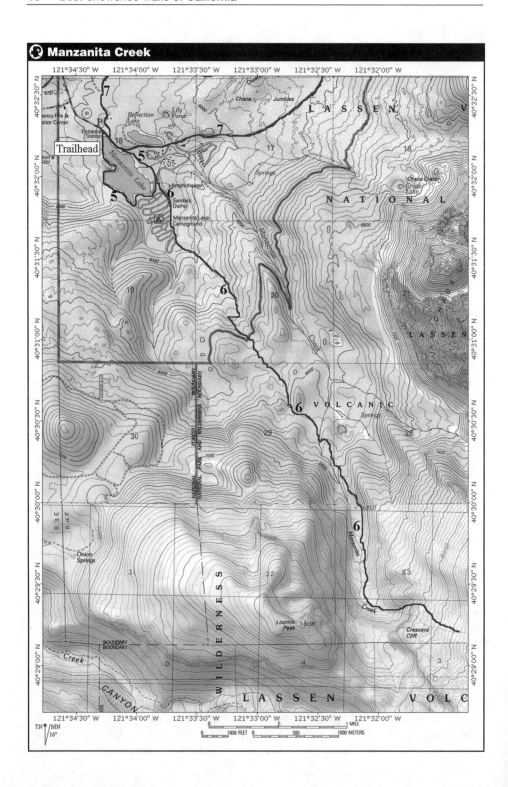

and find the summer trailhead approximately 25 feet up the road, and just over 1.5 miles from the park entrance station.

Initially, the route of the Manzanita Creek Trail is fairly easy to follow along the course of the abandoned fire road through scattered forest. Soon the trees, mainly Jeffrey pines and white firs, begin to thicken, and the swath cut through the trees more clearly identifies the route of the trail. You continue on a steady, mild-to-moderate climb until the terrain eases and you have a glimpse of Lassen and Loomis peaks through the scattered trees. This easy stretch leads to a gap overlooking the Manzanita Creek drainage. From the gap, a mild 0.25-mile climb leads to the bridge across the creek.

Once across the creek, the route follows the east side of the drainage through moderate forest cover until you reach the first of the meadows in the upper canyon, approximately 4.5 miles from the park entrance station. Above you lies the dramatic face of Crescent Cliff.

FYI: Avoid the slopes below Loomis Peak during avalanche conditions.

Warm-ups: See Trip 5

Lassen Peak as seen from the Manzanita Creek Trail

TRIP **7**

Nobles Emigrant Trail Loop

Duration: Three-quarter day
Distance: 6 miles loop trip
Difficulty: Easy to moderate
Elevation: 5870/6265
Map: *Manzanita Lake* 7.5′ quadrangle

Introduction: Long before the Lassen Park Road was improved in 1931, pioneers traveled from northeastern California to the upper Sacramento Valley on a wagon route discovered by prospector William H. Nobles in 1851. Convinced of the superiority over Peter Lassen's road built in 1847, Nobles secured financial backing for improving this natural route and opened the road to settlers in 1852. Once the transcontinental railroad was completed in 1869, Nobles' Emigrant Trail fell out of favor as a major emigrant route, as did the majority of pioneer trails. The old roadway is still quite visible today, and hikers have the opportunity to travel over this historic route that roughly parallels the Lassen Park Road.

Winter enthusiasts can enjoy the first 3.25 miles of the Nobles Emigrant Trail from Manzanita Lake to Sunflower Flat on a marked route, returning to the lake on the snow-covered Lassen Park Road. Most of the trail passes through quiet forest, which thins enough occasionally to allow fine views of Chaos Crags and Lassen Peak. The first part of the journey is a moderate, 2.3-mile climb across the southeast flank of Table Mountain to Nobles Pass, followed by a steady descent to Sunflower Flat. From the flat the route follows the easy route of the Lassen Park Road back to Manzanita Lake. For solitude seekers, the Nobles Emigrant Trail sees far less winter use than the short, easy trail around Manzanita Lake (Trip 5).

How to get there: From Highway 44, approximately 13 miles southwest of Old Station and 44 miles northwest of Susanville, turn onto Highway 89. Travel down 89 to the parking area near the entrance station.

Description: The Nobles Emigrant Trail begins about 150 feet beyond the Manzanita Lake entrance station on a service road branching north from the Lassen Park Road marked service road only. Periodically placed yellow reflectorized markers will help guide you along the route as you follow this gently graded, snow-covered roadway past a maintenance building, continuing on a winding course for 0.5 mile until the road curves east. Here the grade of the Nobles Emigrant Trail increases as you climb

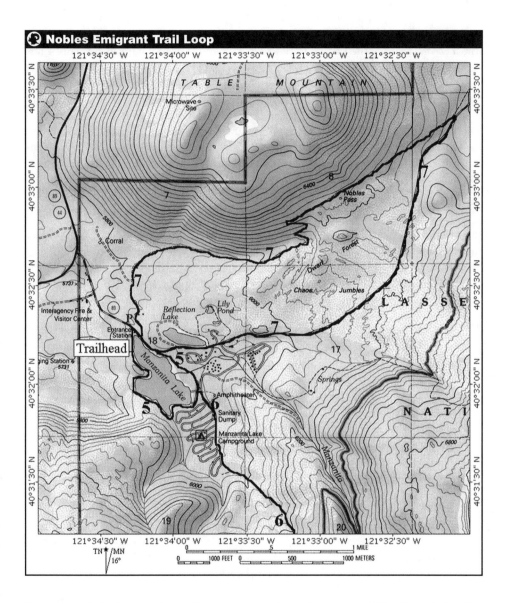

Nobles Emigrant Trail Loop

through a light forest of ponderosa pine, lodgepole pine and Shasta red fir. You ascend at a mild-to-moderate rate up a drainage swale for a brief time until the trail leads you up along the hillside. Through the trees you can see Chaos Crags and a part of Lassen Peak to the south.

At 1.5 miles from the trailhead you begin a series of switchbacks that take you up a steep hillside. Once you have surmounted the hill, the grade eases as you stroll through scattered fir and pine. One-third mile of easy snowshoeing beyond the end of the switchbacks brings you to a short, moderate climb up to Nobles Pass, 2.33 miles from the trailhead.

Beyond Nobles Pass the route makes a continuous descent through moderate forest cover down to the Lassen Park Road, 3.25 miles from the trailhead. This intersection is just below Sunflower Flat.

Turning southwest, you follow the Lassen Park Road back toward Manzanita Lake, climbing briefly for 0.3 mile. A level stretch of highway precedes the descent that will take you back to the starting point. Near where the descent begins you encounter a lighter forest that grants fine views of Chaos Crags to the south. Soon, Lassen Peak begins to peek out from behind the north shoulder of the Crags. Near the 5-mile mark you reenter thick forest and a short distance farther begin to glimpse the Manzanita Lake Campground on your left through the trees. Follow the gentle grade of the road past the Loomis Ranger Station, the Loomis Museum, and Reflection and Manzanita lakes to the parking area, which closes the 6-mile loop.

FYI: If you are considering reversing the description and following the Lassen Park Road to Sunflower Flat as the first leg of your journey, the junction between the trail and the road is extremely difficult to discern (even in summer this trail junction is not marked). Therefore, you should observe the description as written, following the marked trail to Sunflower Flat and returning along the Lassen Park Road.

Warm-ups: See Trip 5.

TRIP 8

Devastated Area

see map
on page
51

Duration: One-half to three-quarter day
Distance: Varies: 2-4.5 miles round trip
  (spring trip)
Difficulty: Easy to moderate
Elevation: 6455/8000
Map: *West Prospect Peak* & *Reading Peak* 7.5′ quadrangles

Introduction: The desire to observe a volcanic landscape in process was one of the driving forces behind the creation of Lassen Volcanic National Park. Certainly, one of the best areas from which to witness some of the destruction that volcanic forces are capable of creating is the Devastated Area, on the northeast slope of Lassen Peak. On May 19th, 1915, hot lava spewed forth from Lassen Peak, melting the deep

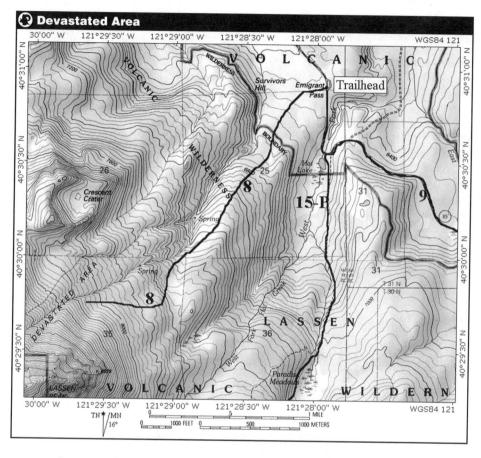

snowpack accumulated from the previous winter's storms. The resulting mass of slush and rock, 0.5-mile wide and 20 feet deep, hurtled down the mountainside, spilling into the canyons of Lost and Hat creeks. Three days later, Lassen Peak erupted, sending a desiccating cloud of vaporized lava and super-heated gas down the course of the mudslide, flattening every tree still standing in its path, creating a swath of destruction 1.25 miles wide and 5 miles in length. The resulting destruction was aptly named the Devastated Area. After 85 years, the sight is not quite as devastated as it once looked, with scattered lodgepole and Jeffrey pines springing up out of the sandy soil. The smattering of short conifers still allows recreationists to view the beautiful surroundings without too much obstruction.

If snowshoers are able to reach the Devastated Area, they can chart their own path across the winter landscape, enjoying a continuous view of the northeast side of Lassen Peak. Most of the winter, an 11-mile journey from Manzanita Lake up the Lassen Park Road is required just to reach the starting point. However, at the conclusion of winter, the Park Service begins plowing the roadway, and usually completes this stretch sometime in early spring. Adequate snow conditions at 6500 feet typically last another 4 to 6 weeks, providing an extended season for snowshoers and skiers alike, who can enjoy the amenities of the Devastated Area without the 11-mile approach.

How to get there: From Highway 44, approximately 13 miles southwest of Old Station and 44 miles northwest of Susanville, turn onto Highway 89. Travel down Highway 89 about 0.5 mile to the entrance station and proceed up the Lassen Park Road for another 10.5 miles to the parking lot at the end of the plowed road.

Description: From the parking lot, cross the highway and work your way up toward Lassen Peak on top of the left-hand bank of Lost Creek. A scattered forest of young lodgepole and Jeffrey pines allows near continuous views of the peak and the surrounding countryside. The moderate slope continues up toward Lassen Peak for a couple of miles until the terrain becomes steeper near the 8000-foot level. From there, retrace your steps to the trailhead.

FYI: Avoid the area below the steeper slopes of Lassen Peak's northeast side when avalanche conditions are unstable.

Warm-ups: See Trip 5.

T R I P 9

Devastated Area to Summit Lake

see map on page **53**

Duration: Three-quarter day
Distance: 7.5 miles round trip (spring)
Difficulty: Easy to moderate
Elevation: 6455/6685
Map: *West Prospect Peak & Reading Peak* 7.5' quadrangles

Introduction: During the spring season, the snow-covered Lassen Park Road offers an easy route from the Devastated Area to Summit Lake. The route of the roadway is easily discernible and the grade of the climb never exceeds moderate. Although the close proximity of the lake to the road makes Summit Lake a tourist magnet in summer, the frozen lake offers a pleasant destination during the win-

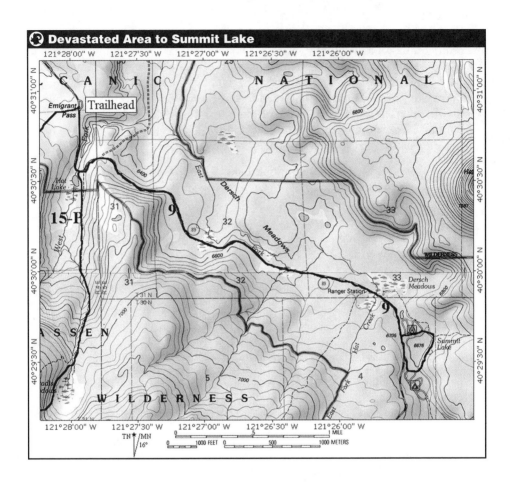

ter. Chances are you will have to share the lake with only the trees around its shore on most winter days. The Lassen Park Road beyond Summit Lake provides access into the heart of the park's backcountry, but the road climbs at a much steeper pitch beyond the lake.

How to get there: From Highway 44, approximately 13 miles southwest of Old Station and 44 miles northwest of Susanville, turn onto Highway 89. Travel down 89 about 0.5 mile to the entrance station and proceed up the Lassen Park Road for another 10.5 miles to the parking lot at the end of the plowed road.

Description: From the Devastated Area parking lot, proceed up the snow-covered extension of the Lassen Park Road toward Reading Peak on a moderate ascent through a young lodgepole-pine and red-fir forest. Not quite a half-mile from the trailhead the road drops briefly around a curve, crossing the drainage of the West Fork of Hat Creek just north of Hat Lake. Beyond the creek the road resumes the ascent as you wind around into a denser covering of forest. The climb continues through the trees until you reach two small pockets of Dersch Meadows at 1.5 miles and 2 miles.

You proceed along the road on a mild-to-moderate climb through light forest as the grade of the road eventually increases. Follow the road on a winding course to another piece of Dersch Meadows at 2.75 miles. Soon you pass the Summit Lake Ranger Station on your left and shortly afterward come to the northeast shore of Summit Lake. Turn down the access road for the Summit Lake North Campground, work your way around the east shore of the forest-lined lake to the access road for the Summit Lake South Campground, and follow that road back to the main highway. From there retrace your steps back to the trailhead.

FYI: A fine extension to the trip to Summit Lake is the 1.25 -mile climb from the lake to the top of Hat Mountain.

Warm-ups: See Trip 5.

T R I P 10

Sulfur Works Loop

Duration: One-half day
Distance: 2 miles round trip
Difficulty: Easy
Elevation: 6735/6995
Map: *Lassen Peak* 7.5′ quadrangle

see map on page 56

Introduction: A trip to the Sulfur Works is perhaps one of the best ways for newcomers to become acquainted with Lassen Volcanic National Park in the winter. The short route follows the easy grade of the Lassen Park Road through open terrain, allowing splendid views of the topography beyond the southwest entrance to the park. Such a close destination gives winter visitors the most accessible glimpse into the geothermal activities for which the park is famous. As billed, the Sulfur Works provides all the sights, sounds and smells associated with the fumaroles and mud pots that appear periodically throughout the Lassen area. Beginners and families should enjoy the opportunity to get a glimpse of this active geological area without expending a great deal of time or energy. Even for the more experienced, the route to the Sulfur Works provides a quick and easy journey to an interesting lunch spot.

How to get there: From Highway 36 near Morgan Summit, turn north onto Highway 89. This junction is approximately 5 miles east of Mineral and 25 miles west of Chester. Follow 89 north to the Southwest Entrance of Lassen Park and continue up the road to the plowed parking area 5.5 miles from the 36/89 junction.

Approaching the steaming Sulfur Works in Lassen Volcanic National Park

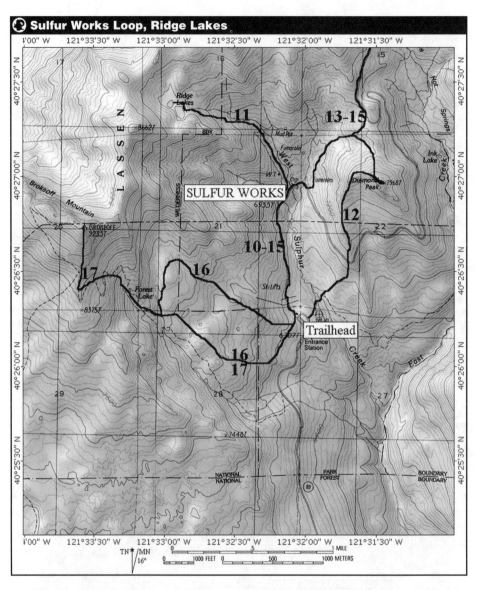

The Southwest Entrance station is manned during daylight hours on weekends, but is generally unoccupied during the week. When a ranger is not present you can self-register, which will require exact change ($10 per vehicle for a 7-day pass). On weekdays you can acquire change or purchase yearly permits at park headquarters in Mineral during office hours, 8:00 to 4:30 Monday-Friday.

Restrooms with running water are available at the Lassen Chalet near the parking lot, but the rest of the building has been closed to winter use since the ski park was abandoned in the early Nineties. Snow camping is allowed at the nearby Southwest Walk-in Campground for $10 per night.

Description: Begin your trip by snowshoeing up the mild grade of the Lassen Park Road northbound from the Lassen Chalet, quickly passing the site of the abandoned ski area. The open terrain allows pleasant views of the surrounding countryside as you parallel the West Sulfur Creek drainage. As you continue up the road towards the Sulfur Works you should be able to spy steam emanating from the various fumaroles scattered around this geothermal area. Actually, before you see the steam you more than likely will smell a faint odor of rotten eggs, which is actually hydrogen sulfide escaping into the air. Near the 0.75-mile mark you cross a bridge over a tributary of West Sulfur Creek and then quickly come to the Sulfur Works.

When conditions are stable you may be able to wander along the course of the short trail that loops around the area. Stay on the marked path of the boardwalk at all times. If park officials have deemed the snow to be unstable surrounding the Sulfur Works you may have to observe the geothermal activity from the safety of the road. Warning signs should be posted when potential instability is present.

Once you have enjoyed the Sulfur Works, begin your return to the parking lot by following the Lassen Park Road a short distance beyond the Sulfur Works around a curve to the south. Find a convenient place from which to leave the road and descend to the east bank of Sulfur Creek. Follow the drainage back south toward the Lassen Chalet. Northeast of the parking lot, you must cross the snow-covered bridge spanning the creek and then climb up the steep hillside to your car.

FYI: Park employees usually begin plowing the Lassen Park Road sometime in early spring, beginning at Manzanita Lake and continuing to the Devastated Area. Once that section is clear, they turn their attention to the terrain above the Southwest Entrance, plowing the first mile up to the Sulfur Works. Check with park headquarters on the conditions of the road if you're planning a trip in late winter or early spring.

Warm-ups: Watering holes and eateries are few in this area, especially during the week. If you're heading west from the park, breakfast, lunch or dinner can be had at the Lassen Mineral Lodge, but usually only on weekends and holidays. For those in search of overnight accommodations, the motel is open all year, and the owners may make the restaurant available during the week for groups with reservations. The facility is located in the small community of Mineral, 5 miles west of the 36/89 junction. For more information, call (530) 595-4422 or visit their website at **www.minerallodge.com**.

TRIP **11**

Ridge Lakes

Duration: One-half day
Distance: 3.5 miles round trip
Difficulty: Moderate
Elevation: 6735/7975
Map: *Lassen Peak* 7.5′ quadrangle

see map on page 56

Introduction: The first half of your journey to Ridge Lakes follows the gentle grade of the Lassen Park Road, gaining a mere 200 vertical feet in 0.75 mile. The second half is a different story altogether as 1000 feet of elevation must be overcome in the course of a 1-mile climb. The route is supposedly marked but you will probably experience less frustration if you forget about the markers and find your own way along the narrow ridge to the lakes. Once at the lakes you have the option of climbing higher to the crest of the ridge above for fine views of nearby Brokeoff Mountain and Mt. Diller, as well as the surrounding terrain.

How to get there: From Highway 36 near Morgan Summit, turn north onto Highway 89. This junction is approximately 5 miles east of Mineral and 25 miles west of Chester. Follow 89 north to the Southwest Entrance of Lassen Park and continue up the road to the plowed parking area 5.5 miles from the 36/89 junction.

The Southwest Entrance station is manned during daylight hours on weekends, but is generally unoccupied during the week. When a ranger is not present you can self-register, which will require exact change ($10 per vehicle for a 7-day pass). On weekdays you can acquire change or purchase yearly permits at park headquarters in Mineral during office hours, 8:00 to 4:30 Monday-Friday.

Restrooms with running water are available at the Lassen Chalet near the parking lot, but the rest of the building has been closed to winter use since the ski park was abandoned in the early Nineties. Snow camping is allowed at the nearby Southwest Walk-in Campground for $10 per night.

Description: Begin your trip by snowshoeing up the mild grade of the Lassen Park Road northbound from the Lassen Chalet, quickly passing the site of the abandoned ski area. The open terrain allows pleasant views of the surrounding countryside as you parallel the West Sulfur Creek drainage. Near the 0.75-mile mark, you cross a bridge over a tributary of the creek just before encountering the Sulfur Works.

As soon as you cross the first bridge, veer away from the road and climb up the narrow ridge between the two branches of West Sulfur Creek. You continue to climb moderately steeply up the ridge as it bends northwest and then west toward Ridge Lakes. The two small lakes lie at the head of an open basin, 0.25 mile southeast of a prominent saddle in the ridge above.

FYI: Avoid the slopes south of the lakes when avalanche danger is present.

Warm-ups: Stover's St. Bernard Lodge is about the only restaurant anywhere close to Lassen Park that remains open during the winter for any days besides the weekends. Located 14.5 miles east of the 36/89 junction, the inn serves steak, prime rib, seafood and chicken dishes at moderate prices for dinner and famous "St. Bernard" burgers for lunch. The relocated building was originally constructed in 1912 and the decor, including lace tablecloths, kerosene lamps and a wood-burning stove, hearken diners back to a bygone era. The antique, full-service bar will appeal to those in search of a hot drink—try a "St. Bernard," a mixture of hot chocolate and peppermint schnapps with a dollop of whipped cream. The lodge is open every day but Tuesdays and Wednesdays for dinner, with lunch available on the weekends. Call (530) 258-3382 for reservations or more information.

TRIP 12

Diamond Peak Loop

see map
on page
60

Duration: One-half day
Distance: 3.25 miles loop trip
Difficulty: Moderate to difficult
Elevation: 6735/7968
Map: *Lassen Peak* 7.5' quadrangle

Introduction: Much of the terrain in the south end of Lassen Park provides great scenery without the obstruction of dense forests. The view from the summit of 7968-foot Diamond Peak has to rank as one of the best park vistas so close to a trailhead during the winter season. Standing atop the knife-edge summit ridge, snowshoers will appreciate the gorgeous surroundings, which include some of the park's more dramatic peaks.

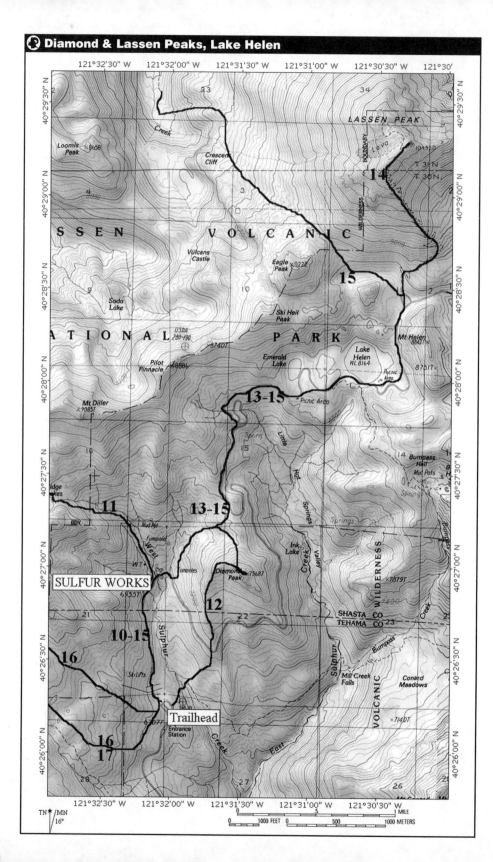

After the first mile along the Lassen Park Road, the climb is technically challenging thanks to some steep slopes and a summit ridge that is quite narrow. There is some avalanche potential here as well, so ascents of Diamond Peak should be attempted only by experienced parties and only when conditions are stable.

How to get there: From Highway 36 near Morgan Summit, turn north onto Highway 89. This junction is approximately 5 miles east of Mineral and 25 miles west of Chester. Follow 89 north to the Southwest Entrance of Lassen Park and continue up the road to the plowed parking area 5.5 miles from the 36/89 junction.

The Southwest Entrance station is manned during daylight hours on weekends, but is generally unoccupied during the week. When a ranger is not present you can self-register, which will require exact change ($10 per vehicle for a 7-day pass). On weekdays you can acquire change or purchase yearly permits at park headquarters in Mineral during office hours, 8:00 to 4:30 Monday-Friday.

Restrooms with running water are available at the Lassen Chalet near the parking lot, but the rest of the building has been closed to winter use since the ski park was abandoned in the early Nineties. Snow camping is allowed at the nearby Southwest Walk-in Campground for $10 per night.

Description: Begin your trip by snowshoeing up the mild grade of the Lassen Park Road northbound from the Lassen Chalet, quickly passing the site of the abandoned ski area. The open terrain allows pleasant views of the surrounding countryside as you parallel the West Sulfur Creek drainage. Near the 0.75-mile mark, you cross a bridge over a tributary of the creek just before encountering the Sulfur Works.

Remaining on the Lassen Park Road, you leave the Sulfur Works geothermal area following a curve. Just past the bridge crossing of the last tributary of West Sulfur Creek, find a convenient spot from which to scale the hillside to the north of the curve. You climb up the moderately steep hillside well above the creek on an arcing ascent that ultimately veers away from the drainage and bends east toward Diamond Peak Saddle, 0.3 mile north of the summit of Diamond Peak. Rather than go all the way to the saddle, turn south and begin a steeper climb up the lightly forested hillside on the north side of Diamond Peak. As you near the top, try to find the easiest spot from which to gain the narrow, summit ridge and then carefully follow the ridge to the top of the mountain. As you approach the ridge keep a wary eye out for the cornices above and then avoid that edge once on the crest.

The view from the knife-edged summit of Diamond Peak is truly spectacular, a sweeping 360° vista of the terrain encompassing the southern end of the park. Although the parking lot is only 1 air mile away, there exists a sense of remoteness atop this isolated aerie that belies mere distance. Notable landmarks seen from the top include Lassen Peak, the crown jewel of the park, as well as Brokeoff Mountain, Diller Peak, Eagle Peak and Mt. Conard. A part of Lake Almanor is also visible off in the distance.

After enjoying the views, you should begin your descent by heading northwest along the summit ridge and then following the extension of the ridge as it arcs around to the south. The descent route continues to be blessed with fine views until you're halfway back to the parking lot, where a smattering of trees begin to inhibit the vistas. About 0.75 mile from the summit you intersect the Lassen Park Road where it meets the crest of the ridge. You cross the road and head down through open terrain toward the West Sulfur Creek drainage, aiming for the bridge across the creek. Once over the creek you make the steep climb up the hillside to the parking lot and the conclusion of your adventure.

FYI: There is a marked route from the Sulfur Works to the saddle north of Diamond Peak which skiers use to shave off nearly 2 miles of travel along the Lassen Park Road and which is very similar to a part of the route described here. However, as with most marked routes within the park, following the markers can be a exercise in frustration. Chances are you will see plenty of tracks ascending the hillside if your visit is well after the last snowfall.

Another reason skiers use this bypass is to avoid the avalanches that oftentimes spill across the Lassen Park Road directly east of Diamond Peak. However, avoiding the road does not insure total safety, as avalanches have been know to occur in areas along this route as well.

Warm-ups: See Trip 11.

A view of Mt. Diller from the summit of Diamond Peak

TRIP 13

Lake Helen

see map
on page
60

Duration: Full day
Distance: 7.5 miles round trip
Difficulty: Moderate
Elevation: 6735/8185
Map: *Lassen Peak* 7.5' quadrangle

Introduction: This trip offers snowshoers a great way to experience some of the best scenery Lassen Park has to offer. Lake Helen was named in tribute to the first woman known to have scaled 10,457-foot Lassen Peak, Helen T. Brodt, in 1864. Situated below the southern slopes of Lassen Peak, the picturesque lake affords superb views of the namesake mountain. Along the way various other park landmarks are visible, including Brokeoff Mountain, Mt. Diller, Diamond Peak and Eagle Peak. In addition, the route passes Sulfur Works and offers the possibility of a side trip to Bumpass Hell, two of the park's most famous active geothermal areas. For those in search of an overnight or multi-day adventure, a basecamp at Lake Helen is a grand place from which to explore the heart of the park.

Although this route follows the Lassen Park Road for most of the way, there are a couple of areas that will require some routefinding. The first is the bypass between Sulfur Works and Diamond Peak Saddle, which saves nearly 2 additional miles of snowshoeing by forsaking the road. The second occurs in the area above Little Hot Springs Valley, where finding any trace of the road is difficult by midwinter. Fortunately, most of the terrain is open, which allows snowshoers to locate landmarks fairly easily, making navigating these two sections reasonably straightforward. However, that same open terrain may present additional problems if the weather turns sour, producing high winds or whiteout conditions. Get an accurate weather forecast before setting out on any journey into the Lassen high country!

Parties fortunate enough to have decent weather who are willing to accept the modest routefinding challenges should find great enjoyment in the journey to Lake Helen. The scenery along the entire route, through both the West and East Fork Sulfur Creek drainages and around Lake Helen is superb and awe-inspiring.

How to get there: From Highway 36 near Morgan Summit, turn north onto Highway 89. This junction is approximately 5 miles east of Mineral and 25 miles west of

Chester. Follow 89 north to the Southwest Entrance of Lassen Park and continue up the road to the plowed parking area 5.5 miles from the 36/89 junction.

The Southwest Entrance station is manned during daylight hours on weekends, but is generally unoccupied during the week. When a ranger is not present you can self-register, which will require exact change ($10 per vehicle for a 7-day pass). On weekdays you can acquire change or purchase yearly permits at park headquarters in Mineral during office hours, 8:00 to 4:30 Monday-Friday.

Restrooms with running water are available at the Lassen Chalet near the parking lot, but the rest of the building has been closed to winter use since the ski park was abandoned in the early Nineties. Snow camping is allowed at the nearby Southwest Walk-in Campground for $10 per night.

Description: Begin your trip by snowshoeing up the mild grade of the Lassen Park Road northbound from the Lassen Chalet, quickly passing the site of the abandoned ski area. The open terrain allows pleasant views of the surrounding countryside as you parallel the West Sulfur Creek drainage. Near the 0.75-mile mark, you cross a bridge over a tributary of the creek just before encountering the Sulfur Works.

Remaining on the Lassen Park Road, you leave the Sulfur Works geothermal area following a curve. Just past the bridge crossing of the last tributary of West Sulfur Creek, find a convenient spot from which to scale the hillside to the north of the curve. You climb up the moderately steep hillside well above the creek on an arcing ascent that ultimately veers away from the drainage and bends east toward Diamond Peak Saddle, which is 0.3 mile north of the summit of Diamond Peak. Regain the road at the saddle near a horseshoe curve, nearly 1.75 miles from the parking lot.

Resume your climb along the Lassen Park Road as you make an ascending traverse high across the hillside above Little Hot Springs Valley and the East Sulfur Creek drainage. You reach a set of 3 hairpin turns, beginning 2.5 miles from the trailhead, which can be bypassed by climbing steeply north directly up the slope from the first turn to the continuation of the road above. Back on the highway, proceed east up the road, angling across the head of the drainage. Continue up the road as it bends north and climbs out of Little Hot Springs Valley on the way toward Emerald Lake. Beyond the bend the topography makes discerning the actual path of the Lassen Park Road difficult, but the course of the highway becomes obvious again near the east end of Lake Helen. If you plan on visiting Emerald Lake, head north and find the lake tucked into the steep slopes of Ski Heil Peak; if not, head directly northeast on a moderate climb toward Lake Helen.

Frozen Lake Helen lies 0.25 mile directly east of smaller Emerald Lake, 3.75 miles from your starting point. The circular lake fills a glacier-carved basin in the shadow of Lassen and Eagle peaks. With an elevation over 8000 feet, Lake Helen accumulates an enormous snowpack in all but the driest of winters, which sometimes reaches a depth of over 30 feet. If you happen to visit the park in summer you may see visitors sliding down lingering snowbanks well into August.

Winter parties interested in snowcamps will find suitable sites near both Lake Helen and Emerald Lake. The nearby terrain offers a wealth of additional opportunities for multi-day adventures, including climbs of nearby peaks and journeys to other remote destinations. Lake Helen is a popular basecamp for snowshoers and skiers attempting the route from the Southwest Entrance to Manzanita Lake along Lassen Park Road (see Trip 15).

FYI: Even though this trip minimizes the exposure, a number of known avalanche paths are crossed. Proceed into the backcountry only when conditions are stable. Current avalanche information is usually posted on the wall inside the Lassen Chalet. The map contained within the park newspaper obtained at the entrance station will give you a very general idea of where avalanches are common.

Warm-ups: The all-year resort community of Chester provides a full range of services to the visitors and residents of nearby Lake Almanor. The 25-mile drive east from the 36/89 junction can hardly seem convenient, but a delightful meal at Cynthia's may actually be worth the trip. The restaurant and bakery offers artistically prepared dishes with an innovative flair for breakfast, lunch and dinner that are sure to please the most discriminating palate. Cynthia's is located in the heart of Chester at 268 Main Street. Reservations are suggested for dinner: (530) 258-1966.

TRIP 14

Lassen Peak

see map
on page
60

Duration: Full day or overnight
    (Three-quarter day for spring ascent)
Distance: Varies: 13 miles round trip from Lassen Chalet
    (4 miles round trip from summer trailhead—spring only)
Difficulty: Extreme for one-day trip
    Difficult for overnight trip
    (Moderate to difficult for spring ascent)
Elevation: 6735/10457
    (8430/10457 for spring ascent)
Map: *Lassen Peak* 7.5′ quadrangle

Introduction: The Lassen Peak Trail is one of the two most popular trails in the park (the other being the trail to Bumpass Hell). A typical summer day will see hundreds of hikers strung out along the path, appearing like a parade of ants to the gaping tourists at the trailhead parking lot. Winter, with the long approach and less temperate weather, changes this scene dramatically, with only a hearty few rising to the challenge of a winter climb. For the avid mountaineer undaunted by the potentially harsh conditions, a trip to the summit of Lassen Peak can be the crowning achievement of a visit to Lassen Volcanic National Park. One thing is for sure, successful summiteers will not have to fight for a space to sit and enjoy the incredible 360° vista from the top of the peak, as is often the case in summer.

Any attempt on Lassen Peak in the winter is not for the fainthearted. When the Lassen Park Road is closed at the Lassen Chalet, the trip is generally done as an overnight outing requiring a snowcamp somewhere along the way, unless everyone in your party is in great condition and able to complete the 13-mile round trip in one day. Avalanche potential must be considered along with the possibility of inclement weather. Windy conditions should be expected and extremely high winds are not uncommon during the course of a normal winter. Compounding these problems is the altitude, resulting in less oxygen and more exposure to ultraviolet rays. Even so, Lassen Peak is one of the most majestic mountains to climb in all of California, with unparalleled scenery along the way and an extraordinary view from the summit.

How to get there: From Highway 36 near Morgan Summit, turn north onto Highway 89. This junction is approximately 5 miles east of Mineral and 25 miles west of Chester. Follow 89 north to the Southwest Entrance of Lassen Park and continue up the road to the plowed parking area 5.5 miles from the 36/89 junction.

The Southwest Entrance station is manned during daylight hours on weekends, but is generally unoccupied during the week. When a ranger is not present you can self-register, which will require exact change ($10 per vehicle for a 7-day pass). On weekdays you can acquire change or purchase yearly permits at park headquarters in Mineral during office hours, 8:00 to 4:30 Monday-Friday.

Restrooms with running water are available at the Lassen Chalet near the parking lot, but the rest of the building has been closed to winter use since the ski park was abandoned in the early Nineties. Snow camping is allowed at the nearby Southwest Walk-in Campground for $10 per night.

Description: Begin your trip by snowshoeing up the mild grade of the Lassen Park Road northbound from the Lassen Chalet, quickly passing the site of the abandoned ski area. The open terrain allows pleasant views of the surrounding countryside as you parallel the West Sulfur Creek drainage. Near the 0.75-mile mark, you cross a bridge over a tributary of the creek just before encountering the Sulfur Works. In spring, you can wait for the road to be plowed and shorten your trip by beginning your climb from progressively opened trailheads at the Sulfur Works, Bumpass Hell or Lassen Peak parking areas.

Remaining on the Lassen Park Road, you leave the Sulfur Works geothermal area following a curve. Just past the bridge crossing of the last tributary of West Sulfur Creek, find a convenient spot from which to scale the hillside to the north of the curve. You climb up the moderately steep hillside well above the creek on an arcing ascent that ultimately veers away from the drainage and bends east toward Diamond Peak Saddle, which is 0.3 mile north of the summit of Diamond Peak. Regain the road at the saddle near a horseshoe curve, nearly 1.75 miles from the parking lot.

Resume your climb along the Lassen Park Road as you make an ascending traverse high across the hillside above Little Hot Springs Valley and the East Sulfer Creek drainage. You reach a set of three hairpin turns, beginning 2.5 miles from the trailhead, which can be bypassed by climbing steeply north directly up the slope from the first turn to the continuation of the road above. Back on the highway, proceed east up the road, angling across the head of the drainage. Continue up the road as it bends north and climbs out of Little Hot Spring Valley on the way toward Emerald Lake. Beyond the bend, the topography makes discerning the actual path of the road difficult, but the course of the highway becomes obvious again near the east end of Helen Lake.

From Lake Helen continue up the Lassen Park Road, climbing up the slope across the west face of Mt. Helen to the summit trailhead. From the vicinity of the trailhead ascend northeast up the slope toward the southeast ridge of the peak. Even though clumps of mountain hemlock appear across this hillside in the summer, only the tallest of these trees will be poking through the depths of an average winter's snowpack. The moderate climb continues until a steeper ascent faces you along the ridge. Hidden beneath the snow in this area are dwarfed whitebark pines, the last conifers able to handle the harsh environment on the fringe of the alpine zone.

The summer trail makes a tight, zigzagging ascent up the ridge at a nearly continuous 15% grade, but with the path buried by the accumulated snowfall you may elect to head straight up the ridge or wind back and forth toward the summit. Either way, the climb is fairly steep and arduous. One consolation for the hearty effort is the improving views of nearby Brokeoff Mountain and Mt. Diller and of Lake Almanor to the southeast and eventually a part of Eagle Lake beyond. As you continue up the mountain, between gasps you can try to visualize the location of ancient Mt. Tehama. Geologists theorize that the summit of the 11,000-foot volcano was just 2 miles to the south-southwest and that Mt. Conard, Diamond Peak, Brokeoff Mountain, Mt. Diller and Pilot Pinnacle are remnants of the volcano's slopes.

Eventually, the grade eases as the ridge meets the broad summit area, where you turn northeast and make the final push toward the summit rocks. Magnificent Mt. Shasta and the Trinity Alps appear to the west. Be prepared for stiff winds along this stretch. Continue across the broad summit area to a position just southwest of the summit rocks. From there you will have to select the least difficult approach up the short steep slope to the top of the 10,457-foot peak and the truly impressive 360° vista.

As the highest point for many miles in any direction, Lassen Peak provides a bird's-eye view of the northern California landscape. Mt. Shasta is the dominant landmark to the north, shining majestically in the deep-blue winter sky, towering over all other geographical features and standing almost 4000 feet higher than your present elevation. To the west are the snowcapped peaks of the Yolla Bolly, Trinity Alps and Marble Mountains. To the south, snowy ridges proceed across a seemingly unending series of mountains, with the Sierra Buttes reigning above the surrounding countryside. Massive Lake Almanor and more distant Eagle Lake complete the panorama of notable landmarks.

FYI: Climbing any of the Cascade volcanoes in winter can be a daunting task, requiring excellent physical condition, proper equipment and mountaineering experience. Check with park officials for current weather, avalanche and snow conditions before embarking on a climb of Lassen Peak.

Warm-ups: See Trips 10-13.

TRIP 15

Lassen Park Traverse —Southwest Entrance to Manzanita Lake

see map
on page
69,71

Duration: Varies–multi-day shuttle trip
Distance: 11.5 miles one way via Manzanita Creek
          19.5 miles one way via Paradise Meadows
          (9.5 miles one way to Devastated Area–spring only)
          29 miles one way via Lassen Park Road
Difficulty: Difficult
Elevation: 6735/8500/5915
Map: *Lassen Peak, Reading Peak, West Prospect Peak & Manzanita Lake 7.5'*
      quadrangles

Introduction: A traverse of Lassen Volcanic National Park would be the highlight of any winter season for experienced snowshoers. The range of scenery one is exposed to along the way is incomparable, unforgettable and extraordinary. A parade of towering peaks, deep canyons, hydrothermal features and frozen lakes highlight the journey. When time is not of the essence, Lassen Park provides an abundance of interesting diversions along the length of the traverse as well.

In stark contrast to summer, the fact that the park is virtually deserted in the winter goes without saying, allowing snowshoers to have the area all to themselves. One may stand alone at famous landmarks where summer sees hundreds of autos or

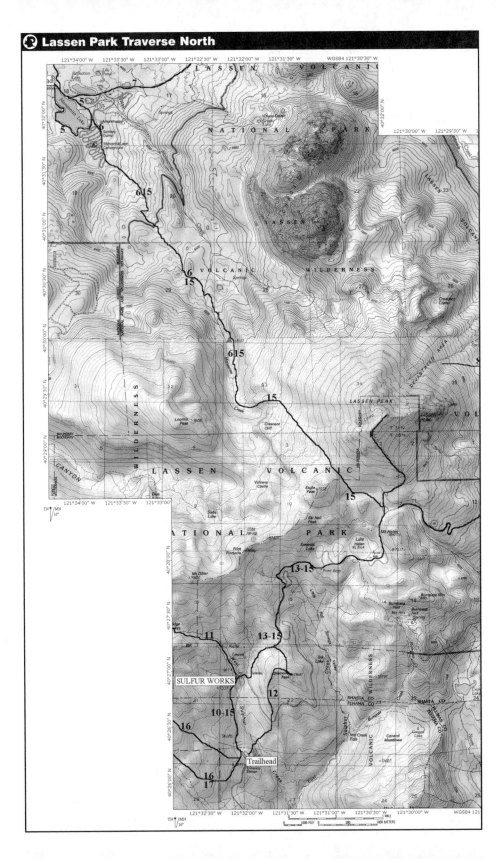

tourists in the exact same locations. Those who crave solitude for their wilderness journeys will not be disappointed with Lassen Park.

The lure of unparalleled beauty and unrivaled solitude aside, any traverse of Lassen Park is a major undertaking which should be attempted only by parties skilled in winter travel and survival. Good physical condition, proper equipment and a stretch of decent weather are additional prerequisites. Since avalanches are common within the park, parties should be aware of the potentially hazardous areas they will cross and the current conditions before embarking on any trip into Lassen's backcountry.

One of the first decisions to be made when planning a traverse of Lassen Park is by what route the attempt will be made. A number of options present themselves. The least amount of routefinding required will be found along the Lassen Park Road, but the price for that ease is the greatest total distance, 29 miles. Some of that length can be shortened by following the cutoff between the Sulfur Works and Diamond Peak Saddle and the cutoff through Paradise Meadows, leaving a total distance of 19.5 miles. However, this nearly 10-mile savings requires a modest amount of navigation. The most difficult option is also the one that necessitates the greatest routefinding skill: the route over the saddle between Eagle and Lassen peaks, around Crescent Cliff and down Manzanita Creek is the shortest distance, at 11.5 miles, but is by far the most challenging alternative. The coming of spring provides an additional option when park employees plow 10 miles of road between Manzanita Lake and the Devastated Area. The combination of a shorter journey with longer days and the potential for better weather makes this an intriguing possibility.

Whatever route you choose, you must possess the requisite navigational skills, the appropriate maps, and a working compass (a GPS may be helpful as well). Rather than a detailed description for each option, you will find a general description for the two alternatives that I think are the most interesting. No matter which way you decide to go, you must have no doubt in your ability to find your own way safely through the backcountry.

How to get there:

Southwest Entrance: Follow directions in Trip 10 to the parking lot near the Lassen Chalet.

Manzanita Lake: Follow directions in Trip 5 to the parking area near Manzanita Lake.

Devastated Area: Follow directions in Trip 8 to the parking area near Emigrant Pass.

Description:

Manzanita Creek Route: Follow directions in Trips 10, 13 and 14 to the trailhead for the Lassen Peak Trail.

Leave the road and head northwest, passing a small knob on your left, toward the saddle between Eagle and Lassen peaks. Traverse across the south, avalanche-prone slopes to the saddle and then work your way northwest toward Manzanita Creek. The crux of the route lies ahead because you must

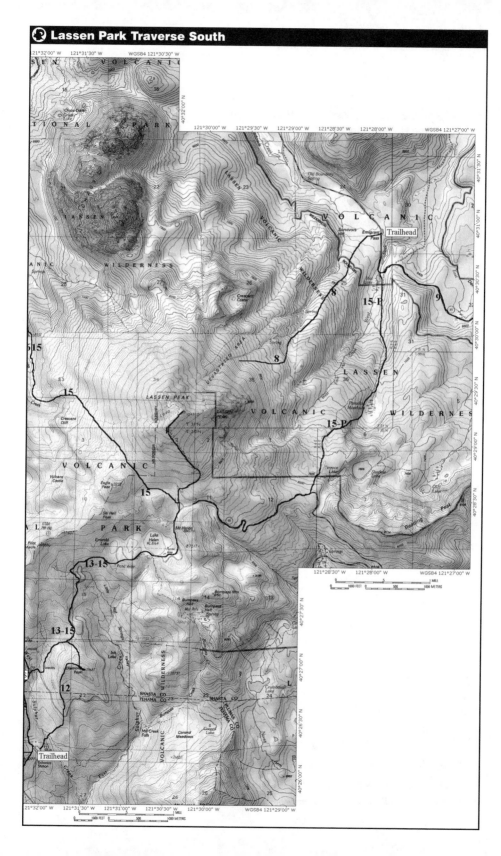

avoid the steep slopes of Crescent Cliff by passing above them and then descending a ridge directly north of the cliffs. Work your way down the ridge to the east side of Manzanita Creek and then follow the route of the hiking trail north through the drainage, reversing the route as described in Trip 6.

Paradise Meadows Route: (shown as route "15-P" on the map on page 70). Follow directions in Trips 10, 13 and 14 to the trailhead for the Lassen Peak Trail.

Continue up the Lassen Park Road for 0.3 mile to the high point of the road at 8500 feet. From there, head down the highway for another 1.75 miles to the site of the Terrace Lake trailhead, at the base of Reading Peak's west ridge. Leave the road and head north for 1 mile to the south edge of Paradise Meadows. You proceed north from Paradise Meadows following the drainage for another mile until you locate a convenient place to cross the creek. Once across, continue another 0.5 mile or so to where you reconnect with the Lassen Park Road. Follow the highway another 0.5 mile to the springtime Devastated Area trailhead or 10.5 miles to Manzanita Lake.

FYI: Any overnight trip into the backcountry of Lassen Park requires a backcountry permit, obtainable at park headquarters in Mineral between 8 a.m. and 4:30 p.m., Monday through Friday. Permits can also be arranged by calling (530) 595-4444, ext. 5134.

Warm-ups: See Trips 5, 10-13.

10,457-foot Lassen Peak from the Lassen Park Road

TRIP **16**

Forest Lake Loop

see map
on page
74

Duration: One-half day
Distance: 2.5 mile loop trip
Difficulty: Moderate
Elevation: 6735/7555
Map: *Lassen Peak* 7.5′ quadrangle

Introduction: Forest Lake sees relatively few visitors in the summer as the shallow lake offers no swimming or fishing and has a rather healthy population of mosquitoes. The lake appears to be so uninviting that no official path leads to the shore, in spite of the fact that the lake lies one tenth-mile off the Brokeoff Mountain Trail. The only redeeming qualities the forgotten body of water seems to possess are the early season display of wildflowers and the backdrop of rugged cliffs descending from Brokeoff Mountain. Winter seems to improve the plight of Forest Lake somewhat as the mosquitoes are gone and no one in their right mind is disappointed in the shallowness of a frozen lake or the corresponding lack of swimming and fishing possibilities. However, the snowy season isn't entirely kind either, as the marked Nordic trail through dense forest can be extremely hard to follow at times. While staying on the marked trail may be a challenge, finding your own way to the lake is not particularly difficult, and becoming permanently lost is next to impossible as all the terrain slopes back downhill to the highway.

The logical question is, "Why go to Forest Lake at all?" The obvious answer for the recluse among us is, "Because no one else does." Solitude is available here in sufficient quantities, but most snowshoers are looking for attributes beyond mere isolation. Even though Forest Lake is not the most scenic destination accessible from this end of the park, the forested journey is pleasant enough and occasional clearings do provide nice views of rugged Brokeoff Mountain. The 2.5-mile loop is short enough to offer a manageable distance for a morning or afternoon excursion, and it presents something of a routefinding challenge without the possibility of suffering the difficult consequences that being off-route on other trips might present. In less than ideal conditions the mostly forested loop offers protection from the elements when traveling in more exposed sections of the park would not be particularly pleasant.

How to get there: From Highway 36 near Morgan Summit, turn north onto Highway 89. This junction is approximately 5 miles east of Mineral and 25 miles west of

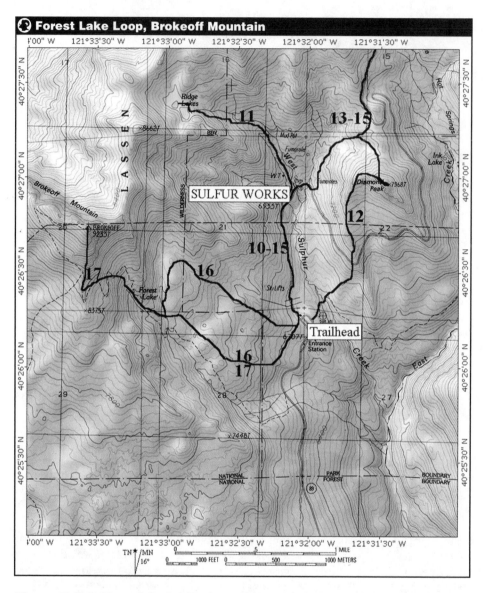

Chester. Follow 89 north to the Southwest Entrance of Lassen Park and continue up the road to the plowed parking area 5.5 miles from the 36/89 junction.

The Southwest Entrance station is manned during daylight hours on weekends, but is generally unoccupied during the week. When a ranger is not present you can self-register, which will require exact change ($10 per vehicle for a 7-day pass). On weekdays you can acquire change or purchase yearly permits at park headquarters in Mineral during office hours, 8:00 to 4:30 Monday-Friday.

Restrooms with running water are available at the Lassen Chalet near the parking lot, but the rest of the building has been closed to winter use since the ski park was abandoned in the early Nineties. Snow camping is allowed at the nearby South-west Walk-in Campground for $10 per night.

Description: At the beginning of the unplowed section of Lassen Park Road, immediately head south away from the road and into the trees. Look for faded orange and red markers identifying the marked trail to Forest Lake. Approximately 100 yards from the road you encounter the loop junction. Bear left at this junction, roughly paralleling the highway for a while until you reach a seasonal stream. Cross the stream channel and turn uphill to the west, eventually reaching the main channel of the creek which drains Forest Lake. Follow the creek upstream to where it divides into two channels. To reach Forest Lake, continue along the right-hand branch another one tenth mile to the south shore. Snowshoers attempting to reach the summit of Brokeoff Mountain should follow the left branch of the creek.

The return part of the loop heads northeast for about 0.25 mile from the lake before turning generally southeast. Initially the route mildly descends through clearings and scattered forest before a steeper descent takes you through denser forest back to the Lassen Chalet. The last part of the route passes directly south of the slopes of the abandoned Lassen Ski Park.

FYI: Due to the potential difficulties in staying on route, beginners should shy away from this trip in favor of easier routes, such as the one to Sulfur Works.

Warm-ups: See Trips 10-13.

Brokeoff Mountain

Duration: Three-quarter day
Distance: 4.5 miles round trip)
Difficulty: Difficult
Elevation: 6735/9235
Map: *Lassen Peak* 7.5′ quadrangle

Introduction: At 10,457 feet, Lassen Peak has the premier views of any to be had within the park. However, the vistas from the summit of Lassen Park's second highest point are nearly as wonderful. Where Brokeoff Mountain wins over Lassen Peak is the distance required to reach those respective views. The trip to Lassen Peak is 4 miles longer (except in spring when the road is plowed), not to mention the additional 1200-foot elevation gain. Peak baggers will marvel at the expansive vista available from Brokeoff Mountain's wee summit, which takes in a vast area of the surrounding landscape as well as nearby park landmarks, including the Lassen massif.

Even though the journey is relatively short, the ascent provides plenty of challenges for snowshoers of any level. The first obstacle to surmount is the routefinding dilemma one faces in attempting to follow the southern part of the Forest Lake Nordic Trail (see Trip 16). However, following that actual route is not essential to success as snowshoers can simply head straight toward the south ridge of Brokeoff Mountain instead. The next task is to surmount the steep slopes below the ridgecrest, which are at a high enough angle to test the skills of most travelers. On the crest of the south ridge, strong winds and less than ideal snow conditions may be the last hurdles to overcome on the final part of the steep ascent up the southwest face of the peak. These difficulties aside, the ascent can be extremely enjoyable when the quality of the snow is good and the weather favorable.

Despite an appellation which has a rather unromantic ring, Brokeoff Mountain is aptly named. Scientists speculate the peak is the highest eroded remnant of the Mt. Tehama volcano, which may at one time have reached an elevation of 11,000 feet. Nearby Mt. Diller, Pilot Peak, Diamond Peak and Mt. Conard also represent remnants of this once-dominant peak. Whatever the geologic origin of Brokeoff Mountain, the views of the peak and those from the summit are splendid.

How to get there: From Highway 36 at Morgan Summit, turn north onto Highway 89. This junction is approximately 5 miles east of Mineral and 25 miles west of Chester. Follow 89 north to the Southwest Entrance of Lassen Peak and continue up the road to the plowed parking area, 5.5 miles from the 36/89 junction.

The Southwest Entrance station is staffed during daylight hours on weekends, but is generally unoccupied during the week. When a ranger is not present, you can self-register, which will require exact change ($10 per vehicle for a 7-day pass). On weekdays you can acquire change or purchase yearly permits at park headquarters in Mineral during office hours, 8:00 to 4:30, Monday-Friday).

Restrooms with running water are available at the Lassen Chalet near the parking lot, but the rest of the building has been closed to winter use since the ski park was abandoned in the early 90s. Snow camping is allowed at the nearby Walk-In Campground for $10 per night.

Description: At the beginning of the unplowed section of Lassen Park Road, immediately head south away from the road and into the trees. Look for faded orange and red markers identifying the marked trail to Forest Lakes. Approximately 100 yards from the road you encounter the loop juntion. Bear left at this junction, roughly paralleling the highway for a while until you reach a seasonal stream. Cross the stream channel and turn uphill to the west, eventually reaching the main chanel of the creek that drains Forest Lake. Follow the creek channel upstream to where it divides into two branches.

You continue along the left-hand stream channel and soon begin to climb more steeply up the hillside. As you climb out of the canyon, the trees begin to thin, allowing views to open up of the rugged southeast face of Brokeoff Mountain directly above and Lassen Peak to the northeast. You continue a steady climb up the steep hillside headed toward the crest of the south ridge of Brokeoff Mountain. Just before you surmount the ridge, the terrain eases slightly, and before long you stand atop the crest of the south ridge of Brokeoff Mountain. Be prepared for windy conditions once you hit the ridgecrest.

At the crest you turn north and follow the ridge to the south face of the mountain and then climb the final 0.25 mile across the nearly bare slope. At an elevation of 9235 feet, the tiny summit of Brokeoff Mountain provides awe-inspiring views, particularly of the continuation of the north ridge as it sweeps around to the summits of Mt. Diller, Pilot Pinnacle, Ski Heil Peak and Eagle Peak, culminating in the climax of Lassen Peak. Beyond the immediate scenery of the park, the 360° vista includes a wide expanse of northern California's landscape.

Once you have sufficiently enjoyed the view from Lassen Park's second highest peak, retrace your steps back to the trailhead.

FYI: Not only should you be prepared for potentially windy conditions on Brokeoff Mountain, but you may want to pack along a pair of crampons and an ice axe for the final part of the ascent if icy conditions are present.

Warm-ups: See Trips 10-13.

CHAPTER 7

Plumas Eureka State Park & Vicinity

Tucked away into a nearly forgotten part of northern California lie the delightful lands of Plumas Eureka State Park. Although this sleepy locale has been discovered by an increasing number of summer devotees drawn by the scenic beauty, regional history, hiking, camping and fishing, the backcountry is virtually deserted when Old Man Winter drops the first flakes of snow upon the striking landscape. Officials boast that Plumas Eureka has something for everyone and such a notion would be hard to argue against, even during the "off-season." For the winter recreationist, the backcountry offers craggy peaks, picturesque lakes, gorgeous panoramas, scenic canyons, hearty forests and even a substantial waterfall.

Plumas Eureka became a state park in 1959 when 5500 acres were set aside, preserving a slice of history as well as providing ample opportunities for recreation. In 1851 a group of nine miners discovered gold on the east flank of Gold Mountain (now known as Eureka Peak). This event triggered a flurry of activity, eventually involving 62 miles of mineshafts, tons of equipment, and a vast assortment of individual miners and mining companies. By the time mining ceased for good in the 1940s, 8 million dollars worth of gold had been claimed. Modern-day miners can discover a treasure trove of information about the old mining days in the museum at park headquarters (call ahead for winter hours). Originally the museum building served as a bunkhouse for the nearby Mohawk Stamp Mill.

Ore for the stamp mill was retrieved from shafts high up the slopes of Gold Mountain and brought down to the mill by means of two gravity-powered tramways. Miners would use the empty ore buckets as transportation up the mountain, and in winter perhaps used this system as the first ski lift in California. Certainly skiing in this area has a long history dating back to 1860, making the area noteworthy for the oldest recorded sport skiing in the western hemisphere. By 1863 "longboarders" were zooming down a 2600-foot run. This spirit has been kept alive at the Gold Mountain Ski Area (founded as the Plumas Eureka Ski Bowl in 1957) by the Historic Longboard Revival Series, where racers dress in period costume including leather boots, and ski on authentic wooden "longboards" while using a single wooden ski pole for balance. Aside from the long-board races, Gold Mountain continues to cater to modern-day alpine skiers and snowboarders with a small-town charm that is a refreshing change from the normal California mega-resort.

Not only does Eureka Peak provide excellent slopes for skiing, but the jagged peak is a worthy 3.25-mile ascent for hearty snowshoers. Along the way to the 7447-foot summit, scenic Eureka Lake presents a picturesque sight at the base of the mountain's steep north-facing cliffs. The sweeping vista from the top is more than enough reward for the strenuous effort. A number of other alpine-looking peaks clustered nearby offer stimulating challenges for peakbaggers and mountaineers alike (the route to the summit of Mt. Elwell is described in Trip 21). The only marked Nordic trail in the park follows the gentle, forested drainage of Jamison Creek on an easy stroll to the mine of the same name. Beyond the mine, an assortment of beautiful mountain lakes are worthy destinations for those who don't mind leaving the security of a marked trail. All the trips described in this chapter offer stunning scenery, whether from atop an airy summit or from the shoreline of a frozen lake. While Plumas Eureka and the nearby Lakes Basin areas are quite popular among summer hikers and backpackers, winter pilgrims can visit these areas with an almost ironclad guarantee of solitude.

Plumas Eureka State Park is a veritable island oasis for snowshoers and cross-country skiers, for outside the park's boundaries lies one of the most heavily traveled snowmobile areas in the state. Fortunately, park status provides a haven for human-powered recreationists searching for the peace and tranquility of a non-mechanized winter environment, which are in short supply in the public lands surrounding the park.

Location: Plumas Eureka State Park is approximately 50 miles northwest of Truckee and 20 miles east of Quincy.

Access: Access to Plumas Eureka State Park is from Plumas County Road A14, which leaves State Highway 89 about 1 mile south of the junction between State Highways 89 and 70. The county road is routinely plowed through the historic community of Johnsville to the parking lot for the Gold Mountain Ski Area.

Amenities: The resort town of Graeagle offers year-round access to gasoline, groceries and limited dining opportunities. Full service communities are Portola, 10 miles east on Highway 70, Quincy, 20 miles west on Highway 70, and Truckee, 50 miles southeast on Highway 89.

Season & Weather: Away from the higher altitudes of California's two premier Cascade volcanoes, Mt. Shasta and Lassen Peak, northern California suffers from a lack of easy access to high-elevation areas. Plumas Eureka State Park is no exception, as most destinations, aside from the summits of the peaks, range between 5000 and 6500 feet. Consequently, snow seasons are generally confined to the true months of winter. In an average year, look for decent snow conditions from sometime in December through March.

PERMITS
Day Use & Overnight Use: Permits are not required for travel within the State Park.

MAPS
Lakes Basin, Sierra Buttes &
Plumas Eureka State Park Recreation Guide
1:31,680, 1999, paper
Plumas & Tahoe National Forests

Plumas National Forest
1:126,720, 1996, paper
Plumas National Forest

STATE PARKS/FOREST SERVICE
Plumas Eureka State Park
310 Johnsville Road
Blairsden, CA 96103
(530) 836-2380

Plumas National Forest
Beckwourth Ranger District
P.O. Box 7
Blairsden, CA 96103
(530) 836-2575

Gold Mountain Ski Area
(530) 836-2317

WEBSITES
Plumas Eureka State Park
Gold Mountain Ski Area
Plumas Ski Club

www.parks.ca.gov
www.skigoldmountain.org
www.plumasskiclub.org

Restored buildings of the Jamison Mine in Plumas Eureka State Park

TRIP 18

Jamison Mine

see map
on page
82

Duration: One-half day
Distance: 2.75 miles round trip
Difficulty: Easy
Elevation: 5160/5350
Map: *Johnsville* & *Gold Lake* 7.5′ quadrangles

Introduction: If you're looking for an easy trip requiring just a few hours to complete, then look no further than the trip to Jamison Mine. During the 1880s around $25 million worth of gold was extracted from numerous shafts sunk in and around Eureka Peak (known as Gold Mountain during the mining boom). Today Plumas Eureka State Park occupies 6700 acres surrounding Eureka Peak and the Jamison Mine, including some of the prettiest backcountry scenery in northern California. A comfortable way to sample a taste of the park is to follow the marked route of a gently graded road the short distance up Jamison Creek canyon to the site of the Jamison Mine. A number of restored buildings are found at the site of this once prosperous mine.

How to get there: From State Highway 70 turn south on State Highway 89, approximately 10 miles west of Portola and 20 miles east of Quincy, following signed directions for PLUMAS EUREKA STATE PARK, GRAEAGLE and BLAIRSDEN. Travel down Highway 89 for 0.9 mile to a junction with Plumas County Road A14 and turn northwest, following another sign reading PLUMAS EUREKA STATE PARK. Follow Road A14 for 4.75 miles to the parking area along a plowed shoulder on the north side of the road opposite the signed trailhead. If you reach park headquarters you have gone 0.5 mile past the trailhead.

Eastbound travelers on Highway 70 can shave off nearly 3 miles of the description above by turning south 0.6 mile before the junction with Highway 89. Follow a paved road past the Ranger Station, across the Middle Fork Feather River and to a junction with Road A14 at the tiny community of Mohawk, 0.6 mile from Highway 70. From this junction the trailhead is 3.6 miles westbound up A14.

Description: A number of signs mark the beginning of the trail to Jamison Mine above the south side of the highway. Proceed along the gently graded, snow-covered road paralleling the highway for a very short distance, to where the road bends

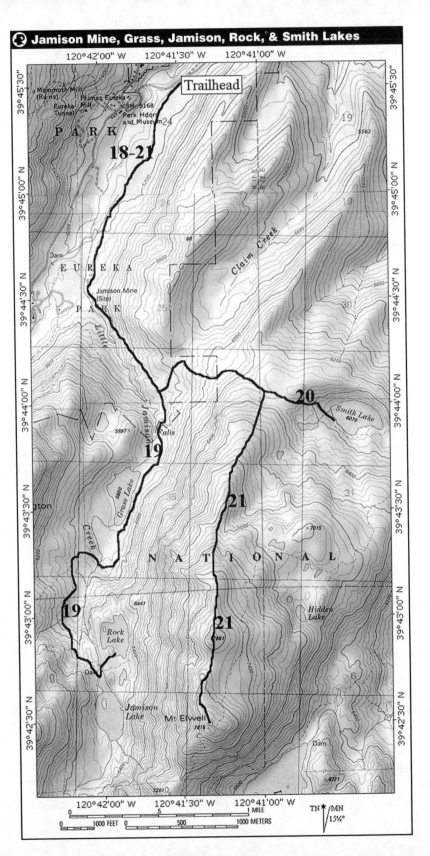

Jamison Mine, Grass, Jamison, Rock, & Smith Lakes

southwest. Continue up the road through a light, mixed forest of cedar, fir and pine which allows occasional glimpses of Eureka Peak to your right and Mt. Washington ahead. The road follows the canyon of Jamison Creek, but at a healthy distance away from the stream. Just beyond where the grade of the road increases slightly, you reach the first of the buildings associated with the Jamison Mine. A short distance farther up the drainage, more buildings appear as the marked ski trail ends. After inspection of the restored structures, retrace your steps back to the trailhead.

FYI: To vary your return, you could cross Jamison Creek via a bridge and follow the road west of the creek back to park headquarters. From there you would have to walk 0.5 mile along the highway back to your car.

Warm-ups: The Iron Door in Johnsville is a fine restaurant; unfortunately it is closed from November through April. However, you can catch a pleasant meal for break-fast or lunch at the Mohawk Cafe, 3.5 miles down the highway. Open year-round, the cafe offers delectable dishes during the hours of 7:30 a.m. to 3:00 p.m. (closed on Tuesdays). For more information call (530) 836-0901. If you come to this tiny com-munity too late for the Mohawk Cafe, you can wet your whistle at the Mohawk Tavern, a funky little bar that has a sign on the outside identifying the old structure as the Mohawk Convention Center and City Hall.

TRIP 19

Grass, Jamison & Rock Lakes

Duration: Three-quarter day
Distance: 8.5 miles round trip)
Difficulty: Moderate
Elevation: 5160/6305
Map: *Johnsville* & *Gold Lake* 7.5′ quadrangles

see map on page 82

Introduction: Three delightful lakes provide an attractive temptation for experenced snowshoers looking for a scenic sampling of the Lakes Basin Recreation Area. Sum-mer hikers are quite familiar with this region, but winter visitors constitute only a

Mt. Washington makes a fine backdrop for frozen Rock Lake

fraction of those who travel to Grass, Jamison or Rock lakes during the warmer half of the year. The first part of the journey, within the boundary of Plumas Eureka State Park, follows the easy grade of a marked trail into the site of the Jamison Mine (see Trip 18). The backcountry within Plumas Eureka State Park and the Lakes Basin Recreation Area beyond sees little use, and what limited traffic this particular route does have will be seen on this initial stretch of easy Nordic trail. After that, snowshoers are on their own as they must navigate their way along the snow-covered hiking trail up Little Jamison Creek canyon. Less than a mile above the mine, an additional treat is the opportunity to view Jamison Falls, a 60-foot cascade which plunges into a scooped-out bowl of rock. Once you reach the lakes farther up the canyon, fine views of Mt. Washington and Mt. Elwell add drama to the picturesque surroundings.

How to get there: From State Highway 70 turn south on State Highway 89, approximately 10 miles west of Portola and 20 miles east of Quincy, following signed directions for PLUMAS EUREKA STATE PARK, GRAEAGLE and BLAIRSDEN. Travel down Highway 89 for 0.9 mile to a junction with Plumas County Road A14 and turn northwest, following another sign reading PLUMAS EUREKA STATE PARK. Follow Road A14 for 4.75 miles to the parking area along a plowed shoulder on the north side of the road opposite the signed trailhead. If you reach park headquarters you have gone 0.5 mile past the trailhead.

Eastbound travelers on Highway 70 can shave off nearly 3 miles of the description above by turning south 0.6 mile before the junction with Highway 89. Follow a paved road past the Ranger Station, across the Middle Fork Feather River and to a junction with Road A14 at the tiny community of Mohawk, 0.6 mile from Highway 70. From this junction the trailhead is 3.6 miles westbound up A14.

Description: Proceed along the gently graded, snow-covered road paralleling the highway for a very short distance, to where the road bends southwest. Continue up the road through a light, mixed forest of cedar, fir and pine, following the course of Jamison Creek. Just beyond where the grade of the road increases slightly, you reach the first of the restored buildings of the Jamison Mine. Proceed past more structures to the end of the marked ski trail.

Depending on the snow depth, you may be able to locate trailhead signs marking the beginning of the summer trail to the lakes a short distance past the sign marking the end of the cross-country ski trail. Continue up the canyon beyond the initial mine structures, passing some more buildings and following the trail above the wooded bank of Little Jamison Creek. You make an angling ascent up across the hillside, emerging into scattered forest high above the creek. Near the 2-mile mark from the highway, you reach a junction with the route over to Smith Lake (see Trip 20).

The moderate climb continues as you proceed up the drainage for another 0.25 mile, reaching an overlook from where you can view Little Jamison Creek Falls spilling into a small bowl of beaten-out rock. Away from the falls, you wander alongside the creek on a gentle climb for 0.3 mile to the north shore of Grass Lake.

Above the west shore, Mt. Washington rises up precipitously over 1500 vertical feet above the surface of Grass Lake. While admiring the view, you may observe the results of small avalanches across the steep east face of the peak. During summer, this lake is one of only five where backpackers can legally camp in the Lakes Basin Recreation Area; the lightly forested shores above Grass Lake would make an equally attractive base camp for further winter explorations.

A weathered old snag perched above Little Jamison Creek Canyon

Proceed around the east shore of Grass Lake and continue up the canyon on an easy grade, passing through light forest and then a small clearing dotted with pine, aspen and fir. Soon, where you encounter the steep cliffs of the rocky headwall 0.25 mile beyond the lake, the canyon narrows. To avoid the cliffs you curve west, cross Little Jamison Creek, and then begin a moderate climb up less imposing terrain on the west side of the creek. Your climb takes you high above the creek, to where before long you encounter the stream coming down from Wades Lake, 3.5 miles from the trailhead.

Beyond the creek you make a 0.5-mile, curving ascent southeast over a low ridge to the north shore of Jamison Lake. Surrounded by widely scattered lodgepole pine and nestled into a depression at the base of a precipitous 1500-ft. slope that climaxes at the summit of Mt. Elwell, the lake is narrow at the north end and widens toward the south. A small island adds further interest to the character of the frozen lake.

To visit Rock Lake, head northeast from the outlet of Jamison Lake and travel the short distance to the south shore. This lake occupies a deep basin near the edge of the steep headwall you encountered 0.25 mile up the canyon from Grass Lake, permitting excellent views down the Little Jamison Creek drainage of distant peaks and ridges. Rock bluffs provide an attractive counterpoint to the icy surface of the lake. Isolated pines scattered here and there lend an austere ambiance to the winter scene.

After enjoying the lakes, retrace your steps to the trailhead.

FYI: Many additional opportunities are available for further wanderings in this area, including those described in Trips 20-21. A base camp near the lakes or along Little Jamison Creek would provide a fine launching point for an overnight or a multi-day adventure.

Warm-ups: If you plan your trip for any month but January, when the restaurant is closed, you can enjoy some of northern California's finest cuisine in one of the most unlikely locations. In the tiny community of Blairsden, the Grizzly Grill Restaurant & Bar, under the artistic direction of owner/chef Lynn Hagen, serves a wide selection of delectable dishes at moderate prices in a relaxed mountain atmosphere. Lynn must prefer the slow pace of the Sierra after a distinguished culinary career in the Napa Valley and San Francisco. Open for dinner only, the Grizzly Grill's menu and extensive wine list will appeal to the most discerning of palates. Call (530) 836-1300 for hours and reservations, or drool over their menus at **www.grizzlygrill.com**.

TRIP **20**

Smith Lake

Duration: Three-quarter day
Distance: 6.5 miles round trip
Difficulty: Moderate
Elevation: 5160/6080
Map: *Johnsville* & *Gold Lake* 7.5′ quadrangles

Introduction: During summer all that stands between Smith Lake and a horde of admirers is the slight effort necessary to hike an easy 1-mile trail. As a result, the picturesque lake has become a very popular destination for hikers, backpackers, anglers and sightseers alike. However, winter has a way of altering summer realities. When snow carpets the mountains and buries the trails, reaching Smith Lake becomes a greater undertaking, which only a few hearty souls seem willing to assume. During those shorter days of winter a quiet solitude falls upon a region that bustles with recreational activity during the other half of the year. Still, if it were not for the ban on snowmobiles within Plumas Eureka State Park, perhaps peace and quiet would not be the expectation of snowshoers making the 3-mile-plus trip into Smith Lake. Even though the lake itself lies just outside the park boundary and is thereby open to mechanized visitors, snowmobilers typically ignore the area for destinations farther up Gold Lake Road.

The route to the lake begins by following the easy, marked Nordic trail to Jamison Mine as described in Trip 18. Beyond the mine snowshoers must navigate their way along the route of the summer trail up the drainage of Little Jamison Creek and then over a forested ridge to Smith Lake. As with many of the other lakes in this area, Smith would make a fine base camp for those seeking overnight or multi-day journeys.

How to get there: From State Highway 70 turn south on State Highway 89, approximately 10 miles west of Portola and 20 miles east of Quincy, following signed directions for PLUMAS EUREKA STATE PARK, GRAEAGLE and BLAIRSDEN. Travel down Highway 89 for 0.9 mile to a junction with Plumas County Road A14 and turn northwest, following another sign reading PLUMAS EUREKA STATE PARK. Follow Road A14 for 4.75 miles to the parking area along a plowed shoulder on the north side of the road opposite the signed trailhead. If you reach park headquarters you have gone 0.5 mile past the trailhead.

Eastbound travelers on Highway 70 can shave off nearly 3 miles of the description above by turning south 0.6 mile before the junction with Highway 89. Follow a paved road past the Ranger Station, across the Middle Fork Feather River and to a junction with Road A14 at the tiny community of Mohawk, 0.6 mile from Highway 70. From this junction the trailhead is 3.6 miles westbound up A14.

Description: Proceed along the gently graded, snow-covered road paralleling the highway for a very short distance, to where the road bends southwest. Continue up the road through a light, mixed forest of cedar, fir and pine, following the course of Jamison Creek. Just beyond where the grade of the road increases slightly, you reach the first of the restored buildings of the Jamison Mine. Proceed past more structures to the end of the marked ski trail.

Depending on the depth of the snow, you may be able to locate trailhead signs marking the beginning of the summer trail to the lakes a short distance past the sign marking the end of the cross-country ski trail. You continue up the canyon beyond the initial mine structures, passing some more buildings, following the course of the trail above the wooded bank of Little Jamison Creek. You make an angling ascent up across the hillside emerging into scattered forest high above the level of the creek. Near the 2-mile mark from the highway, you reach the unmarked junction with the route which continues up Little Jamison Creek to Grass, Jamison and Rock lakes (see Trip 19).

Turn away from Little Jamison Creek and climb up the hillside for 1 mile on an arcing eastward ascent that leads to a lightly forested saddle. From there a 0.25-mile

Winter brings serenity to Smith Lake

descent leads to the west shore of Smith Lake. Twenty-one-acre Smith Lake hides in a deep bowl at the end of a long ridge that trends north from the summit of Mt. Elwell. The shoreline is graced with a light, mixed forest.

Retrace your steps to the trailhead.

FYI: Many of the other trips described in the Plumas Eureka State Park & Vicinity section can be combined with the Smith Lake trip. See Trips 19 and 22 for more information.

Warm-ups: The Fros-Tee near Graeagle, at the junction between Highway 89 and the Johnsville Road, provides weekenders with an opportunity to score an old-fashioned burger and fries that used to be the drive-in standard before the advent of fast food chains.

If you're searching for a morning option, the Village Baker in the small community of Blairsden is a great place to carbo-load or to pick up some treats for the trail. Call (530) 836-1009 for details.

TRIP 21

Mt. Elwell

see map on page **90**

Duration: Full day
Distance: 9 miles round trip
Difficulty: Difficult
Elevation: 5160/7818
Map: *Johnsville* & *Gold Lake* 7.5′ quadrangles

Introduction: Gaining the top of 7818-foot Mt. Elwell is not technically demanding from a mountaineering standpoint, but a good dose of stamina is required in order to reach the summit and obtain the supreme views. A nearly continuous climb coupled with a bit of routefinding through a light forest makes this a trip for moderately experienced snowshoers in reasonable shape. Initially, the route follows the drainage of Little Jamison Creek past the Jamison Mine and over toward Smith Lake. Just before reaching the lake, snowshoers turn south and gain the long ridge that eventually leads to Mt. Elwell. Fine views occur periodically from bare spots along the ridge, but the highlight is the summit vista, where all of the Lakes Basin and Gold

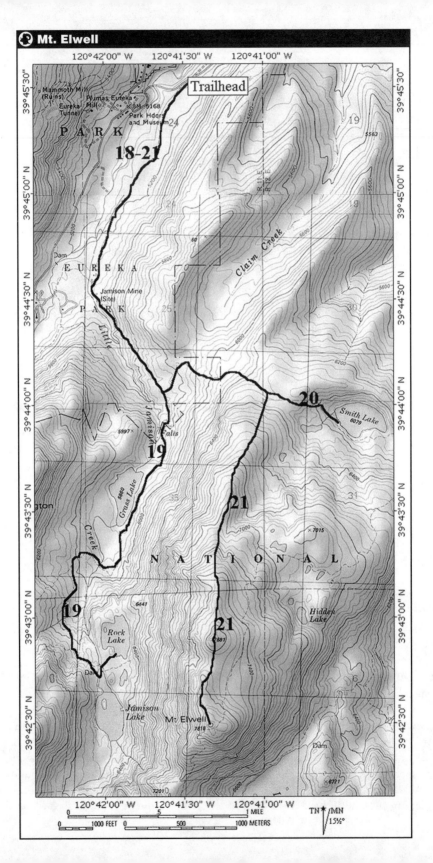

Lake areas are visible, along with the rugged bulwark of Sierra Buttes and the airy vertex of Lassen Peak. Light winter use of Plumas Eureka State Park and the surrounding area guarantees plenty of solitude, particularly beyond the Jamison Mine.

How to get there: From State Highway 70 turn south onto State Highway 89, approximately 10 miles west of Portola and 20 miles east of Quincy, following signed directions for PLUMAS EUREKA STATE PARK, GRAEAGLE and BLAIRSDEN. Travel down Highway 89 for 0.9 mile to a junction with Plumas County Road A14 and turn northwest, following another sign reading PLUMAS EUREKA STATE PARK. Follow Road A14 for 4.75 miles to the parking area along a plowed shoulder on the north side of the road opposite the signed trailhead. If you reach park headquarters you have gone 0.5 mile past the trailhead.

Eastbound travelers on Highway 70 can shave off nearly 3 miles of the description above by turning south 0.6 mile before the junction with Highway 89. Follow a paved road past the ranger station, and across the Middle Fork Feather River to a junction with Road A14 at the tiny community of Mohawk, 0.6 mile from the highway. From there, the trailhead is 3.6 miles westbound up A14.

Description: Proceed along the gently graded, snow-covered road paralleling the highway for a very short distance, to where the road bends southwest. Continue up the road through a light forest of cedar, fir, and pine, following the course of Jamison Creek. Just beyond where the grade of the road increases slightly, you reach the first of the restored buildings of the Jamison Mine. Proceed past more structures to the end of the marked ski trail.

The summit of Mt. Elwell provides a splendid vista

Depending on snow depth, you may be able to locate trailhead signs marking the beginning of the summer trail to the lakes a short distance past the sign marking the end of the cross-country ski trail. Continue up the canyon beyond the intial mine structures, passing some more buildings and following the trail above the wooded bank of Little Jamison Creek. You make an angling ascent up across the hillside, emerging into scattered forest high above the creek. Near the 2-mile mark from the highway, you reach an unmarked junction with the route over to Smith Lake.

Turn away from Little Jamison Creek and climb up the hillside for a mile on an arcing eastward ascent that leads to a lightly forested saddle. From the saddle, turn south and begin a moderately steep climb up the nose of the forested ridge that extends north from Mt. Elwell. After the initial ascent the grade eases to more of a moderate climb as you gain the crest and proceed along the ridge through a light forest that inhibits your views. You briefly climb out of the trees at a bald knob, where you have the first of many wide-ranging vistas. Notable landmarks such as Beckwourth Peak, Sierra Valley and the distant ranges of the Dixie and Diamond Mountains appear to the east, as well as Eureka Peak and Mt. Washington immediately to the west, and Smith Lake directly below.

Away from the knob you enter back into light red-fir and western-white-pine forest and continue up the ridge on a mild ascent until you encounter steeper slopes 0.5 mile north of Peak 7681 as shown on the Gold Lake topo map. Nearer to the peak the grade eases again as you reach an elevation high enough to support the presence of mountain hemlock. Breaking out of the trees, you reach the slope directly east of Peak 7681, where the rugged pinnacles of Sierra Buttes spring into view, a mere 8 air miles to the south. Other points of interest appear in virtually every direction, but even better views from the summit of Mt. Elwell beckon you to continue.

You drop into a saddle and then begin the climb along the summit ridge of Mt. Elwell. The ridge is narrow in spots and you will have to select your route carefully as you make your way to the top. From the 7818-foot summit you have incredible views in all directions, including the canyon of Little Jamison Creek where Rock and Jamison lakes lie directly below. Off in the distance to the north, the top of Lassen Peak pierces the sky, at 10,457-feet the highest point for 300 miles between Mt. Shasta and the higher peaks around Lake Tahoe. The most impressive view is arguably that of the Sierra Buttes, seemingly near enough to reach out and touch.

Before you leave the airy surroundings atop Mt. Elwell, you must head the short distance over to the southern high point in order to obtain the supreme view of the Lakes Basin region. From this high point you suddenly realize that the Lakes Basin is well named as a bevy of frozen lakes spreads out before you. Immediately below is Long Lake, at 147 acres the largest lake in the basin not accessible by a road, surrounded by a number of smaller lakes and ponds. Armed with a copy of the *Gold Lake* topo you can while away an hour identifying all the lakes and other landmarks scattered across the countryside. Just beyond Lakes Basin is Gold Lake, over three times the size of Long Lake.

Once you have enjoyed the views from Mt. Elwell, retrace your steps to the trailhead.

FYI: Most of the snow-covered terrain in this part of California is snowmobile country, which becomes painfully obvious from the vantage atop Mt. Elwell. Seemingly every lake, meadow and ridge within sight is crisscrossed with tracks, especially if your trip corresponds with an extended period of good weather without a recent snowfall. Plumas Eureka State Park is a sanctuary for snowshoers and skiers away from snowmobiles.

Warm-ups: Some places are just so quirky they must be experienced. The Mt. Tomba Inn Dinner House, 0.5 mile east of Cromberg on Highway 70, is just such a place. If John Wayne apparitions were anywhere near the number of Elvis sightings, this would be the place the Duke would be seen having dinner. His memorabilia cover the walls and many of the entrees bear the names of his movies. The Duke was definitely a presence, but his persona alone couldn't have sustained this restaurant out in the middle of nowhere for over 30 years—the food happens to be excellent. Prawns are the house specialty, but as you might imagine, beef reigns supreme in cowboy country. The Duke would surely approve of the substantial portions as well. Accompaniments include homemade soup, salad, bread, potatoes or rice, coffee and dessert. Dining at Mt. Tomba requires a healthy appetite and a touch of whimsy. Call (530) 836-2359 for winter hours (normally open Friday through Sunday nights, but may be closed in either January or February).

TRIP **22**

Eureka Lake & Peak

Duration: Three-quarter day
Distance: 6.5 miles round trip
Difficulty: Moderate to difficult
Elevation: 5490/7286 or 7447
Map: *Johnsville* 7.5′ quadrangle; *Lakes Basin, Sierra Buttes and Plumas Eureka State Park*, Plumas & Tahoe National Forests

see map on page **95**

Introduction: A dramatically picturesque lake and absolutely incredible views combine to make this trip an ideal snowshoe adventure. In winter Eureka Lake is as pretty as any lake you will find in the northern Sierra, particularly any lake that is only 1.25 mile from a trailhead. And finding a better wide-ranging view from the top of twin-summited Eureka Peak is equally hard to imagine. In spite of the fact that the route begins with an ascent of the ski slopes at Gold Mountain Ski Area, the backcountry above offers a sense of remoteness not easily duplicated near some of California's more popular ski areas.

Beginners may not want to climb the steep incline of the ski area and some moderately steep terrain above the lake, or they may balk at the need for the modicum of routefinding required to successfully navigate the route, but intermediate and advanced snowshoers should delight in the rigors of this trip. Part of the journey beyond the lake crosses a slope that may be avalanche prone under the right circumstances, requiring that you keep tabs on the condition of the snow before venturing above the lake. Even if you decide not to go all the way to the top of Eureka Peak, Eureka Lake itself would make a more than adequate destination.

How to get there: From State Highway 70, turn south on State Highway 89, approximately 10 miles west of Portola and 20 miles east of Quincy, following signed directions for PLUMAS and BLAIRSDEN. Travel down Highway 89 for 0.9 mile to a junction with Plumas County Road A14 and then turn northwest. Follow Road A14 past the Plumas Eureka State Park headquarters and through the historic town of Johnsville to the end of the road at the Gold Mountain Ski Area parking lot.

Description: Leave the parking area and follow the plowed path up to the base of the Gold Mountain Ski Area. From the base, make a steep ascent up the hillside, avoiding the groomed ski slopes by following the snow-cat track to the top of the hill (near the terminus of the old poma lift, construction of a modern chairlift is planned for the spring of 2001 which will extend skier access higher up the mountain). Widely scattered firs and pines on the edge of the ski slopes allow inspiring views of Eureka Peak and the surrounding countryside during the ascent. Once you reach the top of the old poma lift, locate the snow-cat track corresponding to the road which wraps around Peak 6284 and leads to Eureka Lake. After the steep climb up the ski slope the road provides a welcome change, making a nearly level traverse around the hill to the lake.

Just before you reach the lake, the road comes alongside the drainage of Eureka Creek and the dramatic north face of Eureka Peak pops into view. Soon you reach picturesque Eureka Lake nestled beneath the rugged rocks of Eureka Peak, 1.25 miles from the parking lot. A smattering of conifers add splashes of green, accenting the snow-covered slopes above the surface of the frozen lake. The thought of obtaining the summit of Eureka Peak from here appears to be a bit daunting, but the standard route proves to be easier than it looks.

To reach the peak you must first travel across the top of the dam and over the outlet of the creek. Beyond the stream you begin a moderate climb up through light forest. Initially, faded triangular snow markers appear sporadically nailed to trees, which may assist in your following the route of the summer hiking trail, but eventually they seem to disappear. After 0.5 mile you break out into the open and begin a moderately steep angling traverse across a hillside. Along the traverse you have nice views down to the lake and out to the distant hills and ridges. The lack of vegetation on this slope and the downhill-leaning nature of some of the small conifers indicate that this area may be prone to avalanches under the right conditions, so pro-

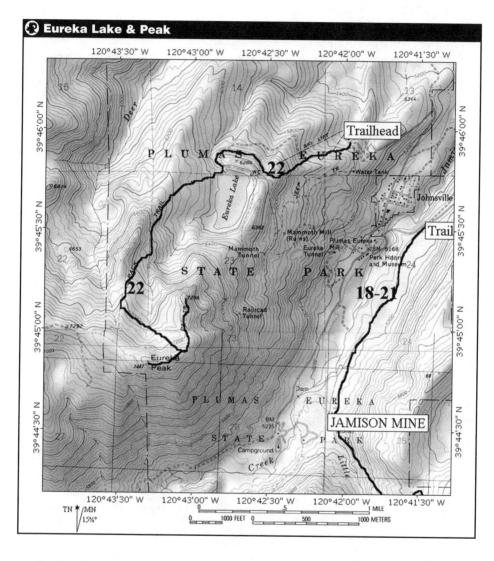

ceed only when the snow is stable. Once across the open hillside you reenter red-fir forest and start to climb more steeply.

Near the 2.5-mile mark you bend southeast and head toward the saddle between the twin summits of Eureka Peak. A moderately forested climb brings you to the base of the steep slope leading up to the summit ridge. Make a zigzagging ascent up the steep slope until the grade eases near the crest. Nearing the top of the ridge you must decide which summit you wish to visit first.

Whichever summit you chose, follow the ridge and then climb the short steep slope up to the top. The north summit of Eureka Peak offers a dramatic 360° panorama including distant Lassen Peak and the nearby summit of Mt. Washington, as well as Eureka Lake directly below you. However, perhaps the most impressive aspect of this view is the expansive terrain of northern California spread out in all directions. The vista from the south summit, which is 161 feet higher, is nearly as impressive, with the added attraction of views down into the Lakes Basin area.

FYI: Gold Mountain Ski Area has the quaint, small-town charm that most of California's premier resorts abandoned long ago. If you like to ski or board, consider spending a day on the uncrowded slopes in conjunction with your snowshoeing experience. Although the resort previously operated on weekends only, after completion of the new lift in 2001 the operators are planning to offer weekday skiing as well. For further information check out the web page at **www.skigoldmountain.org**.

Warm-ups: Although you wouldn't refer to the fare at the Lost Sierra Cafe in the Intorf Lodge at Gold Mountain as haute cuisine, you can catch a reasonably priced breakfast or lunch at the rustic ski lodge. Even if all you desire is to warm up with a cup of hot chocolate or coffee, you can do so while relaxing in front of the large iron fireplace.

A view of Eureka Lake from the slopes of Eureka Peak

CHAPTER 8

Sierra City Gold District

The Sierra Buttes are one of northern California's premier landmarks. Standing alone on the horizon above the surrounding terrain, the numerous vertical parapets that make up the 8591-foot aerie are visible from many northern California mountaintops, all the way from summits around Lake Tahoe to Lassen Peak. However, no sight is more impressive than the first view one obtains from near its base—the bulwark of precipitous cliffs rising straight up out of the landscape 4400 feet above Sierra City. Nestled amid a rolling sea of lesser forested hills, the rugged rocky cliffs of the Sierra Buttes stand out in regal majesty, unparalleled in magnificence. Such mountain drama seems out of place amid the neighboring, more common terrain. While the Sierra Buttes dominate the skyline, the mountain lakes nearby are what lure the majority of summer visitors.

Scattered around the Sierra Buttes and the Lakes Basin Recreation Area are numerous scenic mountain lakes that are the goal of many a hiker and backpacker. In fact, the area is so popular that camping is allowed at only a few of the backcountry lakes. The rest of the lakes outside of the backcountry harbor numerous resorts and campgrounds that serve vacationers from spring through fall. Once snowfall heralds the arrival of winter, the area becomes an extended playground for winter enthusiasts. The lakes freeze over, the hills develop a white winter coat, and the Sierra Buttes appear even more impressive, with a fresh dusting of powder clinging to the crevices and ledges of their sheer face. With the advent of winter and a reduced number of visitors, this area is blessed with a plethora of scenic destinations. However, there exists one major shortcoming—snowmobiles.

Outside of a 4-square-mile area north of Yuba Pass and a thin ribbon of land bordering the North Yuba River, this region is the northern part of a huge tract of Tahoe National Forest, extending south to Lake Tahoe, that is legally open to over-snow-vehicles (OSV). On a sunny winter weekend the Gold Lake Road and Yuba Pass parking areas are filled to overflowing with pickup trucks or SUVs, their trailers having borne mechanized beasts to these ports of entry into the snow country. Obviously, human-powered winter recreationists can't cover as much ground as a mechanized piece of equipment, but one glance at the Winter Recreation Guide for the Tahoe National Forest reveals a disproportionate amount of land open for snowmobiles. Although the winds of change may be stirring, the Forest Service has previously managed this area under a multiple-use approach, ignoring the realities that safety issues along with peace and quiet are important concepts to snowshoers and skiers. Unfortunately, they have to share some of the routes in this region with noisy, stinky machines. However, there are trails to follow that avoid snowmobiles altogether or for a good part of the trip, and the area is just too beautiful to give up without a fight. With an increase in non-mechanized winter use, perhaps the Forest Service will set aside more areas for snowshoers and skiers in the future.

The lure of gold brought a swarm of miners to this mountainous area of the northern Sierra in the last half of the 1800s. The Young American Quartz Mine operated on the north slope above Sardine Lake, producing an average monthly yield of $20,000 between 1884 and 1893. After the gold had been played out and the boom ended, Sierra County returned to the remote and nearly forgotten region it had been before, when the only human visitors were Native Americans seasonally following the spring migration of game from the lowland valleys into the high mountains. Although parties visited the area on horseback as early as the 1850s, use didn't increase much until the advent of the automobile, when a more mobile population of recreationists began to discover the potential of the exquisite back-country beyond Sierra City. With an abundance of scenic mountain lakes and a bounty of recreational opportunities, the area became a magnet for outdoor enthusiasts of all persuasions. Today these picturesque lands within Sierra County sustain a thriving resort community.

Location: The Sierra City Gold District is approximately 45 miles northwest of Truckee and approximately 85 miles northeast of Auburn.

Access: The principal access is via State Highway 49. All trailheads in this chapter are just a short distance off this highway.

Amenities: Downieville, 13 miles west of Sierra City, is the only full-service community during the winter that is anywhere close to the trailheads. Bassetts Station, at the junction with 49 and the Gold Lake Road, offers gasoline, supplies, a small cafe, and a motel. Sierra City has a few establishments that remain open for limited hours during the winter, but most businesses are seasonal. Many of the resorts along the North Yuba River offer lodging at reduced prices during the winter.

Season & Weather: Yuba Pass, at an elevation of 6700 feet, offers recreationists a high starting point assuring reasonably good snow conditions for a potentially lengthy season (Trips 29-32). The two other trailheads, Chapman Creek at 5865 feet (Trip 28) and Bassetts at 5415 feet (Trips 23-27) are considerably lower and prone to more marginal conditions over a much shorter season. During warm winters snowshoers may have to slog their way from these lower trailheads up to better conditions, but cold winters should provide decent snow from December through March. This area generally receives a decent amount of precipitation, but typically experiences wet snow conditions at the lower altitudes.

PERMITS
Day Use & Overnight Use: Permits are not required for entry into the Tahoe National Forest.

Sno-Park: A Sno-Park permit is necessary for parking at Yuba Pass. Permits can be purchased nearby at Bassetts Station (530) 862-1297, or in the town of Sierraville at Sierraville Service Country Store (530) 994-3387.

MAPS

Lakes Basin, Sierra Buttes and Plumas Eureka State Park, Recreation Guide
1:31,680, 1999, paper
Plumas & Tahoe National Forests

Tahoe National Forest and Lakes Basin, Winter Recreation Guide
1:84,480, 2000, paper
Tahoe National Forest

FOREST SERVICE

Downieville Ranger District	Sierraville Ranger District	Forest Supervisor
North Yuba Ranger Station	317 S. Lincoln Street	Tahoe National Forest
15924 Highway 49	P.O. Box 95	631 Coyote Street
Camptonville, CA 95922	Sierraville, CA 96126	Nevada City, CA 95959
(530) 288-3656	(530) 994-3401	(530) 265-4531

IMPORTANT PHONE NUMBERS

Avalanche Report	(530) 587-2158
Sno-Park Permit Information	(916) 324-1222

WEBSITES

Tahoe National Forest	www.r5.fs.fed.us/tahoe
Avalanche Report	www.r5.fs.fed.us/tahoe/avalanche
Sno-Park Information	www.ohv.parks.ca.gov/SVRAs/snopark

TRIP **23**

Sierra Buttes

see map
on page
101

Duration: Full day
Distance: 12.5 miles round trip
Difficulty: Difficult
Elevation: 4690/8591
Maps: *Sierra City* 7.5' quadrangle

Introduction: The Sierra Buttes at 8591 feet are the highest piece of terra firma for many miles around. Consequently, the view from the lookout is quite impressive, covering a vast area of northern California, from Lassen Peak, 75 miles north to Round Top, 75 miles south. In between are many more notable summits and lesser peaks and ridges. The lookout itself is a fairly stirring sight, perched on a narrow ridge, a part of the structure hanging out into space above the nearly vertical northeast face of the mountain. This aerie is an incredibly scenic spot coveted by many a hiker in the warmer months, but may be unattainable in winter. A series of ladders lead from the base of the cliffs to the lookout at the top. Even when free of snow, the dozens of steep steps will daunt acrophobes, and when encrusted with ice and snow may be too dangerous to climb. Extreme caution is vital when considering the ascent of these ladders in winter.

The 6-mile climb up the Buttes presents a steady, sometimes steep, ascent suitable only for snowshoers in good shape and competent on high-angle slopes. Furthermore, when snow covers the roadway, finding the route may be difficult in spots, requiring some routefinding skill. Spring, with longer days and warmer temperatures, may be the best time for some groups, when the lower section of the road is snow-free, providing parking higher up the mountain, and the snow and ice on the ladders has melted. If one can overcome the distance, the steep ascent, the routefinding and the climb up the ladders, the resulting view from the lookout is well worth the effort.

How to get there: Drive on Highway 49 to the small town of Sierra City and turn north on Butte Street. Travel 0.1 mile to Sierra Buttes Road and then head west for 1 mile to the large flat at the county dump. The road should be snow-free to this point, but may be impassable beyond the flat. If so, park your vehicle here. If conditions allow, you can save some steps by turning sharply right and following the road to a parking spot farther up.

Description: If you had to leave your car at the flat, walk up the road, first briefly east and then northwest to a junction with the Sierra Buttes Mine jeep road. From

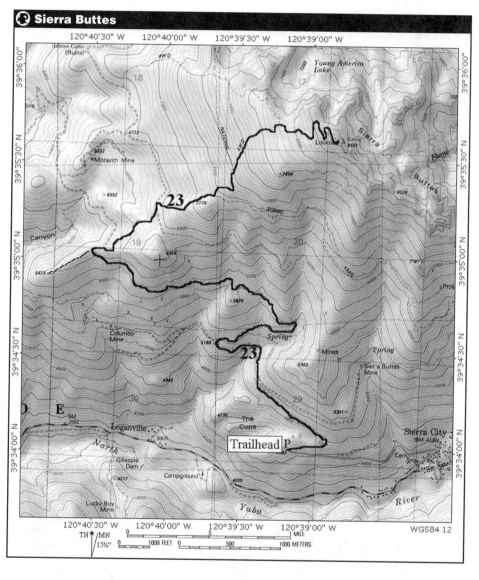

the junction, you continue up the road heading north until the road bends west at a creek. At 1.4 miles from the flat, near a junction with the jeep road to the Columbo Mine, you veer east, climbing moderately for another 0.5 mile until the road curves back to the west, 2 miles from the flat. You proceed generally west along the road for the next 0.5 miles on a steady ascent, passing occasional cedars and ponderosa pines, up to a saddle. An optional 0.3-mile descent from this saddle leads southwest to Point 6433, from where you have a nice view down Ladies Canyon. If you choose not to complete the entire route up the Buttes, this would be a good turn-around point.

From the saddle, the road bends east again and quickly comes to a junction with the road to Monarch Mine on your left. You continue east briefly and then climb northeast through a light forest of white fir, red fir and western white pine. If you have trouble discerning the route of the jeep road through this stretch, you can simply head for the saddle directly north of Point 6924 and then proceed northeast up the slope near the edge of the forest. If you can follow the course of the road, at 4.25 miles from the flat you reach an inconspicuous 4-way intersection. You head east toward a saddle northeast of Point 7179, where in summer you would meet the route of the Pacific Crest Trail. From here, make an arcing, 1.5 mile ascent up the steep slope to the base of the ladders leading to the lookout. As you approach the ladders, the terrain becomes quite steep.

Even when free of snow, the series of ladders leading to the Sierra Buttes lookout are imposing. When encrusted with snow they may be completely unmanageable. Proceed only when conditions are favorable. You may have to be satisfied with the fine view from below the lookout.

FYI: The upper part of Sierra Buttes can be quite wind-prone and the trip should be avoided when high winds are forecast.

Warm-ups: The Sierra Buttes and the North Yuba River region attract vacationers who fill the nearby resorts in summer. Winter is a much quieter time, and the resorts that remain open all year provide comfort and seclusion, sometimes at lower rates. The Sierra Shangri-La, on Highway 49 2.5 miles east of Downieville, offers a big dose of peace and quiet in their guest rooms above the bank of the North Yuba River. Call (530) 289-3455 for reservations or more information.

The dramatic Sierra Buttes as seen from Gold Lake Road

TRIP **24**

Sardine Lakes

see map
on page
104

Duration: Three-quarter day
Distance: 4.5 miles round trip to Lower Sardine Lake
          5.75 miles round trip to Upper Sardine Lake
Difficulty: Easy to Lower Sardine Lake
          Moderate to Upper Sardine Lake
Elevation: 5415/5780
          5415/6020
Maps: *Haypress Valley* & *Sierra City* 7.5′ quadrangles; *Lakes Basin,*
          Sierra Buttes and Plumas Eureka State Park,
          Plumas & Tahoe National Forests

Introduction: The shoreline view of Lower or Upper Sardine Lake backdropped by the sheer cliffs of the Sierra Buttes makes a classic picture-postcard scene. Throngs of summer visitors carried about by their motorized transport pay homage to the stunning scenery every season, far fewer souls make the journey once the winter snows close automobile access along the Gold Lake Road. The scenery is every bit as gorgeous during the winter. In fact, some admirers think that a fresh dusting of snow makes the Sardine Lakes and the Sierra Buttes even more spectacular. The snow-covered ramparts of the Buttes coupled with the frozen lakes do create a compelling winter scene, especially when bathed in sunshine.

To reach such stunning splendor requires only a modest expenditure of energy and next to no routefinding skills as the route follows pleasantly-graded well-defined roads, at least as far as the first lake. Beginning snowshoers in reasonable shape should have little difficulty in reaching Lower Sardine Lake. The remaining almost 0.75 mile to the upper lake follows the course of a jeep road which is moderately steep in parts, but the track is still readily apparent. Aside from the additional mileage and the slightly steeper climb, the route to Upper Sardine Lake is not particularly taxing either.

There exists one potential drawback to this nearly idyllic trip—snowmobiles. The Gold Lake Road and the Lakes Basin region have long been a haven for snowmobilers and OSV travel to Sardine Lakes. Although not a designated route, travel is unfortunately allowed. However, the vast majority of the machines will be left behind at the first junction on the Gold Lake Road and the rest at the junction with the road to Packer Lake, which are both designated OSV routes. Nevertheless, you

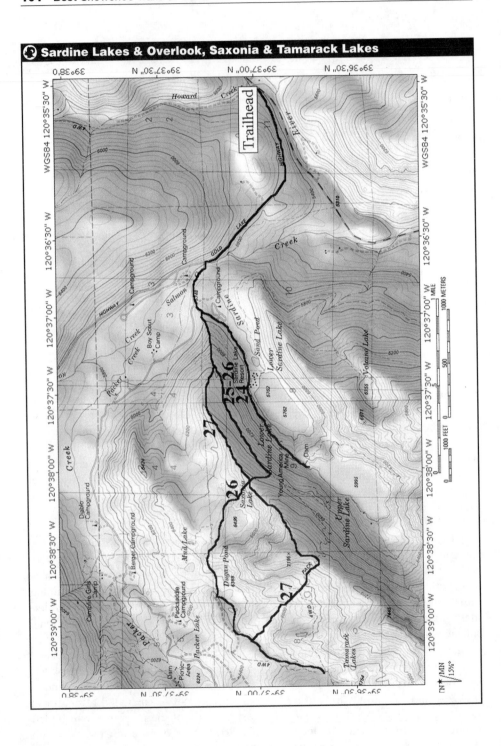

Sardine Lakes & Overlook, Saxonia & Tamarack Lakes

must exercise extra caution, particularly for the first 1.5 miles of the journey. Once you reach the magnificent scenery around the lakes, snowmobiles and the resulting distractions are soon forgotten.

How to get there: Travel on Highway 49 to Bassetts, 5 miles east of Sierra City and 18 miles west of Sierraville, and park in the large OHV staging area parking lot near the beginning of the snow-covered Gold Lakes Road. The parking area has a modern pit toilet. Overnight parking is available at the end of the short plowed section of roadway.

Description: Begin your trip by snowshoeing along the easy grade of the Gold Lake Road through a light-to-moderate mixed forest. Near the 0.5-mile mark, the trees thin and the road bends northwest, permitting dramatic views of the stately Sierra Buttes. Continue to climb mildly to moderately up the road to a junction at 1.25 miles. Following the signed directions to Sardine Lake, turn west at the junction and immediately cross Salmon Creek via the highway bridge.

Beyond the bridge you climb mildly, reaching another junction just past the 1.5-mile mark with a road that heads toward Packer Lake. A short distance beyond the road junction, you encounter the trailhead for the summer route of the Tamarack Lakes Connection Trail.

Continue straight ahead at the junction as the angle of ascent temporarily increases. Soon gentle travel resumes as you pass Sardine Lake Campground and then the Sand Pond Picnic Area. Not long afterward you come to the entrance to Sardine Lake Resort on the east shore of Lower Sardine Lake.

A snowshoer revels in the dramatic sight of the Sierra Buttes from Upper Sardine Lake

The view across the lake of Sierra Buttes can be quite awe-inspiring, particularly if you happen to be here just following a recent snowfall. When fresh powder clings to the crevices and clefts of the rock, glistening and sparkling in the brilliant rays of a clear sunny day, a more beautiful scene is hard to imagine. Whether you take photographs or simply admire the view, respect the private property of the resort while you do so.

To reach Upper Sardine Lake you must find the 4WD road at the Y-junction just before the entrance to Sardine Lake Resort. Climb up the road moderately steeply until the grade eases as you traverse across the south-facing slope above Lower Sardine Lake. The open hillside treats you to more splendid views of the Sierra Buttes and the lake below. As you pass the far end of Lower Sardine Lake, the grade of the ascent increases to a moderate climb that reaches the rock dam at the outlet of Upper Sardine Lake. The view from the upper lake, 1 mile closer to Sierra Buttes, is even more inspiring than the splendid view from the lower lake.

FYI: The terrain surrounding the Sardine Lakes is ripe for further exploration. A snow camp at Upper Sardine Lake would make a fine base camp for additional wanderings, either to other lakes or a summit bid on the Buttes.

Warm-ups: Bassetts Station offers a mini-mart, motel, gas station, and cafe serving the famous Bassetts Burger. The location is convenient, but if you're hankering for more exotic fare, head west down Highway 49 to Sierra City or Downieville.

TRIP 25

Sardine Overlook

Duration: One-half day
Distance: 5.5 miles round trip
Difficulty: Moderate
Elevation: 5415/6455
Maps: *Haypress Valley* & *Sierra City* 7.5' quadrangles; *Lakes Basin, Sierra Buttes and Plumas Eureka State Park,* Plumas & Tahoe National Forests

see map on page 104

Introduction: Few mountains in northern California equal the dramatic appeal of the east face of the Sierra Buttes, particularly in winter. Rising precipitously 2600-feet above the frozen surface of Upper Sardine Lake, the rocky ramparts and cliffs are

A beautiful view of the Sierra Buttes and Upper Sardine Lake from the Sardine Overlook

quite stunning after the dusting of a winter storm. The final mile of this trip rewards travelers with nearly continuous up-close views of the Sierra Buttes as well as both Upper and Lower Sardine lakes.

Snowshoers must share the first 1.25 miles along Gold Lake Road and another 0.25 mile along Sardine Lakes Road with snowmobiles, but the traffic dramatically declines after the Tamarack Lakes Connection Trail junction. Although snowmobiles are not specifically banned from traveling the route to the overlook, the terrain is difficult enough to dissuade the vast majority of users from venturing very far up the route.

How to get there: Travel on Highway 49 to Bassetts, 5 miles east of Sierra City and 18 miles west of Sierraville, and park in the large OHV staging area parking lot near the beginning of the snow-covered Gold Lake Road. The parking area is equipped with a modern pit toilet. Overnight parking is available at the east end of the short section of plowed road.

Description: Begin your trip by snowshoeing along the easy grade of the Gold Lake Road through a light-to-moderate mixed forest. Near the 0.5-mile mark, the trees thin and the road bends northwest, permitting dramatic views of the stately Sierra Buttes. Continue to climb moderately up the road to a junction at 1.25 miles. Following the signed directions to Sardine Lake, turn west at the junction and immediately cross Salmon Creek via the highway bridge.

Beyond the bridge, you climb mildly, reaching another junction, just past the 1.5-mile mark, with a road that heads toward Packer Lake. Veer left at the junction and soon reach the summer trailhead for the Tamarack Lakes Connection Trail.

Head directly up the hillside ahead, climbing moderately steeply across the open slope rather than attempting to follow the zigzagging, ill-defined course of the summer trail. As you reach the crest of the hill, the snow-covered trail will become more obvious as it follows the route of an abandoned jeep road. Once past the steep part of your ascent, the climb abates to a mild-to-moderate ascent along the south side of a lateral moraine. Unobstructed views of the dramatic east face of the Sierra Buttes are your constant companions along this open ridge dotted with an occasional Jeffrey pine. Soon the frozen surfaces of Lower and Upper Sardine lakes pop into view. You continue the climb along the moraine until reaching a junction, directly above the dam at Upper Sardine Lake. Here the course of the Sardine Lake Overlook hiking trail splits from the Tamarack Lakes Connection Trail and begins a 0.3-mile descent to the viewpoint. Beyond this junction the angle of the hillside ahead grows considerably steeper. My recommendation is to be satisfied with the superb view from the junction rather than descending the increasingly difficult terrain to the site of the summer overlook. Either way, once you have taken in the spectacular scenery, retrace your steps to the parking area.

FYI: For interesting trip extensions, see Trips 26 and 27.

Warm-ups: Back in Downieville, the Downieville Bakery and Cafe is a hands-down favorite with locals and travelers alike. During winter you can enjoy breakfast, lunch or dinner from Thursday to Monday in the small cafe (no credit cards). Make sure you snag a loaf of one of Tom Byg's famous breads for the trail. Call (530) 289-0108 for more information.

TRIP 25

Saxonia Lake

see map on page 104

Duration: Three-quarter day
Distance: 6.5 miles round trip
Difficulty: Moderate
Elevation: 5415/6615/6495
Maps: *Haypress Valley & Sierra City* 7.5' quadrangles; *Lakes Basin, Sierra Buttes and Plumas Eureka State Park,* Plumas & Tahoe National Forests

Introduction: Without a road granting shoreline access, Saxonia Lake escapes the summer traffic that nearby popular destinations such as Sardine and Packer lakes receive. Aside from hikers wandering off the beaten path and anglers in search of trout, few visits are made to this nearly forgotten body of water. In winter, when snowfall further complicates access to the lake, even snowmobilers seem to pass it by in favor of other more distant goals. Seemingly ignored by most recreationists, Saxonia Lake offers snowshoers a pleasant opportunity for favorable scenery and relative seclusion. The shoreline is dotted with graceful pines while the frozen lake fills a bowl at the base of scenic cliffs.

The trip to the lake requires only moderate physical effort along with minimal routefinding for an unmarked trail. The terrain is open over nearly the entire route, allowing snowshoers to easily negotiate the entire distance to the lake. The first 1.5 miles follow the well-defined path of the Gold Lake and Sardine lakes roads, and the remaining distance is nearly as straightforward.

How to get there: Travel on Highway 49 to Bassetts, 5 miles east of Sierra City and 18 miles west of Sierraville, and park in the large OHV staging area parking lot near the beginning of the snow-covered Gold Lake Road. The parking area is equipped with a modern pit toilet. Overnight parking is available at the east end of the short section of the plowed road.

Description: Begin your trip by snowshoeing along the easy grade of the Gold Lake Road through a light-to-moderate mixed forest. Near the 0.5-mile mark, the trees thin and the road bends northwest, permitting dramatic views of the stately Sierra Buttes. Continue to climb moderately up the road to a junction at 1.25 miles. Following the signed directions to Sardine Lake, turn west at the junction and immediately cross Salmon Creek via the highway bridge.

Beyond the bridge, you climb mildly, reaching another junction, just past the 1.5-mile mark, with a road that heads toward Packer Lake. Veer left at the junction and soon reach the summer trailhead for the Tamarack Lakes Connection Trail.

Head directly up the hillside ahead, climbing moderately steeply across the open slope rather than attempting to follow the zigzagging, ill-defined course of the summer trail. As you reach the crest of the hill, the snow-covered trail will become more obvious where it follows the course of an abandoned jeep road. Once past the steepest part of the ascent, the climb abates to a mild-to-moderate ascent along the south side of a lateral moraine. Along the open ridge, dotted with an occasional Jeffrey pine, you'll find unobstructed views of the dramatic east face of the Sierra Buttes. At 2.75 miles, you reach the summer trail junction between the Sardine Overlook and Tamarack Lakes Connection trails.

From the vicinity of the junction, angle back to the north and climb up the slope about 0.25 mile to the crest of the ridge above Saxonia Lake. Descend from the ridge, moderately-steeply at times, to the east shore of the lake.

Saxonia Lake occupies a deep bowl at the east base of steep, rocky cliffs that rise up to the summit of Peak 7195. Surrounded by widely scattered pines, the lake presents an enjoyable winter scene that is far enough off the beaten path to receive little use.

FYI: For those who are looking for a nice destination for a snow-camping adventure, Saxonia Lake may be a good choice.

Warm-ups: Catching Mountain Shadows in operation during the schizophrenic winter season, when it's hard to know when an establishment will be open or closed, may be a dubious proposition. If you're fortunate enough to be there when the restaurant is open, you can feast on Beryl Kelley's distinctively British cuisine for breakfast or lunch. If you hanker for something more homespun, Beryl learned how to prepare American fare as a chef for both Packer Lake Lodge and Sardine Lakes Resort. Find Mountain Shadows at 224 Main Street (Highway 49) in Sierra City. Call (530) 862-1990 to see if the lights are on. Credit cards are not accepted.

TRIP 27

Tamarack Lakes

Duration: Three-quarter day
Distance: 8.5 miles round trip
Difficulty: Moderate
Elevation: 5415/7115/6755
Map: *Haypress Valley & Sierra City* 7.5′ quadrangles; *Lakes Basin, Sierra Buttes and Plumas Eureka State Park*, Plumas & Tahoe National Forests

see map on page 104

Introduction: A popular summer destination for two-legged and four-wheeled visitors alike, the Tamarack Lakes see much less traffic during winter. Along the way there are splendid views from vantage points on a 1.5-mile traverse of the ridge separating Sardine and Packer creeks. An optional short climb leads to a 360° vista from the summit of Peak 7195. The most impressive aspect of this vista is the dramatic east face of the Sierra Buttes, a mere 1.5 air miles away. A number of additional landmarks are also visible, including Sardine, Packer and Saxonia lakes.

A summer route, the Tamarack Lakes Connection Trail takes hikers and backpackers across the northwest slope of Sardine Creek Canyon on the way to the lakes. In winter, this steep hillside above Upper Sardine Lake is exposed and potentially treacherous when less than ideal snow conditions are present. Therefore, this description follows a more prudent route along the crest of the ridge before rejoining the summer trail at a saddle directly south of Peak 7195. Although most of the trip passes through open terrain, successfully reaching Tamarack Lakes will require a certain amount of routefinding.

The Sierra Buttes as seen from the Tamarack Lakes Trail

How to get there: Travel on Highway 49 to Bassetts, 5 miles east of Sierra City and 18 miles west of Sierraville, and park in the large OHV staging area parking lot near the beginning of the snow-covered Gold Lake Road. The parking area is equipped with a modern pit toilet. Overnight parking is available at the east end of the short section of the plowed road.

Description: Begin your trip by snowshoeing along the easy grade of the Gold Lake Road through a light-to-moderate mixed forest. Near the 0.5-mile mark, the trees thin and the road bends northwest, permitting dramatic views of the stately Sierra Buttes. Continue to climb moderately up the road to a junction at 1.25 miles. Following the signed directions to Sardine Lake, turn west at the junction and immediately cross Salmon Creek via the highway bridge.

Beyond the bridge, you climb mildly, reaching another junction, just past the 1.5-mile mark, with a road that heads toward Packer Lake. Veer left at the junction and soon reach the summer trailhead for the Tamarack Lakes Connection Trail.

From the vicinity of the trailhead for the Tamarack Lakes Connection Trail, make a moderately steep ascent up the hillside directly ahead toward the crest of the ridge. After 0.25 mile the ascent eases as you gain the actual crest and then climb moderately along the apex of the ridge for the next 1.25 miles. You eventually reach the slope directly south of the summit of Peak 7195, as shown on the *Sierra City* topo map, 3.25 miles from the trailhead. A short climb to the top grants awesome views west to the dramatic eastern face of Sierra Buttes as well as expansive vistas of the surrounding countryside.

From the slope below Peak 7195 make a 0.2 mile descent to a saddle directly south of the summit. From here you turn northwest and descend a lightly forested gully for

0.75 mile to the seasonal creek that drains Tamarack Lakes. Turning south-southwest, you follow this drainage for nearly another 0.5 mile to the first of the Tamarack Lakes. Another 0.2 mile will take you farther up the canyon to the second lake.

Both of the Tamarack Lakes are relatively small, irregularly shaped bodies of water ringed by scattered lodgepole pines. Nestled in shallow basins, the lakes sit near the end of the canyon of Packer Creek below a twin-summited, unnamed rock peak directly northwest of Sierra Buttes. Accessible to OHVs in the summer, the lakes are likewise visited on occasion by snowmobiles during the winter months.

FYI: An interesting variation for your return follows a route past Dugan Pond and Saxonia Lake before reconnecting to your trail up the ridge.

Warm-ups: An overnight stay in one of the four guest rooms at the newly restored Busch & Heringlake Country Inn in historic Sierra City may well be a snowshoers dream come true. Aside from a relaxing glass of sherry in the parlor and an enjoyable continental breakfast, innkeeper Carlo Giuffre offers additional amenities that are unique to the bed-and-breakfast scene. At the helm of the Inn's snowcat, Carlo will ferry his guests deep into the exquisite Gold Lake backcountry and then guide his guests on snowshoe trips into such hard-to-reach destinations as the Salmon Lakes. Following a hot shower back at the inn or a dip in a private jacuzzi, the climax of the day might be one of Carlos favorite dinners served in the downstairs dining room. For reservations, call (530) 862-1501, email Carlo at cgiuffre@cwo.com or send correspondence to 231 Main St., Sierra City, CA 96125.

TRIP **28**

Chapman Creek Loop

Duration: One-half day
Distance: 4.5 mile loop trip
Difficulty: Moderate
Elevation: 5865/6515
Map: *Clio* 7.5' quadrangle

see map
on page
114

Introduction: Chapman Creek offers snowshoers a chance to experience a sense of solitude away from the noise and fumes of snowmobiles so common to much of the terrain in this area. The first half of this loop leads travelers on a moderate climb

The top of the Sierra Buttes as seen from the Chapman Creek Trail

through light forest alongside a secluded drainage. The second half follows the course of an old logging road away from the creek to beautiful views of Deadman and Haskell peaks and the Sierra Buttes. Although the route is not marked, the journey up Chapman Creek follows the obvious course of the drainage and the road back is easily discernible, making the routefinding straightforward. The 4.5-mile distance makes the trip a pleasant half day excursion.

About the only traffic in this area consists of cross-country skiers occasionally following the blue diamonds along the flat 0.25-mile loop around the campground. This loop would certainly provide novice snowshoers or skiers an easy way to try out a new sport. The route up Chapman Creek seems to attract only a few hearty souls throughout the course of the winter, thereby granting a reasonable expectation of peace and quiet. The backcountry north of the loop offers additional opportunities for exploration.

How to get there: Travel on Highway 49, 3 miles east of Bassetts or 3.5 miles west of Yuba Pass to the signed entrance into Chapman Creek Campground. Turn east from the highway, and follow the campground road the short distance to the end of the plowed section, and park as space allows.

Description: From the end of the plowed road a marked trail follows the snow-covered campground loop 0.25 mile back to your starting point. Follow this road for only 0.1 mile to the beginning of the trail alongside Chapman Creek, from where you should leave the loop road and begin the moderate climb up the right-hand (south)

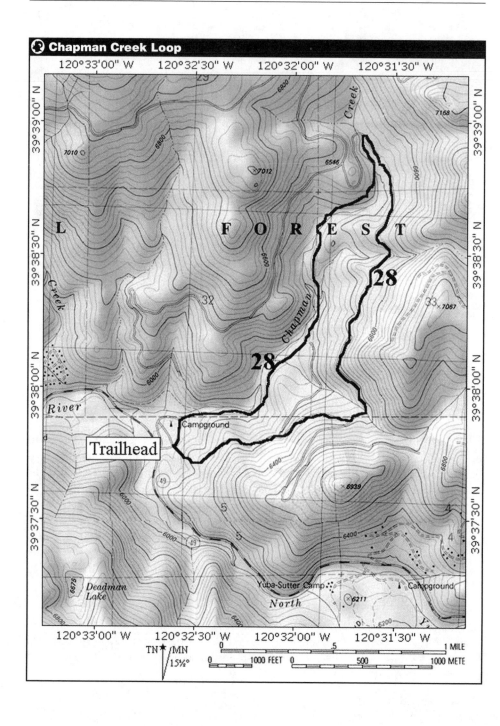

side of the drainage. Depending on the snow depth, you may be able to locate the sign at the start of the trail. If not, the creek drainage should be obvious.

Initially you follow the route of the trail near the bank of Chapman Creek through a light forest of fir and pine, periodically ascending the hillside as you encounter steeper terrain along the stream. You must cross side streams at 0.75 and 1 mile from the trailhead before crossing over the main channel of Chapman Creek just before the 1.5-mile point. You continue up the drainage, passing below a hill to your left. By ascending this hill you can obtain a nice view of Deadman Peak to the southwest and Haskell Peak to the northwest. You cross back over the creek and encounter the snow-covered road near a bridge spanning Chapman Creek at 2 miles from the trailhead.

Leave the creek and follow the route of this road on a mild climb as you bend around to the south. A lighter forest permits glimpses of the surrounding ridges, and eventually Deadman Peak, Haskell Peak and Sierra Buttes pop into view. You continue south along the road until bending southeast to cross a side stream. Just beyond the stream, at 3.5 miles, you encounter a junction.

At the junction, take the right-hand road, heading west, and descend 0.4 mile to another junction, where you should continue straight ahead. Another 0.5-mile of decline leads to the sudden end of the road in the midst of a lightly forested slope. Down the hillside you should be able to locate a swath through the trees for a powerline. Turn northwest and follow this cut 0.1 mile down to your starting point at the end of the plowed section of the campground loop road.

FYI: By utilizing the road system you can create some interesting extensions to your trip. From the bridge over Chapman Creek you can climb a short distance up the hillside to the road and follow it north for a mile to a junction with the Haskell Peak Trail and then southeast to connections with the Lunch Creek and Yuba Pass trails.

Warm-ups: If your trip to Chapman Creek is on a weekend, you may be able to enjoy dinner in the dining room of the Busch & Heringlake Country Inn. Call ahead to (530) 862-1501 to see if innkeeper Carlo Giuffre will be serving. The historic inn, which used to house Wells Fargo, Western Union and an old-fashioned general store, has been completely refurbished. The Inn is in Sierra City at 231 Main Street. For information on lodging see Trip 27.

TRIP **29**

Lunch Creek–
3 Knobs Loop

Duration: One-half to three-quarter day
Distance: 5.5 miles loop trip
Difficulty: Moderate
Elevation: 6465/7425
Maps: *Haypress Valley, Clio, Calpine & Sattley* 7.5' quadrangles;
Tahoe National Forest and Lakes Basin Winter Recreation Guide

*see map on page **117***

Introduction: The Lunch Creek trail system is one of the few places to enjoy the Yuba Pass backcountry sans snowmobiles. Chances are you may hear the distant roar of their engines on nearby designated snowmobile trails, but you do have a reasonable expectation of avoiding their immediate presence. This loop offers a pleasant trip through forested terrain along with the chance for some picturesque views of the terrain north of Yuba Pass, including Deadman Peak, Sierra Buttes and Haskell Peak.

The entire route is marked by blue diamonds, thereby eliminating some of the need for extensive routefinding. However, you will need to pay close attention at the junction 3.5 miles from the trailhead to stay on route.

How to get there: Find the trailhead on the north side of Highway 49, 1 mile west of Yuba Pass or 5.5 miles east of Bassetts. Snowplows create room for about one-half dozen cars near the beginning of the road up Lunch Creek. Additional parking can be had along the shoulder of Highway 49.

Description: From the car, follow the blue diamonds up the moderately graded road a short distance to a road junction. At the junction, turn left (west) and begin a mild ascent across the steep hillside, paralleling Highway 49 below you. You proceed up the road through light forest composed primarily of red fir, with a smattering of lodgepole pine. Near the 0.5-mile mark, the road bends north, and then curves northeast around Peak 6984 (as shown on the Haypress Valley topo). You continue to follow a winding, upward course until you reach the ski-trail junction in a clearing, 1.75 miles from the trailhead.

At the junction, turn northeast, obeying the signed directions for 3 KNOBS TRAIL. The vista improves as you climb moderately across the nearly bare slope. The stunning

Lunch Creek–3 Knobs Loop, Yuba Pass Vista

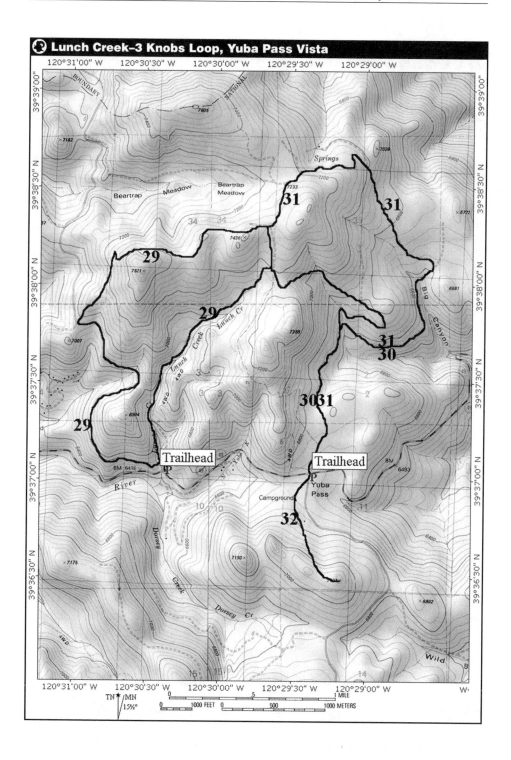

A snowshoer gazes at Deadman Peak from the Lunch Creek Trail

view includes the rugged ramparts of Sierra Buttes, the sheer northeast face of Deadman Peak and the pyramidal profile of Haskell Peak. The views come and go as you travel in and out of the trees, continuing to climb at a moderate to moderately steep grade. You reach an open hillside where the road bends sharply right and then quickly back left across the slope. Now heading east, you make an upward traverse across the first, and tallest, of the three knobs, through widely scattered young trees. The road may be hard to discern through here, so pay close attention to the blue diamonds in order to successfully navigate across this slope. Eventually, the path of the road will become more obvious again.

Past the first knob, the 3 Knobs Trail follows the ridge crest on a brief descent down to a small sloping meadow and then mildly up to the second knob. Gentle terrain leads away from the second knob until a short moderate climb leads to the third knob, shown as Peak 7436 on the Calpine topo. A large rock near the top makes a fine lunch or rest stop. Follow blue markers to the north of the high point, down through the trees for nearly 0.25 mile to the Nordic trail junction, roughly 25 yards before you would intersect the groomed snowmobile route.

A trio of signs at this junction give directions for the 3 Knobs Trail (west—the direction from which you've come—and south—the direction in which you will now be heading) and to the Lunch Creek Trail (east). Although the Lunch Creek Cross-Country Ski Area insert in the Tahoe National Forest and Lakes Basin Winter Recreation Guide shows the snowmobile and Nordic trail sharing a route to the south from this junction, in actuality, the blue-diamond-marked trail parallels the snowmobile route about 25 yards to its west. If you were to proceed along the road, chances are you would miss the point, 0.25 mile south and 3.5 miles from the trailhead, where the Nordic trail veers southwest away from the snowmobile track. Therefore, make sure you follow the blue diamonds south from the junction, avoiding the tendency to travel down the snowmobile route, which ultimately leads to Yuba Pass.

You parallel the snowmobile route for 0.25 mile until the Nordic trail bends southwest through light forest on a moderate descent following a snow-covered road. Continue straight ahead at a junction where a road branches west toward Lunch Creek. Soon you pass below the open hillside of Point 7388 as shown on the Calpine topo and then pass back into light forest as the descent continues. You emerge out onto the crest of an open ridge for awhile before returning to light forest. Proceed along the road as you wind through the trees well above Lunch Creek back to the trailhead, 6 miles from your beginning point.

FYI: Opportunities exist for extending your wanderings by following some of the other trails in the Yuba Pass/Lunch Creek area. However, you will have to face the possibility of sharing some of the trails with snowmobiles. From the junction 1.75 miles from the trailhead, you can continue north, reaching the Haskell Peak snowmobile trail. From there you can either continue north to Chapman Saddle or turn east and then south, following the Haskell Peak Trail to junctions with the Lunch Creek route.

Warm-ups: Riverview Pizza serves great pizza. The fact that they remain open during the winter is another great piece of news. In addition to the pizza, menu items include such Americanized-Italian favorites as spaghetti, calzones and ravioli, as well as hamburgers and hot sandwiches. Find the Riverview on Main Street in Downieville, near the confluence of the North Yuba and Downie Rivers. Call (530) 289-3540 for more information.

TRIP **30**

Yuba Pass Vista

see map on page 117

Duration: One-half day
Distance: 3.25 miles round trip
Difficulty: Easy
Elevation: 6700/6480
Map: *Sattley* & *Calpine* 7.5′ quadrangles; *Tahoe National Forest and Lakes Basin Winter Recreation Guide*

Introduction: An easy stroll with a pleasant view makes this a trip for snowshoers of all levels and abilities. Following the gentle course of an obvious road, the route is marked and well-used, making losing your way next to impossible. In addition, breaking trail probably won't be necessary for the first mile as the road will most likely be groomed. However, the groomer of the trail didn't have snowshoers in mind, but rather snowmobilers, who use this first mile of shared trail to access a variety of routes north and west of Yuba Pass. Therefore, you must exercise caution on the initial stretch of road. Beyond the first mile, leave the noisy, fume-belching beasts behind and continue your easy stroll to the viewpoint amid the peace and quiet of a light forest.

How to get there: On State Highway 49, drive to the Sno-Park at Yuba Pass, 11 miles east of Sierra City. Limited parking is available on the north side of the pass near the trailhead for snowshoers and skiers. The larger parking lot on the south side of the pass is used mainly by snowmobilers. Restrooms are in the south lot.

Description: The groomed track heading north from Yuba Pass is a shared route between human-powered and gasoline-powered recreationists for the first mile. Warning signs are posted for all users to use caution on this multiple-use trail, but you should be alert for approaching snowmobiles at all times, particularly on busy weekends. Initially, you make a mild ascent north away from the pass, made easier by the packed snowmobile track. You continue to climb, cresting a low ridge at the 0.3-mile-mark. Beyond the ridge, a gentle descent leads through light forest to a junction 1 mile from the pass.

Leaving the multiple-use trail behind, you bend east on the signed Nordic ski trail and continue the mild descent for another 0.6-mile, to where the road bends to the north. At the bend, you can follow a minor ridge a very short distance southeast out to the viewpoint.

As you stand at the brink of the hillside, your eyes are drawn to the declivity immediately to the left, aptly named Big Canyon. Plunging steeply south, Big Canyon merges quickly with Turner Canyon, where forested hillsides rise sharply above the stream valley. To the east, you catch glimpses of the large plain known as Sierra Valley.

After enjoying the view, retrace your steps to the car. Make sure you save plenty of energy for the mostly uphill return.

FYI: Remember to observe proper trail etiquette on this route by avoiding stepping on the cross-country ski tracks.

Warm-ups: The cozy Downieville Diner offers home-style cooking and freshly baked desserts. Breakfast and lunch are served from 7 a.m. to 2 p.m. on Thursday through Tuesday, and dinner from 5:45 to 8:30 on Friday, Saturday and Sunday. Find the diner on Main Street. (530) 289-3616.

TRIP 31

Yuba Pass Loop

see map on page **122**

Duration: Three-quarter day
Distance: 6.5 miles loop trip
Difficulty: Moderate
Elevation: 6700/7335
Map: *Sattley & Calpine* 7.5′ quadrangles; *Tahoe National Forest and Lakes Basin Winter Recreation Guide*

Introduction: At 6701 feet above sea level, Yuba Pass offers winter recreationists a fairly good chance of finding decent snow conditions throughout the course of an average season. Since the pass is one of only a few places north of Interstate 80 with such an altitude accessible by automobile, the nearby Sno-Park can be quite a busy place on weekends, particularly when the weather is fair. The terrain to the south is usually dominated by snowmobiles, creating a rather undesirable scenario for those propelled by human power. Unless you have the luxury of a mid-week visit, my suggestion is to avoid the backcountry south of Yuba Pass altogether. However, marked routes to the north of the pass offer snowshoers and skiers alike much better alternatives to the mayhem in the opposite direction,

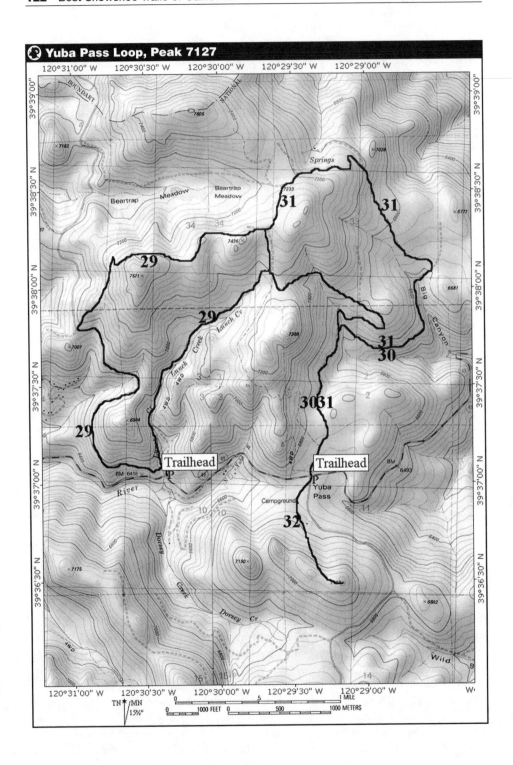

although you still have to share paths with snowmobiles where routes are designated as multiple-use trails.

Since this trip follows an obvious road system marked with blue diamonds for the entire distance, the routefinding is straightforward and relatively easy. Aside from some fine views across Sierra Valley to the range of peaks at the east edge, most of this journey passes through the tranquil setting of a light, mixed forest. After the first mile of multiple-use trail, snowshoers leave the snowmobiles behind. For the next 2.5 miles, you can enjoy the peace and quiet provided by the fir and pine forest, until you intersect the next section of multiple-use trail used for the return to Yuba Pass. For your convenience you can consider different return routes by examining the options below in FYI.

How to get there: On State Highway 49, drive to the Sno-Park at Yuba Pass, 11 miles east of Sierra City. Limited parking is available on the north side of the pass near the trailhead for snowshoers and skiers. Mainly snowmobilers use the larger parking area on the south side of the pass. Restrooms are in the south lot.

Description: Away from Yuba Pass, you make a mild ascent to the north, cresting a low ridge at 0.3 miles. Beyond the ridge, a gentle descent leads through light forest to a junction, 1 mile from the pass.

Leaving the multiple-use trail behind, you bend east on the signed Nordic ski trail and continue the mild descent for another 0.6 mile to where the road bends north. By following a minor ridge a short distance southeast, you can access the view described in Trip 30.

Now head north on the snow-covered road, mildly climbing across the hillside above Big Canyon, following the blue-diamond-marked course of the Nordic ski trail. Soon the road curves northeast as you cross the head of the canyon amid a mixed forest of ponderosa pine and red fir. The steady climb continues as you follow the road around a couple of turns, near the 2-mile mark, before adopting a north-northwest bearing for the next mile. Eventually the gain in elevation allows periodic views to the east across the broad expanse of Sierra Valley to the peaks and ridges at the very fringe of the Sierra.

The road begins to curve again, 3 miles from the trailhead, as you ascend up through scattered fir forest. More views across Sierra Valley appear intermittently until your path adopts a more westerly course. You continue to climb until reaching a junction with the Haskell Peak Trail at 3.5 miles from the trailhead. For a variation on a return route from this point, see FYI below.

From the junction, turn south and mildly climb up the multiple-use trail for 0.25 mile to the high point of your journey and another trail intersection at 3.75 miles from the trailhead, this one with the marked 3 Knobs Ski Trail heading west. For additional variations on return routes from this point, see FYI below.

To return to Yuba Pass you must head south from the junction with the 3 Knobs Ski Trail. Since the next 1.75 mile from the junction is a multiple-use route, you must pay close attention for the possible approach of snowmobiles. You continue south for 0.25 mile until the road bends in a generally southeast direction, making a long winding descent through light forest. Eventually the route curves around to the

A winter trail marker at a junction on the Yuba Pass Trail

intersection with the Nordic ski trail at 5.5 miles from the trailhead, closing your loop.

Retrace your steps 1 mile back to the parking area at Yuba Pass.

FYI: From the junction with the 3 Knobs Ski Trail at 3.75 miles from the trailhead, you can avoid potential encounters with snowmobiles, a least for the first 0.25 mile, by following the marked Lunch Creek Ski Trail, which parallels the road about 25 yards to the west. If you choose this option, make sure that you don't remain on the Lunch Creek trail after the first 0.25 mile, but head west over to the snowmobile route and follow the road back to Yuba Pass.

If you have two vehicles, or if you don't mind the mile-long walk back up Highway 49 to your car, you can alter your return trip by following a trio of routes to the Lunch Creek Trailhead (1.0 mile west of Yuba Pass).

Option 1: (From the junction with the Haskell Peak Trail at 3.5 miles from the trailhead) continue west on the Haskell Peak Trail (a multiple-use trail) through Beartrap Meadow for 1.5 miles to the junction with the Lunch Creek Ski Trail. Turn south and follow the snow-covered road for 0.75 mile to the 3 Knobs Trail junction. Continue on the Lunch Creek route for another 1.75 miles to the Lunch Creek trailhead at Highway 49.

Option 2: (From the junction with the 3 Knobs Ski Trail at 3.75 miles from the trailhead) turn west and follow the 3 Knobs Trail for 1.75 miles to the Lunch Creek Trail. Turn south and continue on the Lunch Creek route for another 1.75 miles to the Lunch Creek trailhead at Highway 49.

Option 3: (From the junction with the 3 Knobs Ski Trail at 3.75 miles from the trailhead). Head west on the 3 Knobs Ski Trail for only about 25 yards to a series of three signs: 3 KNOBS SKI TRAIL (south), LUNCH CREEK SKI TRAIL (east) and 3 KNOBS SKI TRAIL (west). Following the blue diamonds, turn south and follow the marked trail for 0.25 mile and then southwest for another 2 miles to the Lunch Creek trailhead at Highway 49.

Warm-ups: See Trips 23-30.

TRIP 32

Yuba Pass to Peak 7127

see map
on page
122

Duration: One-half day
Distance: 1.75 miles round trip
Difficulty: Moderate
Elevation: 6700/7127
Map: *Sattley* 7.5' quadrangle

Introduction: The terrain south of Yuba Pass is overrun by snowmobiles on weekends. Unless you happen to be in the area on a weekday, you should avoid traveling on the network of roads that carpet the region south of the pass. However, you can escape the motorized madness by heading for the steep, forested hillside of Point 7127 as shown on the Sattley topo map. This short journey quickly leaves the snowmobiles behind and leads snowshoers to a pleasant view of the broad plain of Sierra Valley.

How to get there: On State Highway 49, drive to the Sno-Park at Yuba Pass, 11 miles east of Sierra City. Limited parking is available on the north side of the pass near the trailhead for snowshoers and skiers. Mainly snowmobilers use the larger parking area on the south side of the pass. Restrooms are in the south lot.

Description: Begin your trip by angling southwest away from the well-traveled, snow-covered road that heads south from the Sno-Park. Since the area adjacent to the Sno-Park is relatively flat, chances are you may have to contend with the presence of snowmobiles until the slope becomes steeper. Beyond the level terrain, your goal is to ascend the hill directly south of the parking area, reaching the top of the ridge at the saddle between the true high point at the northwest end and Point 7127 at the southeast end. Dense timber may inhibit you from achieving the most direct route from the beginning of the trip, but you should be able to adjust your bearing as the climb leads through a lighter forest below the crest. Once you reach the ridge top, turn southeast and make the gentle climb up to the top of Point 7127.

To the east, the expanse of Sierra Valley spreads before you, rimmed by snowy peaks at the far east edge of the Sierra. Closer, the cleft of Wild Bill Canyon lies to the southeast, and the hills and ridges obscuring Lincoln valley are directly south.

FYI: To get a view from the true high point of the ridge, you will need technical climbing skills to scale the knife-edged rocky spine that extends to the summit. An easier roue is on the slopes of Peak 7190, 0.6 mile to the west of 7127.

Warm-ups: See Trips 23-30.

CHAPTER 9

Interstate 80 & Vicinity East to Donner Summit

The all-weather highway of Interstate 80 provides access for millions of Californians to one of America's favorite winter playgrounds, Lake Tahoe. After the success of the 1960 winter Olympics at Squaw Valley, Tahoe gained status in the eyes of the world just as an influx of new residents were flocking into the Golden State. As interest in outdoor pursuits reached a crescendo in the "back to the earth" 70s, Tahoe became an exceedingly popular summer venue for a wide range of outdoor enthusiasts. Once the alpine ski resorts expanded and cross-country skiing was discovered by a greater number of Americans, this fervor for the Lake Tahoe area expanded into the winter months as well. Nowadays, hordes of Bay Area and Sacramento residents make the drive each weekend to enjoy their favorite winter pursuits around the lake.

Not all of this attention can be considered favorable. In fact, the ill health of Lake Tahoe recently sparked a presidential-level summit meeting to adopt measures for restoring Lake Tahoe's environment. With substantial federal aid, the challenge has been laid for officials from the various governmental agencies that oversee the area to work together in enacting and carrying out these measures. Hopefully, the health of Lake Tahoe can be restored in the years to come.

Given Tahoe's overwhelming popularity, finding an uncrowded route into the winter backcountry might seem unlikely. However, there are at least 19 potential trips along the I-80 corridor. There may not be a guarantee of solitude provided with each trip, but there shouldn't be a mass of humanity crammed onto any of these routes either. With a number of different trailheads, use is spread over a large area. Nevertheless, the chances of encountering other users is high, so practicing proper trail etiquette is absolutely essential (see Chapter 2).

With so many possibilities, trips range from easy marked routes to strenuous ascents of steep peaks. Picturesque lakes, stunning vistas, beautiful canyons and rugged peaks await the adventurous snowshoer eager to explore the backcountry away from the highway. More than enough snow should be present throughout an average winter since all of these trips lie on the west slope of the Sierra. With easy access, exquisite scenery and abundant snowfall, this area has the potential for many great snowshoeing experiences.

Location: Interstate 80 is the main thoroughfare between Sacramento and Reno, Nevada. The snowshoe trips described in this chapter begin near Yuba Gap and proceed east to Donner Summit.

Access: All trips are easily accessed from exits off of I-80.

Amenities: Since I-80 is such a major transportation link, necessities such as food, shelter, and gasoline are easily obtained at a variety of locations. Major towns with a full range of amenities include Auburn and Truckee.

Season & Weather: The elevation of trailheads ranges from near 6000 feet at Yuba Gap to 7200 feet at Donner Summit. Consequently, the season varies with the elevation. The lower elevations may have decent snow conditions from December through March, while at

A winter scene from the top of the Yuba Gap Viewpoint

Donner Summit there may be plenty of snow through April and on into May.

Since all the trips in this chapter occur on the west slope of the Sierra, storms can be intense at times, especially as one proceeds upward toward Donner Summit. High winds and heavy snows oftentimes accompany even the mildest of storms, so be prepared for inclement weather at all times.

PERMITS

Day Use & Overnight Use: Permits are not required for entry into the Tahoe National Forest.

Sno-Park: Sno-Park permits are required at Yuba Gap (Trips 44-46) and Castle Peak (Trips 57-62). Permits may be purchased near the trailheads at Yuba Gap (530) 389-8241 and Boreal Inn (530) 426-3664.

MAPS
Tahoe National Forest and Lakes Basin, Winter Recreation Guide
1:84,480, 2000, paper
Tahoe National Forest

FOREST SERVICE
Foresthill Ranger District	Truckee Ranger District	Forest Supervisor
22830 Foresthill Road	10342 Highway 89 North	Tahoe National Forest
Foresthill, CA 95631	Truckee, CA 96161	631 Coyote Street
(503) 367-2224	(530) 587-3558	Nevada City, CA 95959-2250
		(530) 265-4531

IMPORTANT PHONE NUMBERS
Avalanche Report   (530) 587-2158
Sno-Park Permit Information   (916) 324-1222
Road Conditions   (800) 427-7623
Weather   (530) 541-1151

WEBSITES
Tahoe National Forest   www.r5.fs.fed.us/tahoe
Avalanche Report   www.r5.fs.fed.us/tahoe/avalanche
Sno-Park Information   www.ohv.parks.ca.gov/SVRAs/snopark

TRIP 33

Yuba Gap Vista

see map
on page
130

Duration: One-half day
Distance: 2.5 miles round trip
Difficulty: Easy
Elevation: 5825/6175
Map: *Cisco Grove* 7.5′ quadrangle

Introduction: A trip with a superb view requiring only a mile of moderate climbing should appeal to even the most inexperienced snowshoer. More adept parties will also be enticed by the promise of such a beautiful vista with such a minimum of

Looking from the summit of Cisco Butte

effort. Atop the crest of a ridge, this trip culminates in a panorama encompassing a vast piece of northern California topography. On a clear Sierra day following a storm, a view all the way to the coastal hills is possible. Following the obvious course of a road all the way to its end, the routefinding necessary for this trip is minimal—another plus for neophytes.

How to get there: Approximately 42 miles east of Auburn, turn off Interstate 80 at the Yuba Gap exit. Following signed directions for sno-park, you head southeast and then east on two-lane road for 0.2 mile to a junction. Continue straight ahead at the junction and proceed another 0.5 mile to the entrance of the Yuba Gap Sno-Park. In the summer months, hordes of campers will recognize this as the entrance to Thousand Trails Campground; winter users bound for Yuba Gap Vista should park in this upper lot near the small general store. Portable toilets are available nearby.

A larger parking area is beyond the gate another 0.25 mile down the plowed road, with access to sledding slopes, snow-play areas, restrooms, concessions, and additional cross-country skiing and snowshoeing opportunities (see Trip 34).

Description: Begin your trip from the upper parking area by following the plowed road eastward for a short distance. Just past the ranger building, find a snow-covered road angling uphill on your left and begin a steady, moderate climb through a light forest of cedar and fir. Periodically, you may notice small blue diamonds nailed to the trees that mark the route for skiers and snowshoers. Nearing the crest of the forested ridge, at 1 mile from the trailhead, you reach a junction with a road angling back to your left (west).

From the junction head west another 0.25 mile to the end of the sparsely forested ridge. From here you have incredible views of the surrounding and the distant terrain. Close at hand is Lake Spaulding, 2 miles northwest but more than a thousand

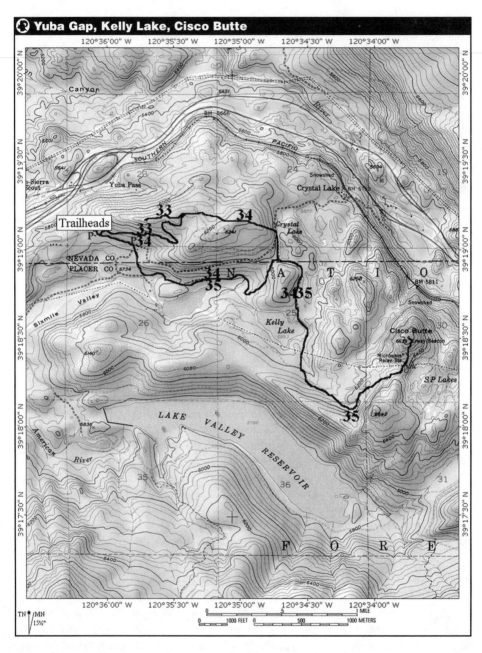

feet below. In the distance, a clear day permits views all the way across the Sacramento Valley to the coastal hills. Diners can enjoy a table with a view by dusting the snow off of one of the many picnic tables scattered around the ridge top.

When you've had your fill of the beautiful vista, retrace your steps to the car or consider extending your day with Trips 34 and 35.

FYI: The general store conveniently located at the Yuba Gap Sno-Park sells Sno-Park permits, either for one day or for the whole season.

Warm-ups: On weekends and holidays only, the grill at the snack shop is open at the Yuba Gap Sno-Park lower parking area. You won't find any delicacies beyond the usual fare of burgers, hot dogs and nachos, but they're hot and close at hand. The small store at the upper lot sells a limited selection of snacks and drinks. If you parked at the upper lot, you will have to produce evidence of a valid Sno-Park permit to get the access code from the store clerk to operate the gate allowing you access down to the lower lot.

TRIP **34**

Yuba Gap Loop & Kelly Lake

see map
on page
130

Duration: Three-quarter day
Distance: 5.5 miles loop trip
(including side trips to
Yuba Gap Vista
and Kelly Lake)
Difficulty: Moderate
Elevation: 5825/6240
Map: *Cisco Grove* 7.5′ quadrangle

Introduction: This trip offers a 5-mile forested loop with only a mile of moderate climbing, the possibility of a 0.25-mile side trip to a fairly spectacular view, and a stop at a pleasantly serene lake. The Yuba Gap loop with added excursions to the Yuba Gap Vista and Kelly Lake offers all of this and more for intermediate-to-advanced snowshoers.

The first item on the itinerary is the awe-inspiring view from the Yuba Gap Vista as described in Trip 33. Beyond the view most of the hard work is over, as the rest of the journey is downhill, level or slightly ascending. The next stop on your excursion is placid Kelly Lake, a medium-sized body of water with a forested shoreline well-suited for a lunch stop. After the lake, the trip continues through more trees, within earshot of a dancing stream and past another pleasant lake before arriving at the lower parking area of the Yuba Gap Sno-Park. On weekends the concession shack offers traditional ski-area snacks guaranteed to ward off any chilliness.

How to get there: Approximately 42 miles east of Auburn, turn off Interstate 80 at the Yuba Gap exit. Following signed directions for the Sno-Park, head southeast and then east on two-lane road for 0.2 mile to a junction. Continue straight ahead at the junction and proceed another 0.5 mile to the entrance of the Yuba Gap Sno-Park. Park in the upper lot near the general store.

Description: Begin your trip from the upper parking area by following the plowed road east for a short distance. Just past the ranger building, find a snow-covered road angling uphill on the left and begin a steady, moderate climb through a light forest. Nearing the crest of the forested ridge, reach a junction with a road angling back to your left (west), 1 mile from the trailhead. If you have the time and the energy, take the extra 0.25-mile journey to the vista point as described in Trip 33.

From the junction, continue to follow the road on a milder grade for 0.1 mile to a junction with a road heading left (north). Although the route ahead is not particularly obvious at this intersection, you should continue straight (east)—the path of the road will quickly become discernible again. A mild climb ensues through light-to-medium mixed forest as you eventually cross a couple of utility cuts and then pass a large concrete-block building associated with the Thousand Trails Campground.

Beyond the building, the road begins a 0.5-mile descent that takes you down to a 4-way road junction, 1.75 miles from the parking lot. The road to your right and left may show evidence of snowmobile tracks as this is the route into privately owned Crystal Lake. Step across this road and continue a short distance to yet another intersection.

To visit Kelly Lake turn left and make a gentle descent past a small unnamed lake. Continue the easy snowshoeing until you reach Kelly Lake, a little more than 0.5 mile from the junction. Kelly is a pleasant, forest-lined lake naturally suited for a rest stop or a lunch break. After taking in the pleasant surroundings, retrace your steps to the last junction.

From the junction you have a couple of options. The most direct path would be to follow the narrow road that heads uphill into the campground. This is the "Central Trail" as shown on the *Yuba Gap Sno-Park Cross-Country Ski & Snowshoe Trail Map*. Although the Central Trail is the most direct route back to your car, the scenery is rather mundane and you miss the chance to grab something warm at the snack shack at the lower parking lot. The preferred option follows the well-traveled trail curving slightly left from the junction. Signs placed by Eagle Mountain Nordic Cross-Country Ski Area reading CISCO TRAIL mark the clearly discernible route.

Proceed from the junction on a mild downhill grade, still through a light-to-moderate mixed forest of cedar and fir. After a bend in the road you should notice another sign for CISCO TRAIL pointing toward a route perpendicular to your road—stay on the road; following the signed directions would take you to the Eagle Mountain Ski Area, which is not close to where you parked your car. Continue the easy snowshoeing along the road and soon, off to your left, you begin to hear the gentle rush of the creek which drains from Kelly Lake—provided that the weather is not frigid enough to halt the stream flow. You pass Sunflower Lake (unnamed on the *Cisco Grove* topo map) and accompanying picnic area and continue along the road, eventually emerging into the lower Yuba Gap Sno-Park.

To return to your car, follow the paved road uphill for another 0.25 mile to the upper parking area.

FYI: The free *Cross-Country Ski & Snowshoe Trail Map* obtainable at the Sno-Park may be a bit confusing in some places, and the USGS topo is old enough not to show all the current roads, so pay close attention to your surroundings at all junctions.

Warm-ups: Not only does the lower Yuba Gap Sno-Park have a very large parking lot, but the area is equipped with restrooms, concession area and grill (open on weekends and holidays), as well as an expansive snow-play area and sledding slopes. Compared to the backcountry you've just snowshoed, this hub of activity can seem a bit overwhelming on weekends. The hot drinks and warm snacks available at the lodge may be a welcome treat after a hearty romp through the woods, in spite of the crowds and the rather plebian fare.

TRIP 35

Yuba Gap to Cisco Butte

see map
on page
130

Duration: Three-quarter day
Distance: 6.5 miles round trip
Difficulty: Moderate
Elevation: 5755/6640
Map: *Cisco Grove* 7.5′ quadrangle

Introduction: The Yuba Gap Sno-Park is one of the busiest centers of winter activity along the Interstate 80 corridor. During weekends of fair weather hundreds of cars crowd into the parking lot, most containing families destined for revelry in the nearby snow-play and sledding areas. However, snowshoers can leave this hubbub behind by following a well-defined, snow-covered roadway into the relative tranquility of the forested terrain beyond the Sno-Park. Although trails originating from the Yuba Gap Sno-Park are equally as popular with snowshoers as with cross-country skiers, the backcountry should provide plenty of peace and quiet away from the crowds.

The journey is fairly easy along the gently graded road for the first 1.75 miles to serene Kelly Lake. Beyond the lake the grade of the road gradually increases for the next 1.25 miles, leading to the final steep 0.25-mile ascent of the rocky hulk of Cisco Butte. The climb to the summit is at a high enough angle to dissuade most beginners unaccustomed to moderately angled slopes, but more experienced parties should be able to surmount this obstacle without too much trouble.

Once at the top of Cisco Butte, snowshoers will marvel at the awe-inspiring vista. The rocky crag protrudes into the canyon of the South Yuba River in relative isolation allowing visitors an unimpaired 360° view. A veritable winter wonderland spreads out in every direction for a truly magnificent panorama. Whatever effort is expended in reaching the summit is quickly forgotten in the midst of the magnificent scenery. A major forest fire recently altered the scenery around Yuba Gap, but despite the charred trees the views are still extraordinary.

How to get there: Approximately 42 miles east of Auburn, turn off Interstate 80 at the Yuba Gap exit. Following signed directions for the Sno-Park, head southeast and then east on two-lane road for 0.2 mile to a junction. Continue straight ahead at the junction and proceed another 0.5 mile to the entrance of the Yuba Gap Sno-Park. Check in at the store near the entrance to buy your Sno-Park permit and get the code for the gate, then proceed another 0.25 mile down the paved road to the lower parking area.

Description: From the lower parking lot, follow the easy grade of the snow-covered road eastward through light-to-medium forest of fir and cedar. Soon, 0.25 mile from the Sno-Park, you come alongside placid Sunflower Lake (unnamed on the *Cisco Grove* topo map). Away from the lake you continue the easy stroll along the roadway within earshot of the stream which flows between Sunflower and Kelly lakes. Nearing the 0.75-mile mark you come to a junction on your right with a ski trail from Eagle Mountain Cross-Country Ski Area marked CISCO TRAIL. For the remainder of the trip to Cisco Butte your snowshoe route along the road will be shared with Eagle Mountain's ski route, so avoid the ski tracks. Continuing straight ahead, at the junction, you soon start to climb a bit more steeply as the road winds around through moderate forest cover. Just before the 1.25-mile mark you encounter a major road intersection.

At the junction continue east, following another sign marked cisco trail, and quickly pass a small unnamed lake visible through the trees to the north. On a mild descent you curve around to the south and reach Kelly Lake, 1.75 miles from the parking lot. Kelly is a pleasant medium-sized lake with a lightly forested shoreline. A picnic area on the northeast shore beckons snowshoers for a brief rest stop.

Away from the lake the grade of the road increases and soon you're climbing at a moderate pace. Still traveling through light-to-moderate forest, the grade eventually becomes moderately steep where the road bends southeast. Continue the ascent as you approach the rocky peak shown as Point 6642 on the *Cisco Grove* topo map, known to locals as Sister Peak. Follow the road as it bends northeast, passing immediately below the peak. The forest begins to thin and the views begin to open up as

From atop Cisco Butte snowshoers have a splendid view east toward Donner Summit

the road assumes more of a winding path. You continue to gain altitude with each step, reaching the crest of the road at 3 miles from the Sno-Park.

The last 0.25 mile to the summit of Cisco Butte is by far the hardest part of the trip. The best path to the top follows the powerlines past the numerous towers, antennas and structures that are spread across the hillside. As you make the climb, each step seems to afford an even more spectacular view, granting visual hints at the incredible view that awaits at the summit. The upper part of the climb above the last powerpole just below the top will be the most difficult to negotiate, but should present few problems to snowshoers experienced with moderately angled slopes. Once you crest the butte you can wander around the flat-topped hill with ease, traveling to each of the 3 high points for the slightly different views.

Perched a thousand feet above the South Yuba River, the unimpaired vista from the summit deserves such superlatives as "awesome and incredible." A clear day allows views east up the canyon to the snowy peaks around Donner Summit and west all the way across the Sacramento Valley to the coastal hills. More immediate landmarks directly across the South Yuba River, such as Lake Spaulding and Signal Mountain, appear to be close enough to touch. Directly below to the west, Kelly Lake, Lake Valley Reservoir and privately owned Crystal Lake are easily recognizable landmarks. On a normal day the wind across the exposed butte will eventually drive you down from the summit toward the protection of the forest. Otherwise you may be inclined to linger on top of Cisco Butte enjoying the exquisite panorama for an extended time. You must eventually pull yourself away from the view and retrace your steps to the Yuba Gap Sno-Park. As you descend from Cisco Butte you will notice Hidden Lakes (shown as SP Lakes on the *Cisco Grove* topo map), directly southeast of the crest of the road.

FYI: Snowshoers with plenty of time and energy can extend their trip by reversing the description in Trips 33 and 34 from the junction 0.5 mile north of Kelly Lake, past the vista point and back to the upper parking lot.

If special overnight accommodations in the heart of the backcountry sounds appealing, access to the lodge of Hidden Lakes Sierra Education Center could be the place for your crew. The facility has been catering to groups during summers since 1986, but with special arrangements is available under limited operating conditions during the snowy season. For more information, contact owner Bill Gallaher at PO Box 8, Emigrant Gap, CA 95715, by phone at (530) 389-2876, or by email at HiddnLakes@aol.com. Check out their website at www.targetearth.org.

Warm-ups: For fare a cut above the food available at the snack shack, head back to the junction 0.2 mile from the freeway interchange and turn south, following signs for Eagle Mountain Cross-Country Ski Center. A mile south of the freeway is the lodge, where you can sample fine California cuisine at the Eagle Mountain Cafe.

T R I P 36

Eagle Lakes

see map
on page
138

Duration: One-half day
Distance: 6.75 miles round trip
Difficulty: Moderate
Elevation: 5600/5440
Map: *Cisco Grove* 7.5′ quadrangle

Introduction: A relatively short journey leads to a network of forested lakes and ponds north of Interstate 80. For the first mile you must travel within a stone's throw of the freeway, but for the remainder of the trip you are in the timbered recesses of the Tahoe National Forest. During summer the road is a popular off-road-vehicle route, but in winter you should have a sense of complete isolation once you turn away from the freeway, due in no small part to the stillness created by the moderate cover of cedar and fir.

A small stream trickles through the snow near the Eagle Lakes Trail

Thanks to this moderately dense forest, obtaining fixes on nearby landmarks is quite difficult, requiring that you have adequate map reading skills beyond the first mile of the trip. Even though you follow a clearly defined road all the way to the lakes, the route is unmarked. To complicate matters, additional roads branch off from the main route, some of which do not appear on the 1981 *Cisco Grove* topo map.

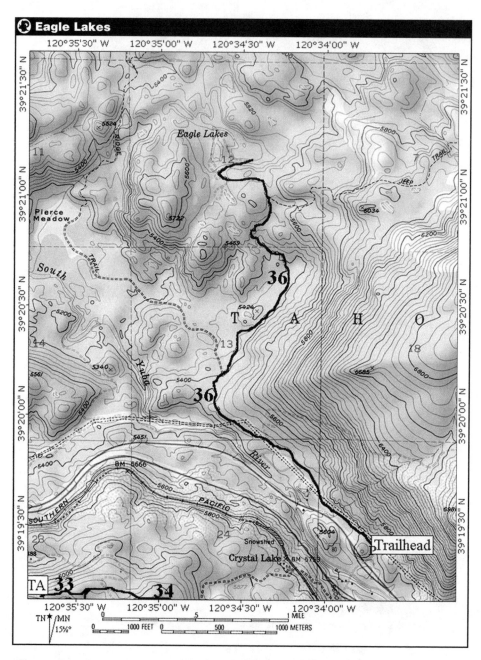

Therefore, although this is not a particularly physically taxing trip, beginners without the requisite navigational experience should not attempt this route.

How to get there: From Interstate 80, take the Eagle Lakes Road exit, drive the short distance north to the end of the plowed roadway, and park as conditions allow.

Description: Follow the snow-covered road north as it makes a short, mild climb and quickly curves northwest. Continue along the road, now on a moderate descent, paralleling I-80 down a powerline swath cut through moderate forest cover of cedar and fir. Near the 0.75-mile mark, you reach an intersection with a road heading left at the entrance to Indian Springs Campground. Soon, following directions on a sign for EAGLE LAKES ROAD, you leave the main road and follow a lesser-used route into the trees for approximately 250 yards. At 1 mile from the parking area you briefly emerge back into the powerline swath before permanently leaving the powerlines and the traffic noise from the freeway behind as the Eagle Lakes Road bends back into the peace and quiet of moderate forest cover.

For the next 0.5-mile you follow the narrow roadway on a mild to moderate descent farther into the depths of the forest. Along the way, at 1.4 miles from the trailhead, you encounter a junction on your left with the road heading toward Pierce Meadow. Continue to follow the main road on a mild grade, ignoring lesser paths that you will periodically encounter. Easy snowshoeing takes you through forested terrain for the remainder of your journey to the lakes.

Retrace your steps to the trailhead, or consider the option in FYI below.

FYI: With elevations below 6000 feet, this trip is best done after a healthy snowfall from a cold Pacific Storm. A good part of the rocky road doubles as a stream carrying meltwater during mild temperatures, creating less than favorable conditions for enjoyable snowshoeing.

Experienced parties can vary their return by accepting the additional challenge of looping back to the car via the road which travels west of the lakes through Pierce Meadow. This route will necessitate more routefinding through forested terrain.

Warm-ups: There's not much around in the way of services, so if you're looking for warm food or hot drink, check out what's available near the Yuba Gap exit (Trips 33-35).

TRIP **37**

Fordyce Lake Road

see map
on page
141

Duration: One and a half days to Woodchuck Flat
Full day to Fordyce Summit & Lake Sterling
Distance: 5.5 miles round trip to Woodchuck Flat
10.5 miles round trip to Fordyce Summit
12 miles round trip to Lake Sterling
Difficulty: Easy to Woodchuck Flat
Moderate to difficult to Fordyce Summit & Lake Sterling
Elevation: 5630/6255
5630/7235/6990
Map: *Cisco Grove* 7.5′ quadrangle

Introduction: A well-graded, readily discernible road awaits to lead you to a variety of destinations. For a short trip suitable for beginners, follow the Fordyce Lake Road on a gentle journey to Woodchuck Flat. Longer variations requiring steeper ascents lead to Fordyce Summit or on to frozen Lake Sterling. Chances are you won't even have to break trail as the road is a favorite of snowmobilers, the only drawback to this trip. Especially when traveling these routes on a weekend keep a watchful eye poised for encounters with the motorized beasts.

How to get there: From Interstate 80, approximately 43 miles east of Auburn, take the Cisco Grove exit and drive the short distance (0.1 mile) north to Hampshire Rocks Road. Turn west and drive 0.1 mile to the site of the old Cisco Grove Sno-Park. Park as conditions permit (see FYI).

Description: Find the Fordyce Lake Road on the north side of Hampshire Rocks Road, diagonally across from the Cisco Grove Sno-Park. Follow the gentle grade of the road up over a rise and then down to a bridge across Rattlesnake Creek. Beyond the bridge the road starts to climb moderately, winding around the west side of the Rattlesnake Creek drainage through a light mixed forest of pine, fir and cedar. Where the road draws closer to the creek, you pass a short but scenic waterfall where the water drops into a small bowl and then cascades over a low rock shelf before continuing to tumble through boulders on its downstream journey.

Away from the falls the road continues up the canyon of Rattlesnake Creek as you travel through mixed forest, generally on a mild climb. Without much fanfare, after 2.75 miles, you reach the campground near the beginning of nearly 0.5-mile-

Fordyce Lake Road, Signal Peak, Rattlesnake Mountain

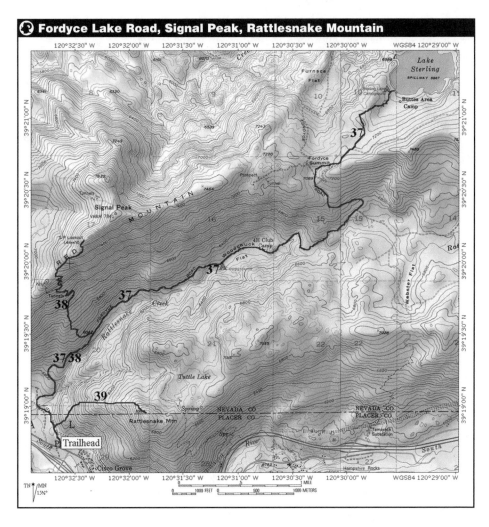

long Woodchuck Flat. The campground would make an excellent base camp for an overnight snowcamp.

Now travel along the mildly graded road around the length of Woodchuck Flat, passing some wooden cabins associated with the 4H camp at the far end. Beyond the flat the road grade increases and you begin a steady 2-mile climb toward Fordyce Summit. As you ascend, the trees thin out to allow partial views back down the canyon and over to Red Mountain and Signal Peak. You continue to climb along the winding road, reaching a road junction just before the 4.5-mile mark. Bear left at the junction, following signed directions to BSA CAMP, LAKE STERLING and FORDYCE LAKE. The right-hand road leads to Lola Montez Lake.

Continue the climb for a little over 0.5 mile, until you reach the next junction at the broad saddle of Fordyce Summit. Don't expect a grandiose view from here, as the forest blocks any chance for a dramatic vista. If Fordyce Summit is your destination, retrace your steps to the trailhead. To go on to Lake Sterling bear right at the junction and follow the road another 0.75 mile down to the southwest shore.

FYI: The Thousand Trails Campground near the trailhead failed to operate. Subsequently the Cisco Grove Sno-Park not operate either. You may have to park your vehicle as conditions allow.

Warm-ups: There's only one restaurant near the next several trailheads. Fortunately, the Engadine Cafe in Rainbow Lodge happens to be that restaurant. Rivaling just about any fare the Lake Tahoe region has to offer, the cafe turns out wonderful meals with a touch of European flair for breakfast, lunch and dinner. The wonderful food is complemented by the rustic but charming decor of the lodge. Since the lodge is owned and operated by Royal Gorge Cross-Country Ski Resort, you don't have to be concerned with whether the restaurant will be open during the winter months. The Sierra Cocktail Lounge and Bar is a great watering hole offering a light menu if you're not ravenous after your spin around the backcountry. You can sip a hot toddy by the mesmerizing fire or sample the history of the region while gazing at the black-and-white photographs lining the walls. If you're looking for a romantic weekend getaway, Rainbow Lodge offers fine bed-and-breakfast packages (2-night minimum; mid-week rates). Reservations are recommended for dinner and Sunday brunch (530) 426-3661. For more information check out their website at **www.royalgorge.com**. Rainbow Lodge is located at 50800 Hampshire Rocks Road, 0.5 mile west of the Big Bend exit. If Hampshire Rocks Road is in good shape, simply drive 2.5 miles east from the trailhead to Rainbow Lodge. If not, take I-80 from Cisco Grove to the Big Bend Exit and double back 0.5 mile to the west.

TRIP 38

Signal Peak

see map on page 141

Duration: Three-quarter day
Distance: 6 miles round trip
Difficulty: Moderate to difficult
Elevation: 5630/7715
Map: *Cisco Grove* 7.5′ quadrangle

Introduction: Back in the days of manned fire lookouts, Signal Peak provided a bird's-eye view of the Yuba River canyon and a vast area of the adjoining Sierra from a stone hut placed at the very edge of the southwest ridge, 125 feet below the summit. Nowadays, snowshoers can follow the route of the old jeep access road on a moderately strenuous climb to the impressive viewpoint. The first half of the journey follows the fairly gentle grade of the Fordyce Lake Road, gaining a mere 450 feet in 1.4 miles. Over the remaining 1.6 miles the elevation gain is an additional 1650 vertical feet up the south-facing slopes of the peak.

The moderately steep climb is well worth the effort as the vista from the old lookout is both expansive and dramatic. A bevy of snow-clad peaks and ridges spread out in virtually every direction. On clear days gazers are treated to a westward view all the way across the Sacramento Valley to the coastal hills. Whatever effort is expended in reaching the lookout is quickly forgotten in the beauty of the impressive vista.

How to get there: From Interstate 80, approximately 43 miles east of Auburn, take the Cisco Grove exit and drive the short distance (0.1 mile) north to Hampshire Rocks Road. Turn west and drive 0.1 mile to the site of the old Cisco Grove Sno-Park and park as conditions allow.

Description: Find the Fordyce Lake Road on the north side of Hampshire Rocks Road, diagonally across from the Cisco Grove Sno-Park.

Follow the road uphill, and at 1.4 miles from Hampshire Rocks Road, locate the indistinct jeep road that diagonals behind you up the hillside to the right. This junction may be noted by a colored plastic streamer tied to a tree, but you shouldn't depend on such a marker being there from year to year. This jeep road junction occurs along a straight stretch of the Fordyce Lake Road where the creek is not far to your right. If you continue past the road to a curve from where you can see Signal Peak, you know that you have gone too far. Locating the obscure beginning of this road may prove to be the most difficult part of the trip.

Fortunately, once you find the beginning of the jeep road the course of the road beyond is fairly obvious. Proceed up the hillside through the dense cover of a mixed forest, primarily cedar, on a moderate to moderately steep climb. As you continue the ascent, the trees begin to thin as scattered pines replace cedars as the dominant conifer. You reach the first switchback, where limited views appear of the terrain across the canyon to the southeast. More switchbacks greet you as the steady ascent continues, the forest thins even more, and the views correspondingly improve. As you zigzag up the mountain, the goal of the climb is soon visible above, the stone lookout hut perched on the very edge of Red Mountain. Proceeding up the hillside, you reach the crest of the ridge near the 2.5-mile mark.

You continue to climb up the spine of the ridge toward the lookout, following a line of old telephone poles. Where you encounter the steep rock cliffs below the stone hut, veer across easier terrain on the right side of the hillside and then climb up to the lookout. The old stone hut has two small rooms, and an old cot easily identifies one as the sleeping quarters for the person who manned the lookout. The other room was heated by an old stove and had a curved observation area that provided an incredible vista of the surrounding terrain.

From the lookout modern-day visitors can gaze at the incredible scenery of the landscape west of Donner Summit. Immediately below appear what look to be toy cars and trains following the serpentine course of the Yuba River on Interstate 80's ribbon of concrete and the twin set of tracks of the Union Pacific Railroad. Immediately before you are Rattlesnake Mountain and Tuttle Lake and directly across the canyon are Cisco Butte, Hidden, Kelly, and Crystal lakes. To the west are Lake Spaulding and the western foothills bordering the massive plain of the Sacramento Valley. Toward Donner Summit a whole procession of snowy peaks adorn the western Sierra. Among the more notable mountains visible are Castle Peak north of Donner Summit, Mt. Judah and Donner Peak south of Donner Pass, Anderson Peak and Silver Peak to the southeast, and Mt. Rose and the Carson Range in the eastern distance. A map of the greater Lake Tahoe region would help in identifying all of the mountains visible from the lookout.

Peakbaggers insistent upon reaching the actual top of Signal Peak can follow the crest of the ridge northeast from the lookout 0.3 mile to the true summit. Signal Peak is aptly named, as the top of the peak is littered with a preponderance of communication towers and buildings. In addition, the view from the top of Signal Peak is not any better than the one from the lookout.

FYI: The climb up the south-facing slope of Signal Peak should be considered only during stable avalanche conditions. Be prepared for stiff winds on the ridge and at the lookout.

Warm-ups: See Trip 37.

TRIP 39

Rattlesnake Mountain

see map on page 141

Duration: Three-quarter day
Distance: 2 miles round trip
Difficulty: Moderate
Elevation: 5630/6959
Map: *Cisco Grove* 7.5' quadrangle

Introduction: A continuously steady, mile-long climb leads to superb views atop a nearly 7000-foot peak. The steep ascent of Rattlesnake Mountain will certainly provide a workout for even the most in-shape of snowshoers. Starting in light-to-moderate forest at the base of the peak, the route eventually breaks out of the trees to fine views that get better with each gain in elevation. Standing on top of the peak, snowshoers are treated to great views of the South Yuba River drainage and surrounding peaks.

How to get there: From Interstate 80, approximately 43 miles east of Auburn, take the Cisco Grove exit and drive the short distance (0.1 mile) north to Hampshire Rocks Road. Turn west and drive 0.1 mile to the site of the old Cisco Grove Sno-Park and park as conditions allow.

Description: Head up the Fordyce Lake Road a short distance until you see a series of powerpoles to your right. At this point leave the road and begin to climb up the forested hillside. The trees will eventually thin around a quarter of the way up the mountain, promising even better views from the summit. The easiest climbing follows the west ridge on a steady ascent to the top.

As billed, the view from the summit of Rattlesnake Mountain is quite impressive. An unobstructed panorama greets you from the top, extending from Castle Peak and other Donner Summit mountains to the east out across the Sacramento Valley to the west. The South Yuba River snakes through the deep canyon 1200 feet below with the thin concrete ribbon of Interstate 80 sinuously following along. Sharing the summit with a handful of weather-beaten trees, you have the fleeting sensation of standing on top of the world.

Route up Rattlesnake Mountain

FYI: Be prepared for the possibility of less than ideal snow conditions at the beginning of the trip, particularly the closer it is to the warmer temperatures of late season. With a starting elevation just over 5600 feet, you may have to struggle up the initial hillside with no snow or very poor snow until you reach better conditions higher up.

Warm-ups: See Trip 37.

The view from atop Rattlesnake Mountain

TRIP 40

Loch Leven Lakes

see map
on page
148

Duration: Three-quarter day
Distance: 5 miles round trip
Difficulty: Moderate
Elevation: 5790/6900
Map: *Cisco Grove* & *Soda Springs* 7.5′ quadrangles

Introduction: Described in an early edition of Jeffrey Schaffer's classic guide *The Tahoe Sierra* as "probably the best constructed trail in the Tahoe Sierra," the path to

An old pine defies the elements near Loch Leven Lakes

Loch Leven Lakes is a very popular summertime trip for hikers. However, a winter excursion along the same route provides the antithesis to the summer experience. Although some cross-country skiers approach High Loch Leven Lake from the east via a marked trail (see Trip 42), few winter enthusiasts accept the challenge of a snow trip following the route of the summer trail.

There are a couple of obstacles to surmount on the way to the lakes. First of all, during years of heavy snows, you may have to shovel some steps into the snowbank at the highway just to get started. In addition, you must cross the frequently traveled Union Pacific Railroad tracks and face the same problem with the snowbank on the far side. This trip also requires some basic routefinding skills, but armed with the necessary expertise reaching the lakes is not particularly difficult.

Along with the solitude, snowshoers will find the Loch Leven Lakes to be quite scenic. Each of the three frozen lakes possesses its own unique charm. The open

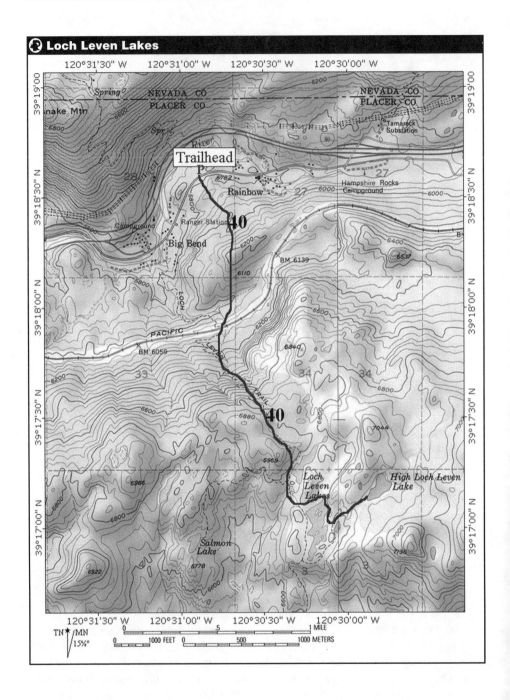

terrain near the beginning of the trip and around the lakes periodically provides fine views of the surrounding countryside.

How to get there: From Interstate 80, take the Big Bend exit (1.5 miles east of Cisco Grove and 6 miles west of the Soda Springs exit). From the exit ramp, follow old Highway 40 (Hampshire Rocks Road) 0.9 mile to the plowed parking area on the north side of the road. A Forest Service block building with a pit toilet is at the west end of the parking area.

Description: On a generally southward course, head directly up the moderately steep hillside amid scattered pines, firs and cedars, attempting to anticipate a course that will result in the least amount of elevation loss on the far side. Beyond the top of the hill, you must descend into deeper forest and, 0.75 mile from the trailhead, cross a creek which eventually feeds into the South Yuba River.

Past the creek, you begin climbing again, quickly reaching a double set of railroad tracks near a trestle. Keep an ear out for approaching trains—those chugging uphill are easily heard, but the ones descending from Donner Pass make far less noise and can sneak up on the unwary. If gaining the slope above the highway was difficult, you may have similar problems negotiating the snowbank on the far side of the tracks.

From the tracks, resume a moderately steep climb south through forest cover of pine and fir. Heading to the right of some bare cliffs, make a steady ascent southeast toward the top of the ridge. Near the crest you have nice views to the north of the Donner Summit area, thanks to a covering of lighter forest. For the next 0.5 mile you will find gentler territory between the top of the ridge and the first of the Loch Leven Lakes. Open, rolling terrain characterizes the area, the granite of summer softened considerably by the snows of winter. From the first lake proceed over a low hump, where you have fine views of the surrounding countryside, to the second and largest of the lakes.

To reach High Loch Leven Lake you must travel another 0.25 mile, bearing east through a notch. If a car shuttle can be arranged, you can put together an interesting extension from High Loch Leven Lake by connecting with the route in Trip 42 and then reversing the description from the lake to the trailhead.

FYI: The location of the summer trailhead is shown incorrectly on the 1955 topo map—the trailhead was relocated 0.5 mile to the east, where the snowshoe description begins.

Warm-ups: Rainbow Lodge is just 0.25 mile east of the trailhead (see Trip 37).

Located near the Big Bend/Rainbow Road exit from I-80, the remodeled Big Bend Visitor Center occupies a restored national historic landmark. The center houses a museum dedicated to the history of transportation in the area. In addition, information is available concerning winter recreation opportunities in the Tahoe National Forest. Call (530) 426-6609 for more details.

TRIP **41**

Matrimony Ridge Vista

see map on page **151**

Duration: Three-quarter day
Distance: 5.5 miles round trip
Difficulty: Moderate
Elevation: 6050/6895
Map: *Soda Springs* 7.5′ quadrangle

Introduction: The usual superlatives one attributes to inspiring views seem inadequate when applied to the vista found at the destination of this trip. The 360° panorama includes northern Sierra landmarks almost too numerous to mention. Bravely clinging to the tenuous soil near the end of an exposed ridge, a weather-beaten Jeffrey pine picturesquely frames the craggy profile of Devils Peak. Beneath the canopy of its overhanging branches at least one couple has taken the vows of marriage, and ever since, the conifer has been known to an ever-expanding group of locals as Matrimony Tree. Even if nuptials are not on your itinerary, the site promises a celebratory experience marrying the modest effort required to reach the tree with a truly stunning vista.

Snow Mountain stands guard over the canyon of the North Fork of the American River

Matrimony Ridge, High Loch Leven Lake

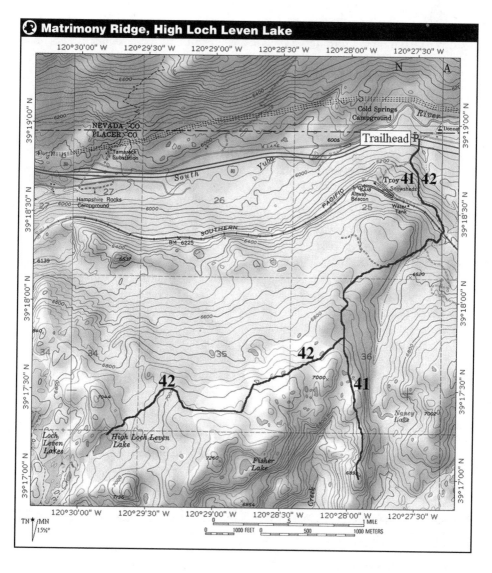

Even so, the 2.75-mile excursion up to this reward is not entirely a bouquet of roses. Although much of the trip passes through sparsely forested terrain and some of the route is marked, you will have to use your routefinding skills to reach Matrimony Tree. In addition, the route intersects the Union Pacific Railroad tracks 0.75 mile from the trailhead, necessitating that you exercise caution when crossing the twin set of tracks, paying particular attention to avoiding the less noisy trains gliding down from Donner Pass. In years of decent snowfall, chances are you will also have to cut steps in order to ascend the far bank above the tracks (don't forget your snowshovel). These cautions aside, experienced snowshoers can successfully consummate their journey to Matrimony Tree with a modicum of effort.

How to get there: Leave Interstate 80 at the Kingvale exit and follow Donner Pass Road west 0.6 mile to an underpass, which is 0.1 mile beyond Donner Trail School. If the beginning of the road under the freeway has been plowed, you can park your vehicle there, otherwise parking is available on weekends back at the school.

Description: Begin your trip by travelling underneath both lanes of the freeway and then climb moderately up the snow-covered road to a Y-junction, 0.2 mile from Donner Pass Road. The junction is about 50 yards beyond an orange steel pole on your right. Turn left (south) and follow this road through scattered forest of pine and fir. You continue to climb at a moderate rate, eventually coming below the double set of railroad tracks at the 0.75-mile mark.

Carefully cross the tracks, keeping an ear out for approaching trains, particularly the muted sounds of those descending from Donner Pass. In normal snow years you will more than likely have to cut steps up the far bank where snowplows have created a steep wall of packed snow. Make the crossing upgrade from a trestle marked 1851 and 1853, where you will see a set of railroad crossing gates next to a small shed. The road crossing is also marked by orange poles on either side of the tracks. A short distance up the road you should see a blue-green sign reading: HIGH LOCH LEVEN LAKES NORDIC TRAIL. Beyond the sign, blue diamonds will help guide you up the road for the next part of your journey.

You travel up the road for nearly 0.25 mile from the railroad crossing, 1 mile from Donner Pass Road, to a marked junction. An obvious reddish-orange sign indicates you are about to cross one of Royal Gorge's network of cross-country ski trails. Nearby, a separate blue-green sign reads FOLLOW THE RAINBOW TRAIL 0.5 MI/0.8 KM. If you were to turn sharply uphill to the right for a very short distance you would encounter yet another sign, across from which is one more sign, reading TRAIL ONE-WAY ONLY DOWNHILL, RAINBOW CONNECTION TO RAINBOW LODGE. If all of this seems confusing, you're absolutely right. The easiest way to proceed is to back up approximately 50 yards from the first set of signs. At this spot, look for a small, rectangular blue sign with white letters, which reads ERA NETWORK REALTY. A Y-junction with a lesser road angling uphill to your right is here—follow this road uphill and proceed. In a short distance you will intersect the convoluted route of quick twists and turns that the signs direct you to follow. Whoever came up with the signed route must have been intoxicated or must take perverse pleasure from having people stumble around like buffoons.

Once on the right track, you climb up this road for 0.25 mile to the broad, lightly forested crest of a ridge and another Y-junction. The route to the right is signed RAINBOW INTERCONNECT TO RAINBOW LODGE 6 KM, but you should proceed straight ahead on the left-hand route marked with every warning imaginable with the exception of "lions, tigers and bears." You continue up the road past a sign delineating your route as HIGH LOCH LEVEN LAKE BACKCOUNTRY TRAIL to where the grade eases. Here the route to Matrimony Ridge leaves the route to High Loch Leven Lake, the continuation of which is described in Trip 42.

Leaving the path of the road, you now head toward the south climbing mildly on the east side of the ridge above a creek drainage. Soon the angle of ascent increases to moderately steep. As you climb, the trees begin to thin and the summit of

A wind-formed pine arches over a snowshoer on Matrimony Ridge

Devils Peak appears to the east above the rise on the opposite side of the drainage below you. Proceed on a southerly course, continuing to skirt the east fringe of the crest, steadily climbing at a moderate rate. The more you climb the less the trees obstruct the increasingly dramatic views, until you reach the virtually bald zenith of the ridge and the incredible climax vista.

Perched at the apex of this unprotected ridge, the weather-beaten form of Matrimony Tree stands in rugged isolation, defying the frequently harsh conditions typical of such exposed promontories found at this elevation in the Sierra. The wind-sculptured, overhanging branches of this Jeffrey pine dramatically frame the rugged profile of Devils Peak, creating a picture-postcard view worthy of any mountain scenery calendar. Not to be outdone, additional snowcapped landforms demand your attention. The ridge delineating the upper boundary of Sugar Bowl Ski Area, which includes such noteworthy peaks as Crows Nest, Mt. Disney and Mt. Lincoln, reigns over the snow-covered terrain to the east beyond Devils Peak. Farther north, the white tips of Castle Peak, Basin Peak and Buzzard Roost pierce the winter sky. Directly south, the massive mound of Snow Mountain dominates the surrounding terrain, including the deep cleft of Royal Gorge, through which course the icy waters of the North Fork of the American River. On clear days, the vista extends beyond the western Sierra, across the Sacramento Valley and all the way to the coastal hills. Be sure to take along a large enough map to help you identify some of the vast array of landmarks visible from this spot.

Once you've had your fill of the fantastic views, retrace your steps to the trailhead.

FYI: Snowboarders and backcountry skiers will love the nearly unlimited possibilities for cavorting down the surrounding slopes. A snowcamp combined with an extended period of fair weather would be the ideal conditions for an incomparable trip.

Warm-ups: See Trip 37.

TRIP **42**

High Loch Leven Lake

see map
on page
151

Duration: Three-quarter day
Distance: 8 miles round trip
Difficulty: Moderate
Elevation: 6050/7025/6865
Map: *Soda Springs* 7.5′ quadrangle

Introduction: Without a marked trail, finding High Loch Leven Lake amid the snows of winter would be a daunting task. Fortunately, a crew of volunteers placed a series of blue diamonds and cross-country skier emblems along this route in 1991, enabling winter users to travel in relative safety to this scenic destination. However, special care should be exercised in a couple of stretches of more difficult terrain. After the initial climb of 600 vertical feet in 1.25 miles, most of the route is fairly gentle, alternating between open benches with pleasant views and light forest. The lake itself is quite scenic, tucked into a rock cleft surrounded by cliffs and slabs on one shore and a forested glade on the other.

The Loch Leven Lakes, close to I-80 and typically blessed with an early season opening in comparison to most Sierra lakes, are popular summer goals for hikers and backpackers alike. Winter has a way of reducing the large number of visitors, allowing snowshoers a reasonable expectation of peace and quiet, both along the route and at the lake. Although there is a marked route to High Loch Leven Lake, the area is not heavily used in winter.

There are some additional safety cautions that should be mentioned in regard to this trip. First, the route crosses the twin set of Union Pacific railroad tracks 0.75 mile from the trailhead. You must exercise extreme care when making this crossing, keeping both eyes and ears attentive to the possible approach of the frequent trains that use these tracks. In addition, during years of decent snowfall you may have to cut steps in the banks on either side of the tracks, so be sure to take a snow-shovel. Lastly, this trip should be undertaken only during periods of decent weather, as you travel through a variety of terrain, a part of which is open and exposed. During foul conditions, becoming disoriented would be easy. Being expert with map and compass would be essential to navigate stretches of this route in inclement weather.

How to get there: Leave Interstate 80 at the Kingvale exit and follow Donner Pass Road west 0.6 mile to an underpass, which is 0.1 mile beyond Donner Trail School.

If the beginning of the road under the freeway has been plowed, you can park your vehicle there, otherwise parking is available on weekends back at the school.

Description: Begin your trip by traveling underneath both lanes of the freeway and then climb moderately up a snow-covered road to a Y-junction, 0.2 mile from Donner Pass Road. Turn left and follow this road on a moderate climb to a double set of railroad tracks at 0.75 mile. Carefully cross the tracks, watching for approaching trains, especially the less noisy ones descending from Donner Pass.

Beyond the tracks, proceed up the road for 0.25 mile to a marked junction, where a mixture of signs creates a certain amount of confusion about how to proceed. Find a lesser road that angles uphill to your right, approximately 50 yards prior to the signed junction. Follow this road uphill and proceed a short distance to an intersection with another road, where the correct route should become more obvious.

Follow this road for 0.25 mile to a Y-junction at the broad, lightly forested crest of a ridge. Continue straight ahead at the junction on the left-hand branch, past a sign delineating the route as the HIGH LOCH LEVEN LAKE backcountry trail. Where the grade eases, the route to Matrimony Tree (Trip 41) veers away from the route to the lake.

You continue straight ahead on the High Loch Leven Lake trail, following the blue triangular markers. The terrain from the junction remains fairly gentle until you resume the moderate climb, passing through a light forest of pine and fir. Soon the grade eases again, nearly 2 miles from the trailhead, as the marked route leaves the road in favor of a lightly undulating traverse across open terrain. You must pay close attention to the placement of the markers through this section in order to stay on route. Aside from a couple of brief interruptions passing through small groves of conifers, you have pleasant views across this exposed stretch of trail. Across the canyon to the northwest is Signal Peak, easily identifiable by the numerous antennas on the summit. After 0.75 mile, near a horseshoe-shaped pond, the traverse across this open plateau ends as you intersect another road, 2.75 miles from the trailhead.

An arrowed sign at the intersection with the road directs travelers to the right (north-northwest) through light forest. Initially you follow a level stretch of road until a lengthy descent brings you to a point, 0.6 mile from the intersection, where the marked route leaves the road and heads cross-country toward the lake. Once again you must pay close attention to the placement of the markers as this part of the route heads across more difficult terrain, weaving around trees and rocks. Eventually, you emerge out into the open once again, well above the northeast shore of High Loch Leven Lake. You have the option of enjoying the view from here or working your way down to the lakeshore.

High Loch Leven Lake is a pretty sight in winter with snow-covered rock slabs and cliffs angling down to the lake on one side and a light forest caressing the edge of the opposite shore. In summer a smattering of tiny islands add a picturesque quality, but in winter the only visible aspect of these islands will be the occasional dead snag poking its gray limbs up out of the snow. Although all of the Loch Leven Lakes are popular destinations for hikers and backpackers, you should be able to enjoy the surroundings with few winter visitors.

FYI: To visit the lower Loch Leven Lakes, head southwest from the upper lake through a narrow gully to the southernmost lake. With a car shuttle, arrangements could be make to combine this route with Trip 40.

Warm-ups: See Trip 37.

TRIP 43

Donner Peak

Duration: One-half day
Distance: 2.5 miles round trip
Difficulty: Moderate
Elevation: 7090/8019
Map: *Norden* 7.5′ quadrangle

see map on page 157

Introduction: Donner Peak is a dramatic looking hulk of a mountain as viewed from various points around Donner Pass. Equally as dramatic is the view from the summit. At 1.25 miles, the distance to the top is minimal but the elevation gain of nearly 1000 feet is fairly steep. Although the hillsides are too precipitous for most cross-country skiers, you may encounter snowboarders or backcountry skiers careening down the north-facing slopes during periods of powder conditions. If you are an accomplished skier/snowboarder and you don't mind carrying the extra weight, such a descent might provide a reasonable, if not exhilarating, alternative to snowshoeing back to the car (remember to avoid the slopes of Sugar Bowl Ski area).

How to get there: From Interstate 80, take the Soda Springs/Norden exit and travel 3.7 miles east on the old Donner Pass Road to the Alpine Skills International parking area at Donner Pass. You may park your vehicle in the lot for a fee. Check in at the front desk in the main building of ASI for a parking permit, which must be displayed on your dashboard to avoid having your vehicle towed.

Description: Begin snowshoeing south-southwest from the parking lot on a slight downhill grade until you reach a convenient spot from which to start up the moderately steep hillside of the northwest slope of Donner Peak. Proceed up the mountain through widely scattered conifers. As you climb, you have very nice views of Lake Van Norden to the west and the peaks of Donner Pass to the north. Before reaching

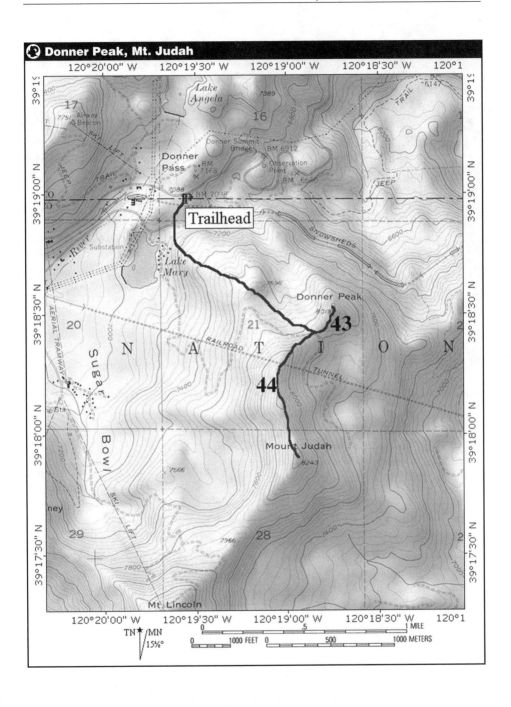

Donner Peak, Mt. Judah

Donner Lake as seen from the summit of Donner Peak

the top of Donner Peak, you must climb over a minor summit, shown as Point 7696 on the *Norden* topo map. A fine vista is at this point, a foretaste of what is to come. Continuing the climb, you pass through a stand of trees on the way to the saddle that separates Donner Peak and Mt. Judah.

Once at the saddle, turn northeast and make the short climb up moderate slopes to the summit rocks. From the top you have marvelous views in all directions. Donner Lake lies at your feet to the east, while massive cornices loom above along the extended ridge of Mt. Judah. An array of peaks spreads out both north and south.

From the summit, retrace your steps back to the saddle between Mt. Judah and Donner Peak and follow your trail back to the parking lot.

FYI: A climb of neighboring Mt. Judah can easily be combined with the ascent of Donner Peak as you have already completed most of the climb by reaching the saddle separating the two peaks. From the saddle an additional 300 feet of steep climbing is all that is necessary to reach the easy snowshoeing along the nearly level ridge crest (see Trip 44).

Warm-ups: Alpine Skills International offers a reasonably priced bunk-and-breakfast package for anyone with their own sleeping bag and $25 (plus tax). For the serious outdoor enthusiast in search of additional training or guided adventures, they also offer a wide variety of winter and summer backcountry programs. Call (530) 426-9108.

TRIP 44

Mt. Judah

see map
on page
157

Duration: One-half day
Distance: 4.5 miles round trip
Difficulty: Moderate
Elevation: 7090/8243
Map: *Norden* 7.5′ quadrangle

Introduction: A grand view awaits the diligent snowshoer willing to make the steep 1150-foot climb up the north side of Mt. Judah to the long, gentle ridge that leads to the summit. From the top, northern Sierra peaks stretch out in virtually every direction. Notable landmarks clearly visible from the summit include nearby Mt. Lincoln, Anderson Peak and Crows Nest along the prominent ridge to the west, and north across Interstate 80 to Castle Peak.

When conditions are favorable you may see a number of backcountry skiers and snowboarders making the climb for the thrill of the descent. If your skills are up to the task, such a descent may provide an exciting return to your vehicle. One note of caution: prevailing westerly winds produce monstrous cornices on the east side of the summit ridge of Mt. Judah, so avoid that edge of the crest.

How to get there: From Interstate 80, take the Soda Springs/Norden exit and travel 3.7 miles east on the old Donner Pass Road to the Alpine Skills International parking lot at Donner Pass. You should be able to park your vehicle in the lot for a fee. Check in at the main building of ASI for a parking permit, which must be displayed on your dashboard to avoid having your vehicle towed.

Description: Begin snowshoeing south-southwest from the parking lot on a slight downhill grade until you reach a convenient spot from which to start up the moderately steep hillside of the northwest slope of Donner Peak. Proceed up the mountain through widely scattered conifers. As you climb, you have very nice views of Lake Van Norden to the west and peaks of Donner Pass to the North. Climb over Point 7696 and pass through a stand of trees on the way to a saddle separating Donner Peak and Mt. Judah.

From the saddle begin climbing steeply up the hillside toward the long summit ridge of Mt. Judah. Aim for a pair of reflectorized signs at the north edge of the ridge. Once on the crest the grade eases considerably as you head for the true summit at the south end. Remember to avoid the cornices along the east edge. Continue along the crest, dropping slightly before you make the last easy climb to the top.

The ridge and the summit of Mt. Judah offer a grand panorama of the north Tahoe countryside. A flurry of activity occurs to the north, including skiers and snowboarders on the ski slopes of Sugar Bowl and Donner Ski Ranch, trains chugging up the long grade toward Donner Pass, and hundreds of cars snaking along Interstate 80 headed for unknown points. The bustling community of Truckee lies to the east beyond Donner Lake. A more remote scene is in the south, where myriad snow-covered peaks stretch along a series of ridges, beckoning the adventurous toward further exploration. For most people, the view from Mt. Judah is a satisfactory reward for a half day's work. After taking in the scenery, retrace your steps back to the car.

FYI: If you find yourself at the summit of Mt. Judah with plenty of energy and time, you can accept the challenge of the more demanding route to Anderson Peak along the ridge heading southeast from Mt. Lincoln. Be forewarned, this adds another 7 miles round trip to your journey.

Those interested in an overnight experience can make arrangements with the Sierra Club to stay at Benson Hut, 0.1 mile north of Anderson Peak. From there, rather than retrace your route, you can continue farther south along the crest until exiting the traverse at Squaw Valley. The 11-mile excursion requires plenty of backcountry savvy, excellent conditioning, and a car shuttle, among other things. For information about renting the hut (you need not be a member) contact the Sierra Club at: Clair Tappaan Lodge
PO Box 36
Norden, CA 95724
(530) 426-3632

Warm-ups: See Trip 43.

A view of Mt. Judah from Donner Peak

Donner Pass Lakes & Boreal Ridge Loop

see map
on page
162

Duration: One-half day
Distance: 3.25 miles round trip
Difficulty: Moderate
Elevation: 7200/7445
Map: *Norden* 7.5′ quadrangle

Introduction: Aside from the potential routefinding problems, this trip would be rated easy, as the distance is short and the terrain is not particularly steep. However, the densely forested, undulating topography over the first mile can be somewhat confusing, requiring a modicum of navigational ability. For those willing to test their skills, the lakes offer pleasant scenery, and the view from the top of Boreal Ridge is splendid.

How to get there: Just west of Donner Summit take the Castle Peak exit from Interstate 80. Follow signs to the Sno-Park at the east end of the frontage road immediately south of the freeway.

Description: From the east end of the Sno-Park, head into medium forest cover and proceed for a little more than 0.25 mile on a course roughly paralleling the freeway. Near the edge of a clearing, turn southeast and head through somewhat convoluted terrain to a hillside 0.75 mile from the trailhead, from where you should be able to spot Azalea Lake. Descend to the lake, in a basin bounded by rock walls and steep hillsides. Flora Lake is directly south of Azalea through a narrow gap. Both lakes are quite picturesque, providing a serene setting for a rest stop or lunch.

From the second lake, climb south directly over a less-wooded rise and descend to the north shore of Lake Angela, the largest of the three lakes. This lake sprawls across open terrain, providing views of the peaks on the south side of the old Donner Pass Road. The pristine nature of the area is compromised by a massive powerline running along the west and north sides of the lake and a dam across the south end.

The next stage of your loop trip begins at the northwest tip of Lake Angela, from where a gully rises northwest up the hillside. Proceed up this gully, climbing on a

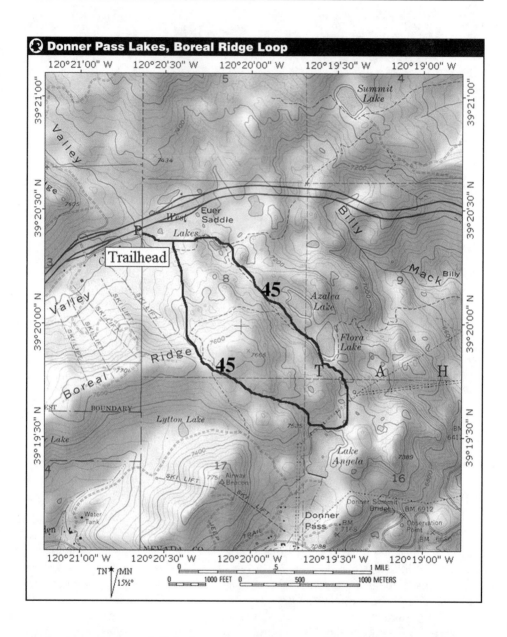

moderate grade through light forest toward the crest of Boreal Ridge. Reach the top directly west of the easternmost high point, labeled 7665 on the *Norden* topo map. From the ridge you have splendid views of the Donner Pass region.

From the top of Boreal Ridge, descend into heavier forest on the north-facing hillside. Intersect your trail from the Sno-Park approximately 0.75 mile from the top of the ridge and retrace your steps back to the car.

FYI: By leaving a car at Alpine Skills International at Donner Pass (see Trip 45 for directions), you can arrange a one-way, 2.5-mile shuttle trip between the Sno-Park on I-80 and the ASI parking lot ($5 parking fee required) on the old Donner Pass Road. However, this plan would eliminate the return trip over Boreal Ridge.

Warm-ups: See Trips 37, 43, 51-61.

Round Valley near Peter Grubb Hut

Peter Grubb Hut & Round Valley

see map on page
165

Duration: One-half day
Distance: 5.25 miles round trip
Difficulty: Easy
Elevation: 7200/7900
Map: *Norden* 7.5′ quadrangle

Introduction: The easy access and short distance to Peter Grubb Hut make this trip extremely popular with skiers and snowshoers alike. Chances are, due to the popularity of this trip, you will be able to follow a packed trail all the way into Round Valley. Staying overnight at the hut provides a comfortable way to explore some of the backcountry to the north, insuring a degree of solitude which will almost certainly be lacking on the trip into the hut. On clear days you have excellent views of Castle Peak and the Donner Summit area from Castle Pass.

How to get there: Just west of Donner Summit take the Castle Peak exit from Interstate 80. Follow signs to the Sno-Park at the east end of the frontage road immediately south of the freeway. To reach the trailhead you must walk back under the freeway to the north side of the westbound off-ramp.

Description: After walking under the freeway to the westbound off-ramp, begin your hike by following a snow-covered road that climbs above the ramp. Quickly the road turns northwest into mixed forest, where a pair of signs direct snowmobiles to the left and self-powered travelers to the right. Soon the route along the road leads to the open meadow of Castle Valley. Excellent views of the west face of Castle Peak appear as you pass slightly above and west of the valley bottom on a mild grade. Unless your trip occurs in the middle of a snow storm, you should be able to follow the tracks of previous snowshoe or ski parties, due to the high popularity of this trip. Otherwise, periodically placed blue markers will help guide you.

    Leaving the meadow behind, you continue to ascend mildly up the valley through light-to-moderate forest cover. Near the head of the canyon, where the loop through Castle Valley heads east (See Trip 47), the grade increases. At 2.25 miles from

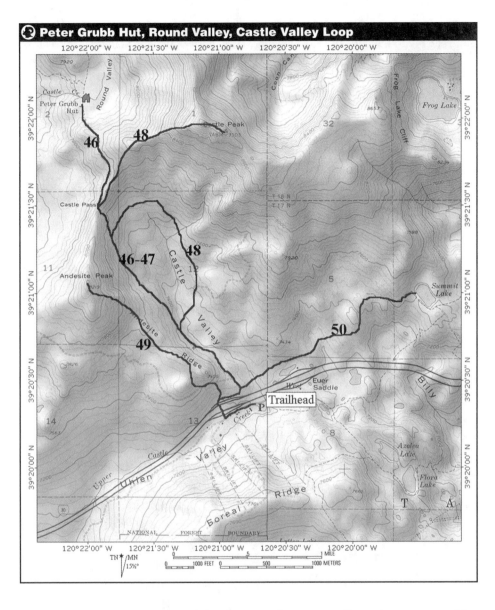

Peter Grubb Hut, Round Valley, Castle Valley Loop

the trailhead you stand on top of Castle Pass, where an excellent vista appears of the peaks and ski areas of the Donner Summit region. The ramparts of Castle Peak loom directly above, while the ski runs of Northstar, Boreal Ridge and Sugar Bowl are clearly seen carpeting the nearby hills.

Avoid the tendency to immediately descend from the pass, which leads to the snowmobile area. Instead, continue along the ridge northeast toward Castle Peak, following some old orange triangular signs marked SIERRA SKI WAY, CASTLE PEAK-NORDEN. Eventually the route leaves the ridge and makes a mild descent through light forest for 0.5 mile to the edge of the hill overlooking beautiful Round Valley. Now descend more steeply to the edge of the valley and work your way over to Peter Grubb Hut.

The hut is a pleasant destination for a half-day outing, or a fine base camp for further explorations into the lonely territory to the north. The gentle, open slopes of Round Valley provide the perfect environment for skiers practicing their kick-and-glide technique.

Retrace your steps back to the trailhead.

FYI: To spend a night or two at the hut, contact the Sierra Club for reservations at:
Clair Tappaan Lodge
PO Box 36
Norden, CA 95724
(530) 426-3632

Warm-ups: See Trips 37, 43, 51-61.

The Sierra Club's Peter Grubb Hut

TRIP **47**

Castle Valley Loop

Duration: One-half day
Distance: 3.75 miles partial loop trip
Difficulty: Easy
Elevation: 7200/7795
Map: *Norden* 7.5′ quadrangle

see map
on page
165

Introduction: By virtue of the 7227-foot elevation and the fairly dependable access of Interstate 80, Donner Summit provides snowshoers and skiers alike with access to some of the best conditions in the Sierra. Fair-weather winter weekends will see plenty of adventurous souls cavorting across the slopes of Boreal Ridge or propelling themselves into the backcountry on the opposite side of the highway. Fortunately, enough options exist to disperse these hearty recreationists across the snow-covered slopes of the Donner Summit region (see Trips 45-50).

Perhaps one of the easiest routes to be enjoyed in this area is the relatively simple jaunt around Castle Valley. Requiring only mild climbing and reasonably straightforward routefinding, combined with a short length, this trip is well-suited to snowshoers of all levels. Blue diamonds will aid in finding the way through the forested sections, but the configuration of Castle Valley should present few navigational problems. In addition, even though most of the route passes through timber, the meadow at the lower end of Castle Valley provides a nice view of dramatically rugged Castle Peak.

How to get there: Just west of Donner Summit take the Castle Peak exit from Interstate 80. Follow signs to the Sno-Park at the east end of the frontage road immediately south of the freeway. To reach the trailhead you must walk back under the freeway to the north side of the westbound off-ramp.

Description: After walking under the freeway to the westbound off-ramp, begin your hike by following a snow-covered road that climbs above the ramp. Soon the road bends northwest into mixed forest, where a pair of signs directs snowmobiles to the left and self-powered travelers to the right. Follow the road along the edge of Castle Valley Meadow, from where you have periodic views of Castle Peak. Leaving the meadows behind, you continue the mild ascent up the valley through forest cover. The grade of ascent increases near the slope below Castle Pass at the head of the valley.

From just below the pass make a slightly descending traverse to the east through the trees to the far side of the drainage of Castle Valley. Continue the descent as the route bends to the south following the east edge of the valley through the forest. At 2.75 miles you break out into open meadows and traverse the clearing for a 0.5 mile until you rejoin the road, thereby closing the loop.

After meeting the road you should retrace your steps for another 0.75 mile back to the Sno-Park.

FYI: Individuals or groups interested in a guided tour in the Castle Peak or other Tahoe National Forest areas can contact Snowshoe Tours with Cathy Works at (530) 273-6876, by email at **info@cathyworks.com**, or by regular mail at 17639 Cindy Lane, Grass Valley, CA 95945. In addition to the guide service, snowshoes, lessons and permits are included in the reasonable fee.

Warm-ups: See Trips 37, 43, 51-61.

A snowshoer below the slopes of Castle Peak near Donner Summit

TRIP 48

Castle Peak

Duration: Three-quarter day
Distance: 6.25 miles round trip
Difficulty: Difficult
Elevation: 7200/9103
Map: *Norden* 7.5' quadrangle

see map
on page
170

Introduction: The rugged ramparts of Castle Peak are a dominant feature of the Donner Summit landscape. At 9103 feet, the peak towers above the surrounding countryside, dwarfing the nearby hills and ridges. Coveted by alpinists and ski-mountaineers alike, the climb to the top provides a stimulating challenge for those up to the task. The first 2.25 miles to Castle Pass as described in Trip 46 are relatively mild, gaining only 725 vertical feet. However, the climb from the pass to the summit is an entirely different story, gaining 1200 feet in a mere 1 mile. Only those comfortable with high-angle slopes should consider climbing above the pass. Once atop the peak the effort is well rewarded by stunning views of the north Lake Tahoe countryside.

How to get there: Just west of Donner Summit, take the Castle Peak exit from Interstate 80. Follow signs to the Sno-Park at the east end of the frontage road immediately south of the freeway. To reach the trailhead you must walk back under the freeway to the north side of the westbound off-ramp.

Description: After walking under the freeway to the westbound off-ramp, begin your hike by following a snow-covered road that climbs above the ramp. Soon the road bends northwest into mixed forest, where a pair of signs directs snowmobiles to the left and self-powered travelers to the right. Follow the road along the edge of Castle Valley Meadow, from where you have periodic views of Castle Peak. Leaving the meadows behind, you continue the mild ascent up the valley though forest cover. The grade of ascent increases near the slope below Castle Pass at the head of the valley. at 2.25 miles from the trailhead. you stand on top of Castle Pass, where an excellent vista appears of the peaks and ski areas of the Donner Summit region.

From the 7930-foot pass head moderately steeply up the west ridge of Castle Peak. Higher up the ridge, bear slightly north of the ridge line and follow the less precipitous slopes toward the summit. Nearing the top, turn southeast to the true summit at 9103 feet. Depending on the conditions, some parties may feel more comfortable ascending the final pitch sans snowshoes. From the top of Castle Peak you

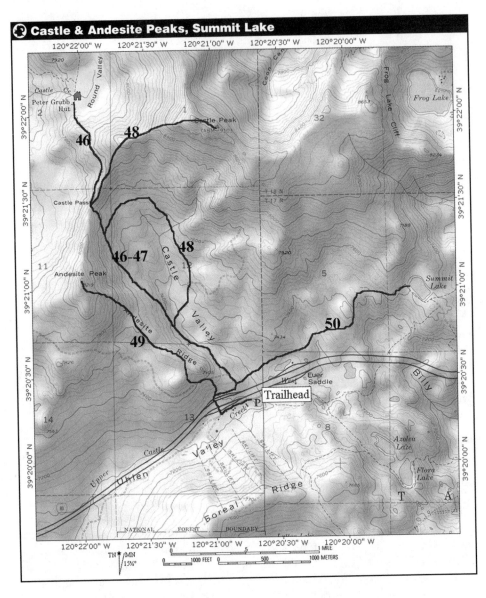

have extraordinary views of the Donner Summit region as well as north to Sierra Buttes and south to the peaks of Desolation Wilderness.

When you have had your fill of the spectacular scenery, retrace your steps to the trailhead.

FYI: If you prefer not to retrace your steps, with a little navigation you can descend the southeast ridge of Castle Peak and loop back to the trailhead.

Warm-ups: See Trips 37, 43, 51-61.

Castle Peak

TRIP **49**

Andesite Peak

Duration: One-half day
Distance: 3.5 miles round trip
Difficulty: Moderate
Elevation: 7200/8219
Map: *Norden* 7.5′ quadrangle

see map on page **170**

Introduction: The ascent to Andesite Peak is a reasonably short hike to fantastic views of the northern realm of the Lake Tahoe region. The vistas are nearly as good as those from the summit of Castle Peak, which requires an additional 3 miles and 900 vertical feet to reach. Except for a couple of steep slopes, one near the beginning and one at the end, the trip would be classified as easy, since the navigation is fairly straightforward—gain the ridge and follow it to the top. A lack of popularity will almost guarantee an uncrowded journey. Certainly you should see fewer people than on the Castle Peak route.

How to get there: Just west of Donner Summit take the Castle Peak exit from Interstate 80. Follow signs to the Sno-Park at the east end of the frontage road immediately south of the freeway. To reach the trailhead you must walk back under the freeway to the north side of the westbound off-ramp.

Description: After walking under the freeway to the westbound off-ramp, begin your hike by following a snow-covered road that climbs above the ramp. Immediately leave the road and head directly up the tree-covered slope below Andesite Ridge. After 0.1 mile, you will intersect a road heading west. Follow it a short distance, until you find a convenient place from which to begin a curving ascent of the steep slopes below Point 7605 shown on the *Norden* topo map. The immediate goal is to reach the top of Andesite Ridge just below and northwest of Point 7605.

Once the ridge is gained, the grade eases considerably as you stride northwest along Andesite Ridge. The scattered forest allows for sublime views of Castle Peak and the Donner Summit area. Straight ahead lies your goal, Andesite Peak. The next 0.5 mile provides easy snowshoeing across mild terrain, eventually returning to moderate forest cover below the base of the peak. Avoid the extreme east edge of Andesite Ridge and Andesite Peak, as large cornices may be present.

The summit of Andesite Peak

The grade increases dramatically as you approach the last 600 vertical feet to the summit. Initially the route passes through more heavy timber, but your perseverance will be rewarded higher up the slopes as the trees begin to thin again where you have dramatic views of Castle Peak. Continue to ascend until the terrain begins to ease just below the final ridge leading to the broad summit of Andesite Peak.

The 360° view from the summit is quite spectacular. Castle Peak looms majestically to the northeast, while off in the distance in all directions you have an incredible panorama of the peaks of north Tahoe.

Retrace your steps to the trailhead.

FYI: Varying your return to the Sno-Park is possible by descending north to Castle Pass, then reversing the description in Trip 46.

Warm-ups: See Trip 37, 43, 51-61.

TRIP 50

Summit Lake

see map
on page
170

Duration: One-half day
Distance: 4.25 miles round trip
Difficulty: Moderate
Elevation: 7200/7475
Map: *Norden* 7.5' quadrangle

Introduction: The trip to Summit Lake provides a pleasant alternative to the "freeway" leading to Peter Grubb Hut. However, without a marked trail or road to follow, you will have to put your routefinding skills to the test. The open terrain along the way provides some spectacular scenery of the Donner Summit region, and the secluded lake is a worthy destination for snowshoers looking for a peaceful half-day trip away from the crowds.

How to get there: Just west of Donner Summit take the Castle Peak exit from Interstate 80. Follow signs to the Sno-Park at the east end of the frontage road immediately south of the freeway. To reach the trailhead you must walk back under the freeway to the north side of the westbound off-ramp.

Description: After walking under the freeway to the westbound off-ramp, begin your hike by following a snow-covered road that climbs above the ramp. Proceed along the road until it quickly bends northwest. At this point leave the road and head east-northeast, roughly parallel to Interstate 80. Cross the ravine that drains Castle Valley and work your way over to the slope just above the westbound highway rest area.

From above the rest area, begin to head northeast slightly away from the high-way. Although the trip in general does not gain a great deal of elevation, the topography is such that you must work your way over hummocks, across drainages and around minor hills, continually negotiating minor elevation changes. Try to maintain a direct route by following a visual fix on a point at the end of the south-east ridge extending down from Castle Peak. Summit Lake nestles in a shallow basin just below the end of that ridge.

Unless the day is so windy that you need the protection of the trees, you can set a course through open terrain for most of your route to the lake. Out in the open you have excellent views of the Castle Peak and Donner Summit areas, providing plenty of landmarks to help keep you on track, such as Interstate 80 and Boreal Ridge Ski Area. As you make the final approach, the best route stays well above the level of the lake, avoiding some steep terrain to the south that plunges down toward the high-way. Cross the crest of a minor ridge and drop down to the lake, which is surrounded by a moderate forest of pine and fir. Summit Lake, pristine in appearance, provides only relative tranquillity as the din from traffic on Interstate 80 is not completely out of earshot.

FYI: Parking at the westbound rest area of Interstate 80 and beginning your trip from there would save nearly a mile of additional walking over starting from the trailhead at Donner Summit Sno-Park as described. Unfortunately, parking there for recreational purposes is illegal and thereby subject to fine.

Warm-ups: See Trips 37, 43, 51-61.

CHAPTER 10

Truckee & Vicinity

Compared to the west side of the Sierra, recreationists can expect a little more sun, a little less cloudiness, and slightly less snow east of Donner Summit. Since storms move in from the Pacific Ocean and deposit most of their moisture while rising up the west side of the mountains, the east side oftentimes experiences the subtleties of a little bit better weather thanks to this rain-shadow effect. Farther from the megalopolises of Sacramento and the Bay Area, recreationists can expect fewer companions on the trail as well. Even though the relatively easy access via the all-weather highway of Interstate 80 allows winter recreationists to flock into the north Tahoe region in large numbers, the farther east you travel the less pressure is placed on these recreational lands. Therefore, better weather and less crowding should be the expected reward for those valley-dwelling Californians willing to drive the extra distance beyond Donner Summit.

Expansive meadows, forested canyons, airy summits, and grand vistas are all here for the asking. Whether short or long, easy or difficult, there are plenty of trip

View west from Silver Peak

options for snowshoers of all skill levels. Neophytes can stroll easily along the level terrain of a meadow, while experts can tackle tall peaks or traverse high ridges for their impressive views.

The historic town of Truckee is the hub of this region with snowshoe trips scattered around in virtually every direction. Although the Donner Party fiasco took place nearby, more pleasant times fell upon Truckee with the arrival of the transcontinental railroad in 1868. The railroad fostered thriving logging and ice-harvesting industries. Along with the affluence came all the trappings associated with the typical bawdy Wild West town. At the peak of prosperity, Truckee's streets were lined with saloons, gambling halls, and a prosperous red-light district. However, by the 1920s the town had fallen on hard times and remained so until the 1960 Winter Olympics put Tahoe on the map as a winter playground. Ever since the success of the Olympics, the town of Truckee has been on the upswing. Nowadays, a bevy of fine restaurants, shops, and cafes entice strangers just passing through into leaving town with depleted pockets. Imagining those old Wild West days is quite easy when you stroll along the wooden sidewalks through the historic section of town.

Snowshoers wishing to avoid contact with snowmobiles will be quite content with the routes in this chapter. The only two possibilities of an encounter occur on a short span of the route below the west end of Shallenberger Ridge (Trip 52) and on the road to Kyburz Flat (Trip 55), although snowmobiles are forbidden to use this road after February 1st.

Location: Truckee is located alongside Interstate 80, approximately 50 miles east of Auburn.

Access: Interstate 80 provides the principal access to Truckee. From the west end of Truckee, the Donner Pass Road leads quickly to the trailhead for Trips 51 and 52. From the Highway 89 exit in the middle of Truckee, you can travel south to Trips 57-59 and north to Trips 53-56. From the Highway 267 exit at the east end of Truckee, you pass through the historic center of town and travel southeast to the trailheads for Trips 60 and 61 near Brockway Summit.

Amenities: Truckee offers all necessities and many luxuries as well. The Sierra Mountaineer at Bridge and Jibboom Streets (530) 587-2025 is a good source for outdoor equipment.

Season & Weather: In an average winter, snowfall is sufficient in this region for snowshoeing by sometime in December and continuing through the first weeks of April.

As previously mentioned, the weather conditions on the east side of the Sierra should generally be slightly better than on the west side. However, storms can be every bit as intense, so be prepared for foul weather and always obtain an accurate forecast before venturing into the backcountry.

PERMITS

Day Use & Overnight Use: Permits are not required for entry into Tahoe National Forest. A Wilderness permit is not necessary for entry into Granite Chief Wilderness (Trip 59).

Sno-Park: A Sno-Park permit is required for parking at Donner Memorial State Park (Trips 51-52).

MAPS

Tahoe National Forest and Lakes Basin, Winter Recreation Guide
1:84,480, 2000, paper
Tahoe National Forest

FOREST SERVICE

Tahoe National Forest
Foresthill Ranger District
22830 Foresthill Road
Foresthill, CA 95631
(530) 367-2224

Tahoe National Forest
Truckee Ranger District
9646 Donner Pass Road
Truckee, CA 9616-2949
(530) 587-3558

Forest Supervisor
Tahoe National Forest
631 Coyote Street
Nevada City, CA 95959-2250
(530) 265-4531

Toiyabe National Forest
Carson Ranger District
1536 S. Carson Street
Carson City, NV 89701
(775) 882-2766

IMPORTANT PHONE NUMBERS

Avalanche Report   (530) 587-2158
Sno-Park Permit Information (916) 324-1222
Road Conditions   (800) 427-7623
Weather   (530) 541-1151

WEBSITES

Tahoe National Forest   www.r5.fs.fed.us/tahoe
Avalanche Report   www.r5.fs.fed.us/tahoe/avalanche
Sno-Park Information   www.ohv.parks.ca.gov/SVRAs/snopark

Animal tracks along the road to Stampede Reservoir

TRIP **51**

Donner Memorial State Park Loop

Duration: One-half day
Distance: 2.5 miles loop trip
Difficulty: Easy
Elevation: 5935/5975
Maps: *Truckee & Norden* 7.5′ quadrangles

Introduction: The essentially flat landscape of Donner Memorial State Park is a great place for neophytes in need of some easy terrain where they can become accustomed to walking on snowshoes. The gentle topography provides a safe and easy environment for families with children as well. Even for the more advanced snowshoer, the park loop is a fine place to spend a morning or afternoon wandering through the scattered trees and catching glimpses of the lake. Incorporating a visit to the Emigrant Trail Museum along with a meal at one of the many fine establishments of Truckee makes for an excellent outing.

How to get there: From Interstate 80, take the exit for Donner Memorial State Park near the west end of Truckee and follow signs to the Sno-Park.

Description: The Nordic trail begins at the west end of the Sno-Park. Follow the snow-covered road, across the bridge over Donner Creek, avoiding the set cross-country ski tracks, and then move quickly to the marked junction with your return route on a road to the south. From this junction continue west along the road as it follows the curving shoreline of Donner Lake. After a mile you bend around at China Cove and then follow the marked route as it heads east for nearly 1 more mile. You then bend north for 0.25 mile and reach the junction that closes your loop. From there retrace your steps the short distance to the parking area.

FYI: The Emigrant Trail Museum, dedicated in part to the fateful Donner Party mishap, is open from 9 a.m. to 4 p.m. There is a $2 fee for adults and $1 for children (6-12). Sno-Park permits can be purchased at the museum. For more information, call (530) 582-7892.

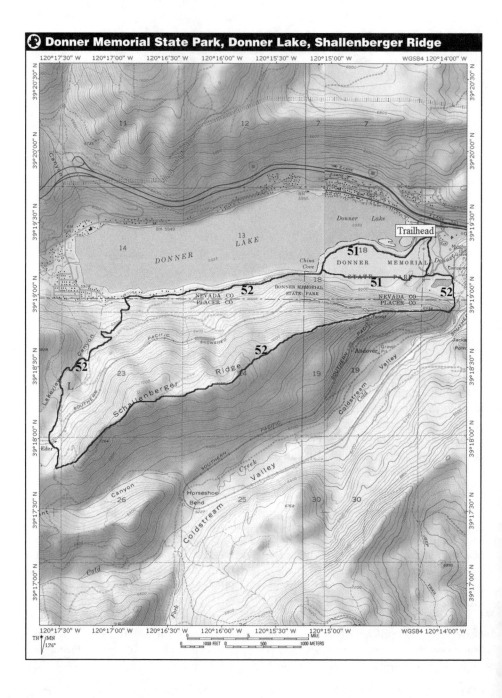

Warm-ups: The Donner Lake Kitchen, on the Donner Pass Road on the north shore of the lake, is a favorite breakfast hangout of locals and out-of-towners on weekends. The rustic cafe serves hearty portions sure to keep your engine stoked on the trail. Some years the cafe closes for a week during the winter. Otherwise you can sink your teeth into their delectable fare seven days a week, from 7 a.m. to 2 p.m. (530) 587-3119.

T R I P 52

Donner Lake – Schallenberger Ridge Loop

see map
on page
180

Duration: Full day
Distance: 9.75 miles loop trip
Difficulty: Difficult
Elevation: 5935/7469
Maps: *Truckee & Norden* 7.5′ quadrangles

Introduction: Modern-day visitors, armed with good equipment, fairly reliable weather forecasts and accurate maps, now flock to an area that was once the site of perhaps the best-known tragedy of the westward expansion. Surprised by November snows, members of the Donner Party holed up at Donner Lake in an ill-fated attempt to survive the harsh conditions of the winter of 1846-47. Out of the 87 who began the trip in Illinois, only 47 were eventually rescued and led to safety over Donner Pass and down to the more hospitable climate in the valleys of California.

A century and a half later, snowshoers can experience the beauty of a winter wonderland that was no doubt lost on these unfortunate pioneers. Donner Lake is beautiful in its own right, but travelers along Schallenberger Ridge enjoy the added treat of stunning views of some of the Tahoe Sierra's most notable landmarks. A mere 2 miles east of Donner Pass, numerous peaks can be seen, including Mt. Lincoln, Anderson Peak and Castle Peak. While visitors confront the bustling human activity in the town of Truckee and the whizzing traffic along the concrete ribbon of Interstate 80, snowshoers may feel as though they are in a different world altogether as they travel along a remote crest.

This trip, like the grisly tale of the Donner Party, is not for the faint of heart. Completing the full journey requires the better part of a day, especially if snowshoers must plod through untracked powder. Although the route is generally straightforward, some routefinding is necessary, especially for the most direct route down Lakeview Canyon. One potential drawback for some may be the 1-mile walk along the plowed section of road on the south shore of Donner Lake between Lakeview Canyon and Donner Lake Park.

How to get there: From Interstate 80, take the exit for Donner Memorial State Park near the west end of Truckee and follow signs to the Sno-Park.

Description: From the Sno-Park, follow the Donner Park Nordic Trail across the bridge over Donner Creek and then quickly to the trail junction. Turn south and proceed along the marked route for approximately 0.3 mile to where the Nordic loop trail bends west. Leave the Nordic trail at this point and work your way east and then south around a pond to the snow-covered road leading into Coldstream Valley. Once upon the road, climb a short distance to where the road crosses the eastern extension of Schallenberger Ridge, nearly 1 mile from the trailhead.

Leaving the road here, climb moderately steeply up the nose of the hill through a light forest of fir and pine. After the initial climb the terrain eases somewhat as you begin to have views through a more scattered forest down into Coldstream Valley and up the canyon toward the ridge between Anderson Peak and Mt. Lincoln. Along the way toward the high point at 7469 feet, you climb through sections of open ridge crest and light forest. Once you reach the apex of Schallenberger Ridge, 3 miles from the Sno-Park, views expand to include Donner Peak and Mt. Judah to the west, Boreal Ridge and Castle Peak to the northwest, Mt. Rose and the Carson

View from Schallenberger Ridge

Range to the east, and a host of other landmarks including Donner Lake, Interstate 80 and Donner Pass Road.

Now you descend along the ridge through light-to-scattered forest to a saddle and then make a short, moderate climb up the hill 0.75-mile west of Peak 7469.

Nearly level walking along the ridge brings you to better views where the trees thin again. Soon the ridge narrows and you make a brief descent into the next saddle before a short climb leads up to Point 7264.

From Peak 7264, you follow the narrow crest of Schallenberger Ridge on a moderate descent toward the broad, forested saddle above Lakeview Canyon. At the saddle you encounter a road, 4.75 miles from the Sno-Park. Unless you are here during or immediately after a storm, there should be plenty of tracks on this route as snowmobilers use this road as a connection between Donner Lake and Coldstream Valley.

You turn north and follow the road on a winding descent for 0.25 mile. As you approach the railroad tracks, the road bends west, paralleling the tracks for 0.5 mile before crossing over and continuing down Lakeview Canyon. Rather than follow the road, carefully head straight across the tracks near Eder, an abandoned railroad stop as shown on the Norden topo map. Once safely across you must negotiate the short, steep slope on the downhill side of the tracks.

Beyond the tracks, make your way north across the gentle terrain to the west branch of the seasonal creek that drains Lakeview Canyon. Find the continuation of the road nearby and follow its winding course down through the canyon to the paved road above the south shore of Donner Lake, 7 miles from your starting point.

For the next mile you will be forced to abandon your snowshoes and walk the plowed road past the homes along the south side of the lake, as the road is kept open for residents during the winter. Once you reach the end of the plowed section, you can don your snowshoes again and proceed on a gentle downhill grade, crossing the western boundary of Donner State Park near China Cove, 8.5 miles from the trailhead.

You proceed through the park for a short distance until reaching a groomed turnaround. Veer north at this point and then follow the north branch of the Nordic loop trail around China Cove and east along the south shore of Donner Lake. Just beyond the end of the lake you encounter a Y-junction, from which you should continue straight for another 250 yards to a T-junction. Closing the loop here, you turn left, following an exit sign, cross the bridge over Donner Creek, and quickly conclude your journey at the parking lot.

FYI: Avoid the north edge of Schallenberger Ridge, where nasty cornices may develop.

Warm-ups: See Trip 51.

Sagehen Campground

see map
on page
185

Duration: One-half day
Distance: 5.5 miles round trip
Difficulty: Easy
Elevation: 6435/6295/6485
Maps: *Hobart Mills* & *Independence Lake* 7.5′ quadrangles

Introduction: The realm of snow-covered terrain north of Interstate 80 along Highway 89 is typically overrun with the noise and stench of snowmobiles. However, in the midst of this terrible blight there are some small parcels of real estate that are off-limits to the mechanized beasts. The short trip to Sagehen Campground is just such an escape. You may have to tolerate snowmobiles for the first 0.25 mile, but after that the forested territory along the banks of Sagehen Creek is free from such modern distractions. This area has been closed not for the benefit of skiers and snowshoers in search of peace and quiet, but to prevent any detrimental effects caused by mechanized equipment to the research being done at the University of California Field Station 2 miles from the highway.

The trip into Sagehen Campground, while not filled with dramatic scenery, is a pleasant stroll through the drainage of Sagehen Creek. The mild grade and well-defined road make this a fairly easy trip for both advanced and beginning snowshoers. For those in search of a greater challenge, making a longer loop trip back to the car is possible via a road open to snowmobiles (see FYI). Sagehen Campground would provide a fine basecamp for exploring the surrounding terrain, including scenic Independence Lake.

How to get there: A small plowed parking area just large enough for about a half dozen cars is on the west side of Highway 89, 7.9 miles north of Interstate 80. This trailhead is 0.2 mile north of the Sierra/Nevada county line.

Description: Begin your trip by heading southwest and then west along the easy grade of a snow-covered road through light forest cover. Approximately 0.25 mile from the trailhead you encounter a junction with the snowmobile route heading north from the Prosser OHV staging area. Continue straight on your road for another 500 feet to yet another junction. Following signs marked ROAD CLOSED 500 FEET and FIELD STATION 2, leave the main road and follow the lesser used road (FS 876-2) that angles slightly left. **Note:** If you were to continue on the main road you would very quickly

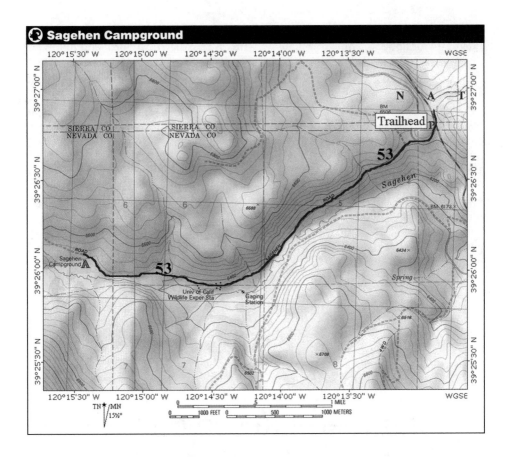

come to one more junction marked for destinations of SAGEHEN CAMPGROUND 4 (right-hand branch) and LITTLE TRUCKEE SUMMIT (left-hand branch). These are both routes open to snowmobiles. If desired, the left-hand road can be combined with the description below for a loop trip (see FYI).

Gratefully, you now leave the snowmobile route and begin a mild descent free from the mechanical beasts. Through pine forest you make a 1.25-mile gradual descent along Sagehen Creek. Another 0.5 mile of gradual ascent takes you past the University of California Field Station. Mechanized travel of all kinds has been forbidden in this area, winter and summer, to avoid disturbing the ongoing scientific studies associated with the field station.

You continue to climb mildly along the road, reaching Sagehen Campground after another mile of snowshoeing. The campground makes an excellent overnight base for further exploration of the surrounding terrain. Options for additional wanderings include trips to Independence Lake and across the Sagehen Hills.

FYI: If you don't mind the possibility that you may encounter snowmobiles, you could avoid retracing your steps by making a loop back to the trailhead, you would have to snowshoe 1.5 miles more than if you just backtracked your original route. To make the loop, begin by heading northwest from Sagehen Campground along FS Road 11-4 for about 0.5 mile to a junction with FS Road 11. Turn north and follow FS Road 11 east for another 3.5 miles to the intersection just west of where you originally turned down FS Road 876-2 to Sagehen Campground. From there, retrace your steps 0.3 mile back to the car.

Note: unfortunately, the complete length of FS Road 11 is not shown on the 1981 *Independence Lake* topo map, but the road cut is obvious all the way and should present little routefinding difficulty.

Warm-ups: Back in Truckee, El Toro Bravo will take the chill out of a cold winter's day with a wide selection of spicy Mexican dishes for lunch or dinner. Along with more traditional fare, the restaurant offers fajitas and seafood specialties like Capitola Snapper and Aptos Grilled Prawns. Once the spicy food raises your core temperature again, you can refresh yourself with a glass of Sangria or a tasty Margarita. El Toro Bravo is on Donner Pass Road at the west end of the historic district of town. (530) 587-3557.

Stampede Reservoir

see map
on page
188

Duration: Three-quarter day
Distance: 6 miles round trip
Difficulty: Easy to moderate
Elevation: 6435/6095/6410
Maps: *Hobart Mills* 7.5′ quadrangles

Introduction: The Sagehen parking area is a fairly popular starting point for skiers and snowshoers alike, particularly those interested in the route past the University of California Field Station to Sagehen Campground (See Trip 54). Unfortunately, away from that particular route, the network of roads west of Highway 89 is exceedingly popular with snowmobilers, considerably diminishing the opportunity for peace and tranquility for self-powered travelers. Fortunately, those in quest of solitude and serenity can find rewards east of Highway 89 as few recreationists of any kind consider the terrain across the highway for their pursuits, in spite of the fact that the scenery is superb.

Stampede Reservoir

The splendid landscape, or at least your ability to view it, is due in part to an unfortunate occurrence. In August of 1960 a forest fire began near the Donner Lake Interchange on I-80 eventually consuming nearly 45,000 acres of timberland. Thousands of "penny pines" were purchased through numerous donations from groups and individuals allowing the Forest Service to conduct a massive reforestation project. Today those ponderosa pines make up a young, widely scattered forest that permits visitors along this route to experience fine vistas of Stampede Reservoir, the surrounding ridges and distant peaks.

If you're searching for stunning scenery along with peace and quiet, then this trip will be hard to beat. Chances are, there won't be a packed trail to follow, as there more than likely would be on the opposite side of Highway 89, but the potential for solitude and the open terrain are more than enough compensation for the extra effort.

How to get there: Follow directions in Trip 53 to the small plowed parking area at the beginning of Sagehen Road (FS 11).

Description: From the parking area, cross Highway 89 and bear north paralleling the highway for just under 0.1 mile, until you find a road heading northeast. Follow the easy grade of this road, periodically marked by orange steel posts, through light ponderosa-pine forest, traversing around a low hill to your right. As you proceed, you have views of the surrounding hills and ridges, thanks in no small part to the relatively young age of the scattered pines planted here after the 1960 fire. At the 0.75-mile mark, where you may notice a couple of posts marking a jeep trail heading south up the hillside, continue straight ahead.

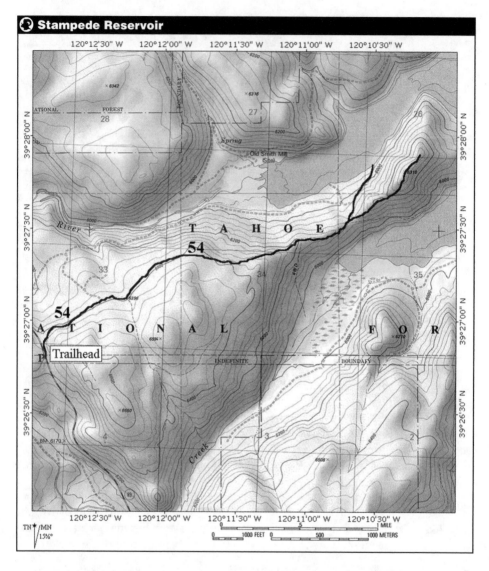

Proceed along the mildly graded road through the widely scattered pines. You may notice a few burned snags still standing, but most of the evidence of the fire has long since disappeared, and most of what does remain is hidden under a blanket of winter snow. After a mile of easy snowshoeing, you get your first glimpse of the Little Truckee River arm of massive Stampede Reservoir nearly 500 feet below surrounded by snow-covered ridges. Mt. Rose and the rest of the Carson Range also burst into view on the southeast horizon. The beautiful vistas continue to improve as you near the crest of your journey, just past the 1.25-mile mark.

From this viewpoint you can visually follow the upcoming route of your journey as the road makes an arcing decline around to the ridge separating the Little

Truckee River arm and the Sagehen Creek arm of Stampede Reservoir. The mile-long moderate descent brings you to a 6095-foot saddle, the low point of the trip.

From the saddle, you begin a mild ascent along the road as it climbs near the crest of the ridge ahead. Directly to your right you have a fine view of the Sagehen Creek drainage emptying into the reservoir, as well as continued views of the Carson Range to the southeast. Nearing the 2.5-mile point, where the road crosses the crest of the ridge, you reach a moment of decision. You can continue along the road as it descends to the lakeshore, or follow the ridge on a moderate climb to the ridge's high point.

FYI: As with all mountain lakes, exercise extreme caution if you venture out onto the surface of the reservoir.

Warm-ups: Wong's Garden is the place in Truckee for Szechuan cuisine. Located at 11430 Deerfield Drive, Wong's open for lunch at 11 a.m. and closes for dinner around 9 p.m. (530) 587-1831.

View from the Stampede Reservoir trail

TRIP **55**

Kyburz Flat

see map
on page
191

Duration: One-half day
Distance: 2 miles round trip
Difficulty: Easy
Elevation: 6275/6375
Maps: *Sierraville* & *Sardine Peak* 7.5′ quadrangles

Introduction: Beginning snowshoers will love this trip, as will families with children and snowshoers not yet in peak condition. The grade is easy, the distance is short, and next to no routefinding is required along the easily discernible road regularly marked with blue diamonds. Once you reach Kyburz Flat, a host of possibilities await for additional wanderings for those who find the easy mile not enough of a challenge (see Trip 56). The scenery is quite pleasant: Kyburz Flat is a vast clearing encased by lightly forested hills, emitting a delightfully pastoral ambiance.

The area is replete with history as well. The Washoe tribe constituted the first inhabitants of the valley nearly 2000 years ago, undoubtedly drawn to the abundant supply of waterfowl that nest in the marshes of Kyburz Flat during springtime. In the 1850s the Henness Pass Road became a major thoroughfare for immigrants traveling to prosperous mining districts on the Yuba and American rivers. After the mining boom the road provided a major link between the towns of Nevada City, California and Virginia City, Nevada. At the beginning of the 20th century, logging and grazing became big business in the valleys and surrounding hillsides.

Presently, human activity around Kyburz Flat is limited to recreation and sightseeing, most of which occurs during the summer months. Fortunately for skiers and snowshoers, snowmobiles are banned after the end of January (to avoid disturbing the waterfowl), leaving the area for people satisfied to travel under their own power during the rest of the winter months.

How to get there: Go 12.7 miles north of Interstate 80 on State Highway 89 and turn right onto the short plowed section of Sierra County Road 450. Watch for a sign reading KYBURZ FLAT prior to the junction. Parking is available for a half dozen or so vehicles.

Description: Begin your journey by following the snow-covered road on a gentle grade, wandering along the edge of a thin ribbon of meadow rimmed by forested

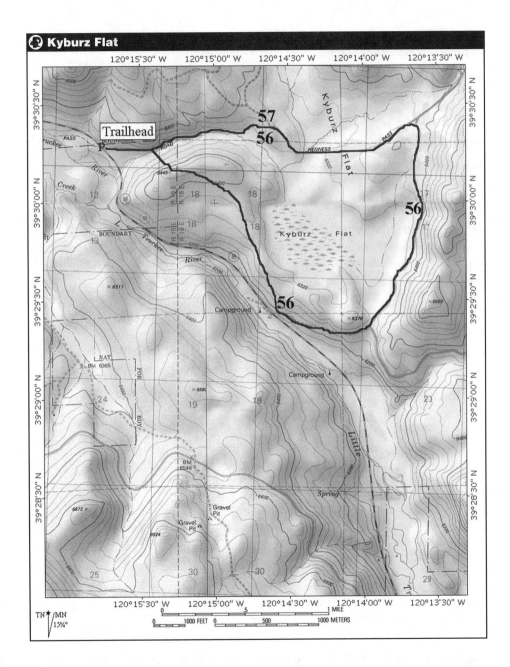

hillsides on either side. Although the route is obvious, blue diamonds attached to trees will help guide you. Where the grade of the road momentarily increases slightly, near the half-mile point, the wide expanse of Kyburz Flat begins to come into view. You traverse a short stretch of light forest before encountering a pit toilet and information board heralding your arrival at the Kyburz Flat Interpretive

Area. Continuing on the Henness Pass Road, you break out into the vast openness of the flat, 1 mile from the trailhead.

FYI: Once you reach the meadows a host of additional opportunities present themselves. You could continue along the marked road network and complete the 5-mile Wheeler Loop, or wander out into the flat, or ascend one of the low hills above the flat for a fine view, or simply return to the trailhead satisfied with the little effort required to reach Kyburz Flat.

Warm-ups: The Cottonwood, high up on the hill south of town at the base of what was once California's first ski jump, is a consensus winner for one of Truckee's top restaurants. You would never guess from the ramshackle appearance of the exterior that the inside of the restaurant is warm and inviting. The slightly eclectic menu changes daily, but always offers a number of delights. While the Cottonwood may be one of Truckee's best dining establishments it is also one of the most expensive. The Cottonwood is just off Highway 267 at 10142 Rue Hilltop at Hilltop Lodge. Call (530) 587-5711 for reservations or more information. You can salivate over the Cottonwood's menu or sample excerpts from several reviews at **www.cottonwoodrestaurant.com**.

TRIP **56**

Kyburz Flat Loop

Duration: Three-quarter day
Distance: 5.5 miles loop trip
Difficulty: Moderate
Elevation: 6270/6450
Maps: *Sierraville, Sardine Peak, Hobart Mills,* &
      Independence Lake 7.5' quadrangles

see map
on page
191

Introduction: Cross-country skiers covet the essentially level, open terrain of Kyburz Flat, particularly since the area is closed to snowmobiles, along with the accompanying noise and pollution, after February 1st. A marked trail entices skiers and snowshoers on the 5-mile Wheeler Loop, which goes around the northern limits of the flat. The trip described below, also a loop, heads in the opposite direction along the east edge of Kyburz Flat before leading west and then north back to the trailhead.

Snowshoers follow the gentle grade of the Henness Pass Road along a thin ribbon of meadows to expansive Kyburz Flat, as described in Trip 55. Waterfowl use this area for nesting purposes in the marshes of spring, but in the winter you may be awestruck by the wide open expanse of snow-covered plain, 2 miles long by 1 mile across. Past the flat, snowshoers complete the loop by wandering through the seclusion of a light-to-moderate pine forest.

How to get there: Go 12.7 miles north of Interstate 80 on State Highway 89 and turn right onto the short plowed section of Sierra County Road 450. Watch for a sign reading kyburz flat prior to the junction. Parking is available for a half dozen or so vehicles.

Description: Follow the gentle grade of snow-covered Henness Pass Road along the fringe of a thin meadow rimmed by forested hillsides. Where the grade of the road momentarily increases slightly, the wide expanse of Kyburz Flat springs into view. Continue on the road through the expansive opening toward the east side of the flat and and a T-junction, 2 miles from the highway.

From the junction, turn south and follow the snow-covered road on a mild climb through light pine forest. After 0.5 mile you see Kyburz Flat on your right, visible through breaks in the trees. Along the forested edge of the flat, the road resumes a nearly level grade. Farther down, ignore a road to your left at a Y-junction, continuing straight ahead (south) on the main road. As you near the south end of Kyburz Flat, a low forested hill appears just beyond the flat to your right (west). Immediately beyond this hill, just prior to the 3.5-mile mark, is an indistinct junction with a road heading west that travels around the south side of the hill through the trees. Keep a close watch for this road as you pass the hill, and when you find the junction, turn west.

Proceed on a mild descent along the roadway as it cuts a narrow swath through light pine forest. After a bit you reach a Y-junction—take the uphill path to the right (the left branch heads down to Highway 89 near the Upper Little Truckee Campground).

Through light-to-moderate pine forest you follow this logging road as it begins a steady climb. Eventually the road seems to disappear amid the moderate forest cover, but just continue the ascent northwest to the top of Peak 6649. From there you can see the thin ribbon of meadow below and the Henness Pass Road on the far side. Work your way down the steep hillside, cross the meadow, and rejoin the road. From there, follow your tracks west back to the trailhead.

FYI: Prior to February 1st, snowmobilers may use the Henness Pass Road through Kyburz Flat, so you may want to avoid this area on weekends until after January.

Warm-ups: The Passage is another favorite Truckee dining establishment, located inside the historic 4-story Truckee Hotel. Restored to Victorian splendor nearly a decade ago, the hotel, restaurant and bar are popular with tourists and locals alike. The Passage serves excellent food for lunch (M-F), Saturday and Sunday brunch, and dinner nightly. The award-winning wine list is highly touted. Find the Truckee Hotel across from the train station at the intersection of Bridge Street and Commercial Row. (530) 587-7619.

TRIP **57**

Silver Peak

see map
on page
195

Duration: Full day
Distance: 9.75 miles round trip
Difficulty: Difficult
Elevation: 6020/8424
Maps: *Tahoe City 7.5'* quadrangle

Introduction: During sunny weather, Silver Peak provides one of the best views of Lake Tahoe in the entire Tahoe basin. Most of the trip follows an easy grade along a snow-covered road, but the last 0.75 mile gains 1000 feet up a steep ridge to the top and should be attempted only by experienced parties. If you don't mind the challenge of high-angle slopes and wind-blasted aeries, Silver Peak rewards you with an unsurpassed vista. Experiencing the awesome view upon reaching the summit on a sunny, windless day creates an idyllic memory. Experienced snowboarders will certainly want to have their gear along for the descent if the snow is stable.

How to get there: Travel south on Highway 89, 5.9 miles from the junction with Interstate 80 in Truckee, to a small plowed area on the west side of the road. This parking area is just south of Pole Creek, diagonally across the highway from a contemporary wooden structure signed olson const co. Park judiciously in the limited area. From the clearing you should be able to see the beginning of the snow-covered road, Forest Road 08, almost paralleling the highway as it heads into the trees.

Description: Follow the road as it winds and climbs away from the highway through moderate forest. If you feel comfortable leaving the security of the established route, you can save some distance by heading directly cross-country rather than following the circuitous path of the road. As the mild climb along the road progresses, you have nice views of the surrounding hills and eventually of Silver Peak itself. After 1.85 miles, you reach a junction with another road on the right, which heads downhill toward Pole Creek (see Trip 58).

Bear left at the junction and continue to follow your road south as it climbs through a mixed forest of pine, fir and occasional cedar. If you want to forgo the road, you can take a more direct course straight over Peak 7403 to the northeast ridge of Silver Peak. Otherwise, remain on the road as it circles the hillside on a mild grade, reaching an overlook just shy of 3 miles from the trailhead. From this

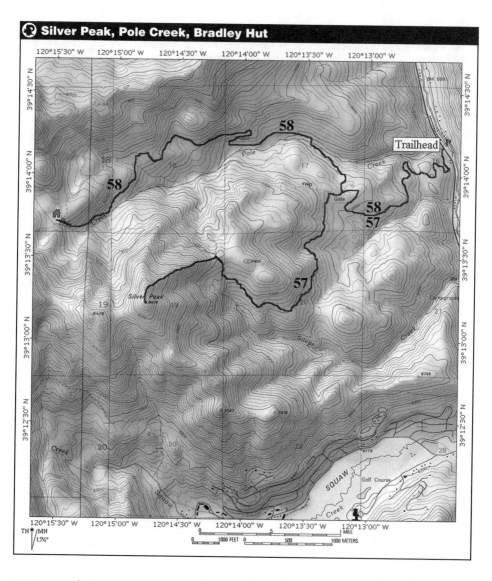

Silver Peak, Pole Creek, Bradley Hut

vantage point, you can gaze southeast across the waters of Lake Tahoe to Freel Peak, the highest mountain in the Tahoe basin. Another 0.75 mile of snowshoeing along the road brings you to the northeast ridge of Silver Peak, 3.75 miles from the trailhead.

Now you leave the gentle grade of the road behind and climb much more steeply up the ridge. As you gain elevation, follow a direct line southwest up the ridge to the summit, except for a pair of rock outcroppings, which should be passed on the right. The final pitch is fairly steep and may be composed of wind-packed snow, so some parties may wish to bring ice axes and crampons during periods of extremely hard snow conditions.

The view from the summit of Silver Peak is spectacular. Lake Tahoe is revealed in all its glory, and the basin's highest peaks provide the perfect backdrop. Thousands of feet below, the busyness of Squaw Valley stands in stark contrast to the remoteness at the summit. You can while away the hours watching brightly clad skiers descending the numerous runs of one of Tahoe's largest resorts.

FYI: Under stable conditions, experienced skiers and snowboarders may want to pack along their gear—the descent of Silver Peak provides outstanding backcountry possibilities.

Warm-ups: If headed back to Truckee, check out the options in Trips 51-56, 60 and 61. For one of the best breakfasts in Tahoe, head down Highway 89 to Tahoe City and the Fire Sign Cafe. A popular Tahoe hot spot since 1970, the cafe is extremely busy on weekends, but the freshly prepared dishes are worth the wait. Not only will you find bacon and eggs, but more exotic fare such as Cape Cod Benedict and dill and artichoke omelets. Lunch (served until 2 p.m.) is also available but breakfast is the main attraction. The restaurant occupies an old home at 1785 W. Lake Blvd., 2 miles south of town. To avoid the long wait on weekends, time your arrival for 7 a.m. when the cafe opens.

TRIP 58

Pole Creek & Bradley Hut

see map on page 195

Duration: Full day
Distance: 10.25 miles round trip
Difficulty: Moderate
Elevation: 6020/7610
Maps: *Tahoe City* & *Granite Chief* 7.5' quadrangles

Introduction: Harold T. Bradley was a university professor and former president of the Sierra Club who, after experiencing the pleasures of the hut system in the Swiss Alps, proposed a similar string of six alpine huts that would span the mountains above Lake Tahoe from Donner to Echo Summit. Only four of the huts were ever realized, the last completed in 1957 within the Five Lakes Basin, directly above what would one day become the Alpine Meadows Ski Area. This final hut was named as a memorial to Harold's late wife Josephine.

In 1984 the inclusion of the Five Lakes Basin within the designated Granite Chief Wilderness created a profound dilemma for the Bradley Hut. Since the legal definition of wilderness is "an area without permanent improvements or human habitation," the existence of the structure was incompatible with wilderness. After much debate, rather than destroy the hut, a plan was worked out to move the structure to the current location along Pole Creek. With the aid of many volunteers, the structure was relocated, refurbished and reopened for the winter of 1998. Today visitors can follow the record of the original construction as well as the eventual relocation through the photographs mounted on the walls in the hut.

The trip to Bradley Hut is a pleasant experience, even for those not anticipating an overnight stay. Following the moderate grade of a snow-covered road, travelers weave their way through light forest for the first 2 miles and then follow the banks of Pole Creek for another 3 miles up into the scenic basin at the head of the canyon. Along the way there are stunning views of 8424-foot Silver Peak. The hut provides a fine basecamp for snowshoers and skiers who want to explore the sloping terrain above the creek or the backcountry beyond. Overnighters must arrange for use of the Bradley Hut (see FYI).

How to get there: Travel south on Highway 89, 5.9 miles from the junction with Interstate 80 in Truckee, to a small plowed area on the west side of the road. This parking area is just south of Pole Creek, diagonally across the highway from a contemporary wooden structure signed OLSON CONST CO. Park judiciously in the limited area. From the clearing you should be able to see the beginning of the snow-covered road, Forest Road 08, almost paralleling the highway as it heads into the trees.

Description: Follow the road as it winds and climbs away from the highway through moderate forest. If you feel comfortable leaving the security of the road, you can save some distance by heading directly cross-country rather than following the circuitous road. After 1.85 miles along the road, you reach a junction.

From the junction, take the right-hand road north on a moderate descent into the drainage of Pole Creek. After you draw near to the stream, proceed up the road on a gentle climb to a wooden bridge. You cross the bridge and begin a moderate climb above the north bank of Pole Creek through widely scattered ponderosa pines. As you continue, the summit of Silver Peak peeks above the tops of the trees to the southwest.

At 3 miles from the trailhead, you begin to climb more steeply as the road switchbacks up the hillside. In another 0.25 mile you reach a junction, where you should follow FS Road 08 as it bends sharply back to the left, heading west again. On the steady ascent, the stately form of Silver Peak makes regular appearances over the next mile through a widely scattered forest. After you cross a feeder creek, work your way over to the main channel of Pole Creek, and follow alongside the stream toward the upper basin. Just past the 5-mile mark you find the newly relocated Bradley Hut near the road on the fringe of the open terrain at the head of the canyon.

The two-story, A-frame cabin with matching outhouse provides temporary shelter for day-trippers. When visiting the cabin observe the posted rules and do your part to insure that this historic legacy will remain intact for generations to come.

FYI: For overnight reservations, or for more information about the Bradley Hut, contact the Sierra Club at: Clair Tappaan Lodge
PO Box 36
Norden, CA 95724
(530) 426-3632

Warm-ups: When the "PIZ" fell off the sign out front, the owner seized the moment and renamed the restaurant ZA's. This momentous occasion aside, great Italian food served at reasonable prices probably has more to do with the overwhelming success of this restaurant than the offbeat name. Space is limited, so you may have to wait for a table, but you won't be disappointed in the food when it comes, or the size of the check, for that matter. Lunch is served from 11 a.m. to 3 p.m. and dinner from 4:30 p.m. till closing. Za's is located in Tahoe City at 395 North Lake Blvd. (Highway 28), across from the fire station. If heading to Truckee, check out Trips 51-56 and 60 and 61.

TRIP 59

Alpine Meadows to Five Lakes Basin

see map
on page
199

Duration: One-half day
Distance: 3.25 miles round trip
Difficulty: Moderate to difficult
Elevation: 6560/7500
Maps: *Tahoe City* & *Granite Chief* 7.5′quadrangles

Introduction: A short but strenuous climb leads to a quiet basin with five small lakes. An extremely popular summer destination, the Five Lakes area is seldom seen during the winter. On a typical winter day, hundreds if not thousands of skiers cavort along nearby ridges and slopes at the upper limits of Alpine Meadows and Squaw

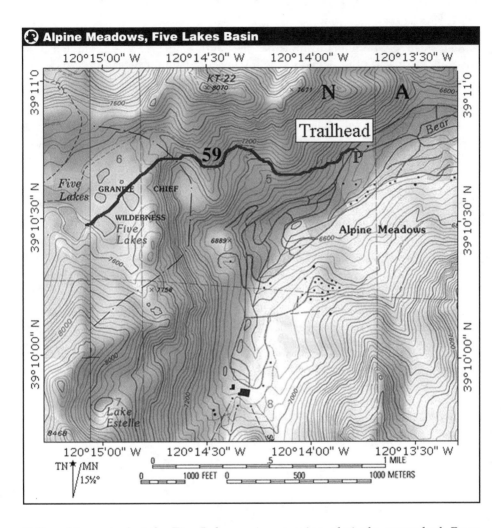

Alpine Meadows, Five Lakes Basin

Valley ski resorts, but the Five Lakes region remains relatively untouched. From Alpine Meadows, a route across the steep mountainside past impassable-looking cliffs and over to the lakes would seem inconceivable, but a route does exist for those who don't mind the steep ascent. Due to the precipitous slopes one must cross and the potential for avalanche, this trip should be attempted only when snow conditions are stable. The high, open terrain provides bird's-eye views of Alpine Meadows during the ascent.

How to get there: Go south on Highway 89, 9.5 miles from the junction with Interstate 80 in Truckee, to the access road for Alpine Meadows. Go up the Alpine Meadows road 2.1 miles to the second of two intersections both marked DEER PARK ROAD. Parking is extremely limited, so try to find a place in a plowed area near this intersection. If parking near the trailhead is impossible, you may have to park in the ski-area parking lot and bum a ride back from an agreeable skier.

Description: Climb up the bank on the north side of the road and begin the moderately steep, continuous ascent across the south-facing hillside through a light covering of fir and pine. A quick visual inspection should reveal that this is not a route to be tried in unstable circumstances—this slope could be prone to avalanches under certain conditions, and nasty cornices loom above you at the top of the ridge. As you gain elevation, pleasant views of Alpine Meadows should calm your spirits. During calm weather, this slope is marked by myriad ski and snowboard tracks, which might further allay any apprehension about the stability of the slope.

Continue the diagonal ascent across the north side of the canyon until you reach a broad gully. Make an angling traverse around the head of this gully and then cross the ridge ahead at the most convenient spot, avoiding the rock cliffs. From the ridge, steady progress brings you to another canyon, where you should turn northwest and climb to its head. Ascend to the low point and then bear south as you travel over gentler terrain beyond the lip of the canyon. A short, gentle ascent brings you to the first of the Five Lakes. The relatively level basin provides easy terrain for exploration of the other lakes.

FYI: Consult the avalanche report before your trip (530) 587-2158. Accurate backcountry information may be hard to come by at the ski area, where your best bet may be the guys in the repair shop.

Warm-ups: The Bridgetender Tavern & Grill will satisfy your hunger and your thirst without busting your wallet. Twenty beers are on tap and the grill offers burgers, sandwiches, salads and appetizers that will fill you up at a reasonable cost. The Bridgetender is in Tahoe City on Highway 89 at Fanny Bridge. (530) 583-3342.

TRIP **60**

Martis Peak

see map
on page
202

Duration: Three-quarter day
Distance: 8 miles round trip
Difficulty: Easy to moderate
Elevation: 7000/8742
Maps: *Martis Peak* 7.5′ quadrangle

Introduction: Martis Peak is a popular trip for skiers and snowshoers alike, and with good reason. The 4-mile climb to the summit is relatively easy, thanks to a predominantly mild grade and a readily discernible Forest Service road, periodically marked by blue diamonds. Most likely, thanks to the popularity of the route, you won't have to break trail, unless you're the first one there after a fresh snowfall. The forested road leads to a restored fire lookout, at one time the only manned outpost in the Tahoe Basin, where you have incomparable views of Lake Tahoe.

How to get there: Reach Highway 267 from Interstate 80 in Truckee, or from Lake Tahoe off Highway 28 in Kings Beach. Travel south from I-80 or north from Highway 28 on Highway 267 to Martis Peak Road, 0.4 mile north of Brockway Summit (9.1 miles from I-80 and 3.6 from Highway 28). Park in the small plowed area on the east side of the highway at the beginning of Martis Peak Road. Parking is limited, especially on weekends, so leave as much room as possible for other vehicles.

Description: Begin your trip by climbing east up the road on a moderate grade through a mixed forest of white fir, ponderosa pine, and lodgepole pine. The grade eases after the first 0.75 mile as you ascend mildly through medium forest cover. Even if tracks have not been set by previous skiers or snowshoers, the alignment of the road is obvious. After proceeding straight ahead for 1.3 miles, you reach a junction and turn sharply left (north), following a brown Forest Service ski marker.

Continue to climb up the road, the mild climb briefly interrupted by a couple of short descents. Pass through a small clearing, over a flat knoll, across another small clearing and back into the forest, where you come to another junction. Follow the road to the right around a sweeping turn and begin a more moderate climb, angling up the hillside. Where the moderate ascent levels, 3.25 mile from the highway, turn 90 degrees left onto a road leading north to the lookout on Martis Peak.

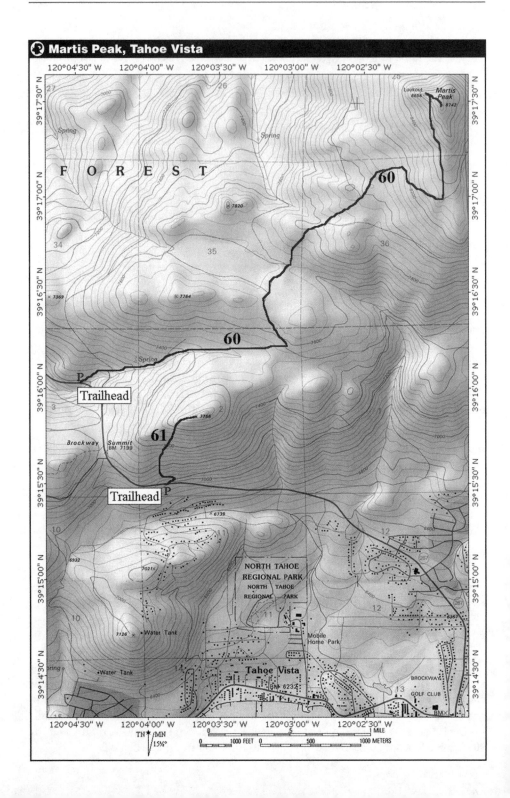

As you make the moderate climb up the road, the forest begins to thin, allowing for some limited views of the surrounding countryside. The grade increases over the last 0.25 mile until you reach the saddle and the Martis Peak fire lookout, 4 miles from Highway 267.

The lookout has been recently restored, thanks to a joint effort involving the California Department of Forestry and the U.S. Forest Service. Improvements to the wooden building include double-paned windows and a linoleum floor. Feel free to use the lookout, but with proper respect for the historical landmark and the hard work necessary for its restoration. Although previous parties have camped in the lookout, you should obey the ban on fires and cooking if staying overnight. The structure provides a wonderful setting for enjoying the supreme view of Lake Tahoe and the neighboring forest land. Near the lookout you will find a picnic table and an outhouse on the wind-blown ridge.

If you wish to reach the actual summit of Martis Peak, you must follow the ridge southeast another 0.1 mile and 86 vertical feet from the lookout to the top of the 8742-foot mountain.

FYI: Taking a pair of cross-country skis for the descent permits a thrilling ride from the summit all the way back to the car.

Warm-ups: The Squeeze Inn offers breakfast aficionados a bounty of unusually named omelets that will surely satisfy the tastebuds of the most finicky diner. Each omelet comes with a choice of sauces along with yummy potatoes and whole wheat toast. A small selection of traditional fare is offered for anti-omelet eaters. The rustic cafe is located in the heart of the historic district of Truckee and is open from 7 a.m. to 2 p.m. (530) 587-9814.

TRIP 61

Tahoe Vista

see map
on page
202

Duration: One-half day
Distance: 1.25 miles round trip
Difficulty: Moderate
Elevation: 7125/7766
Maps: *Martis Peak* 7.5′ quadrangle

Introduction: A short but steep ascent leads to a supreme view of Lake Tahoe and the encircling mountains. In the summer, hikers can follow the newly built Tahoe Rim Trail nearly a mile to a junction with a spur trail up to this wonderful vista. However, snowfall has a way of obliterating well-defined summer trails, and this particular route is no exception. Attempting to successfully follow this trail in winter can be daunting, so this description below forsakes the standard route and climbs directly up the hillside to the top of Peak 7766.

Although the climb begins in dense timber, the route is simple—climb up the slope until you can't climb any higher. Near the top the forest barrier eases, climaxing in a nearly treeless vista from the top of the peak. The view of Lake Tahoe and neighboring peaks is a truly great reward for the relatively brief effort.

How to get there: Drive on State Highway 267, southbound from Truckee or northbound from Kings Beach, to the plowed shoulder just 0.5 mile southeast of Brockway Summit. Depending on the snow depth, you may find hiker emblems or Tahoe Rim Trail signs alongside the highway.

Description: Cross the highway to the northeast shoulder and begin snowshoeing up Forest Road 56 to the summer trailhead for this section of the Tahoe Rim Trail. The TRT bends west from the trailhead, but the snow-covered trail is difficult to discern beyond the beginning of a series of switchbacks that zigzag up the moderately-forested hillside. Therefore, if you don't mind the steep climb, perhaps the simplest way up the slope is a direct climb toward the ridge crest above.

You climb up the hillside moderately steeply through thick ponderosa pines. Even though the timber doesn't allow you to gain your bearings on the initial part of the ascent, the routefinding is straightforward—head for the top. The higher you climb, the less dense the forest becomes, granting a small prelude to the upcoming view from the peak. Once you reach the sparsely forested, long summit ridge, stunning views of Lake Tahoe and the surrounding countryside are a fine reward.

A clear day promises exquisite views of one of California's most prominent natural treasures. Lake Tahoe shimmers in the midwinter sun, surrounded by Sierra peaks on all sides. To the west, Silver Peak presides over the northwest shore. Mt. Tallac dominates the southwest side of the lake, backed by the rugged peaks of Desolation Wilderness. The triangular summit of Freel Peak rises above the southeast shore as the Tahoe Basin's highest summit at 10,881 feet, while the ski runs of Heavenly Valley lie in Freel's shadow. The highest mountain seen on the east side of the lake is Snow Valley Peak. Nearby is Martis Peak, where careful observation reveals the lookout nestled on a ridge immediately northwest of the true summit. Just beyond Martis Peak to the southeast is Mt. Baldy, lying just within the Mt. Rose Wilderness boundary.

FYI: Snowboarders may want to pack along their gear for the thrilling descent. However, caution should be exercised on the lower part of the run through the dense timber.

Warm-ups: One of the old standbys in Truckee is O.B.'s Pub and Restaurant. The rustic decor accented with antiques hints at the over 25 years that O.B.'s has been serving locals and tourists alike. Located in the heart of the historic section of town across from the fire station, O.B.'s serves lunch and dinner daily and brunch on Sunday. (530) 587-4164. Visit their website at **www.obstruckee.com**.

Lake Tahoe as viewed from Tahoe Summit

TRIP **62**

Mt. Rose

Duration: Full day
Distance: 11.25 miles round trip
Difficulty: Difficult
Elevation: 8835/10776
Maps: *Mt. Rose* 7.5′ quadrangle

see map on page **207**

Introduction: Strictly speaking, Mt. Rose is not within California, but lies just across the border in neighboring Nevada. However, for one of the principal peaks in the Lake Tahoe basin, we can bend the rules just enough to include this ascent in a guidebook to California snowshoe routes.

Hundreds of hikers may reach the summit of Mt. Rose on a busy summer weekend, but only a few daring souls accept the challenge of a winter ascent. Views from the third highest peak in the Tahoe basin are sublime, a worthwhile reward for the hearty effort. Most winter enthusiasts are content with more easily reached goals nearby, but the challenge of ascending Mt. Rose appeals to experienced snowshoers. The first half of the trip follows the mellow grade of an access road and then makes an easy descent into Galena Creek basin. The second half is quite steep and subject to less than ideal snow conditions, as well as stiff winds above 9800 feet.

How to get there: From Reno, travel south on U.S. 395 to the Mt. Rose Highway, State Route 431. Head west on S.R. 431 to Mt. Rose Summit, at 8900 feet the highest winter-maintained road in the Sierra. From the summit descend 0.3 mile to the trailhead at the beginning of the access road near a concrete block building, where you may find limited parking for a handful of cars on the westbound shoulder. If parking spaces are unavailable, descend another 0.5 mile on the highway to the Tahoe Meadows trailhead, where you will find a plowed parking area on the eastbound shoulder. On busy winter weekends the parking lot fills quickly, and you might be forced to park on the shoulder of the busy highway.

If you are coming from Incline Village, the Tahoe Meadows trailhead is 7.75 miles east of the junction of the Mt. Rose Highway and State Route 28.

Description: If you were able to park at the trailhead, follow the route of the access road as it climbs on a mild grade above the highway. Those parked at the Tahoe Meadows trailhead lot will have to cross the Mt. Rose Highway and make the short

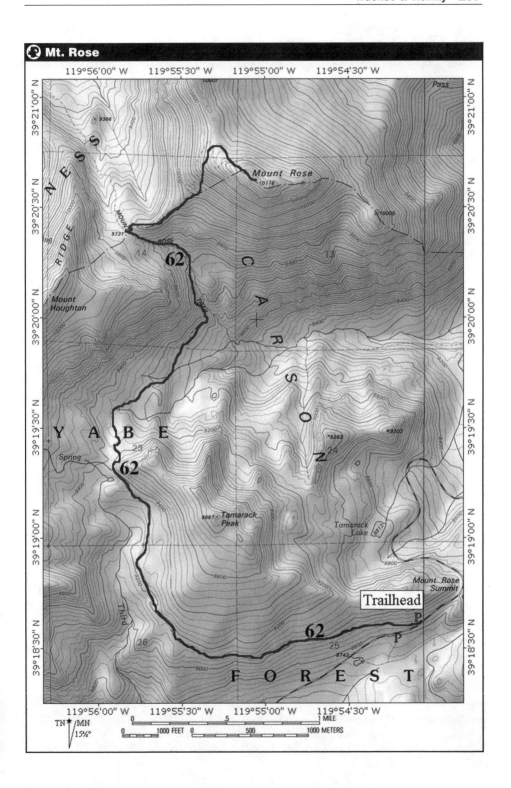

but steep climb up to the access road. At the road, scattered lodgepole pines allow for splendid views of both Tahoe Meadows and Incline Lake below and parts of Lake Tahoe farther west. Unfortunately, the lack of forest may also provide an unobstructed path for the winds that are common to the Mt. Rose area, resulting in wind-packed snow and chilling breezes.

Hike along the access road for about a mile, proceeding west until curving north, leaving the views behind as you enter light forest. Another 1.5 miles of mild ascent lead to the junction of the access road and the Mt. Rose Trail. Without a beaten path on the ground, this junction may not be obvious at first, particularly if the directional signs that guide summer visitors are buried by the winter snowpack.

Leaving the road, the route quickly ascends a low saddle and then drops into the upper basin of the Galena Creek drainage. Traverse around the head of the basin across the main channel of the creek to groves of lodgepole pine, which provide a pleasant locale for a winter picnic and for admiring the beauty of the basin and the snow-tinged cliffs above.

Some years ago, the upper basin of Galena Creek was threatened by the planned development of a destination resort, which would have blighted the beautiful scenery with condominiums and a casino. Fortunately, a land exchange was negotiated between the government and the owners of the property, protecting this marvelous resource.

From the groves of lodgepole pine in the vicinity of the creek, continue to circle northeast around the basin on a moderate descent until crossing the northern branch. From the drainage, make a moderate ascent across an open hillside to a side canyon where you turn northwest up a much steeper grade. At the head of this canyon, you reach the crest of a ridge and turn northeast, heading along the ridge line. If the winds are howling, this is a good place to turn around and head back, as they would only get worse as you neared the summit.

Follow the ridge for 0.5 mile until you encounter the summit massif of Mt. Rose, where the route begins to climb the northwest slope. After gaining 200 feet of elevation, make an ascending traverse toward the broad saddle separating Mt. Rose from Peak 10601. You probably will encounter wind-packed snow conditions in this area, so carefully watch your footing. At the saddle, turn southeast and steeply ascend the final slopes to the summit.

The views from Mt. Rose are quite impressive. On clear days following storms, you may be able to see all the way north to the Cascade volcanoes of Mt. Shasta and Lassen Peak. If the atmosphere is less kind, Sierra Buttes will be the prominent landmark on the northern horizon. To the southwest, Mt. Tallac and Pyramid Peak stand guard over Desolation Wilderness and, to the south, Freel Peak, Jobs Peak, and Jobs Sister dominate the Carson Range. As one might expect, the crystalline waters of Lake Tahoe provide the centerpiece for the grandest of views from the summit.

If the winds are calm on top of Mt. Rose, consider yourself truly blessed. If not, your continued admiration of the views will probably be self-limiting as you urgently seek the less breezy conditions below. However long your stay, the short winter days will ultimately hasten your return as you retrace your steps to the trailhead.

On the route to Mt. Rose in the Carson Range

FYI: As noted in the description, the winds on top of Mt. Rose can be severe. Even if the conditions at the trailhead appear benign, take along plenty of clothing for the potentially windy conditions on the 10,776-foot summit. The second half of the trip can be tedious, depending on the weather and the condition of the snow. Get an early start to avoid returning in the dark.

Warm-ups: Since the recent closure of the Christmas Tree, recreationists traveling the Mt. Rose Highway will have to descend east toward the outskirts of Reno to find a decent eatery or watering hole. Those in search of a cocktail or an upscale dinner can stop at Galena Forest Restaurant and Bar, located 4 miles west of US 395. Open Tuesday to Sunday, diners can savor scrumptious entrees like pistachio encrusted trout with herb cappelinni and creamy lobster sauce, or Moroccan spiced lamb shank. Call 775-849-2100 for reservations.

Snow-sodden snowshoers in search of more plebian fare will enjoy Bully's Sports Bar and Grill in the Raley's shopping center at the northeast corner of the intersection of the Mt. Rose Highway and Wedge Parkway. Voted best sports bar in northern Nevada every year since 1996, Bully's offers a wide array of delectable dishes and beverages. Check out their menu at **www.bullyssportsbar.com**.

CHAPTER 11

South Tahoe, Carson Pass & Vicinity

The land south of Lake Tahoe offers plenty of open terrain from which to view the stunning scenery of snowcapped craggy peaks, frozen alpine lakes and icy canyons. The snows of winter add a touch of majesty to this region that makes parts of this area very popular with winter users, particularly the terrain directly south of the pass. However, there are plenty of options for avoiding the weekend crowds, and this chapter submits seven of them for approval.

With a starting elevation above 8500 feet, Carson Pass provides recreationists with a high-enough altitude to enjoy excellent snow conditions for an extended period during the average winter. While lower areas may be plagued by a lack of snow or by mushy conditions, Carson Pass usually has plenty of good snow in both quality and quantity, two attributes that further lend to the area's popularity with snowshoers and cross-country skiers alike. Many a fine adventure can be enjoyed throughout the long season.

Although Highway 88 provides good access to the lands surrounding Carson Pass, many hikers and backpackers pass over this region in summer in favor of the backcountry of Yosemite to the south or Lake Tahoe to the north. This lack of affection is due to a variety of reasons which are handily taken care of by the snows of winter. Off-road vehicle access, cattle grazing and commercial use combine to detract from some of the natural beauty of the area in summer. However, the hint of winter drives away the cattle, closes the roads and puts an end to some of the commercial exploitation. Once snow arrives in this part of the Sierra, the negative aspects of summer lie forgotten beneath the cleansing presence of the snowpack, and the awesome beauty inherent to the region can be fully appreciated by those willing to step away from their automobiles and venture into the backcountry under their own power. A healthy snowpack transforms the region south of Lake Tahoe into a veritable winter wonderland.

With one exception, the trip to Scotts Lake (Trip 64), access into most of the backcountry south of Lake Tahoe will necessitate the use of the skills of more experienced snowshoers. The terrain is difficult in places and a modicum of routefinding is necessary, since no marked trails are described in this chapter. Three of the trips are ascents of peaks that require parties to feel comfortable climbing moderately-high-angle slopes in order to reach the incredible views from their summits. The remaining trips all lead over rolling terrain to frozen lakes, requiring varying degrees of routefinding and endurance. For groups interested in snow-camping, much of the backcountry is well-suited for it.

Carson Pass, as well as a host of other geographical features, bears the name of Kit Carson, who made his first trip to California in 1829. Between 1842 and 1846 he served as a guide for John C. Fremont's expeditions to California. This expeditionary participation along with his later exploits were popularized in dime novels that made him into a legendary figure of the American West.

While snowmobiling is quite popular in and around Hope Valley east of the pass and from the Iron Mountain Sno-Park west of the pass, snowmobiles are banned around Carson Pass itself. All the routes described in this chapter should be free from the presence of snowmobiles.

Location: Carson Pass is approximately 8.5 miles west of the junction of State Highways 88 and 89, and approximately 100 miles east of Highway 99 in Stockton.

Access: California State Highway 88 provides year-round access to the backcountry near Carson Pass. Pioneer Trail, accessing Trip 63, provides a shortcut to Highway 50 between South Lake Tahoe and Meyers.

Amenities: Opportunities are limited along Highway 88 beyond the full-service communities of Jackson (60 miles west of Carson Pass) and Minden, Nevada (40 miles east of Carson Pass). South Lake Tahoe can be reached by traveling 20 miles north on Highways 89 and 50 from the 88/89 junction.

Season & Weather: As previously mentioned, the high altitude of Carson Pass provides a lengthy season for winter recreationists during an average winter. Snowfall is generally sufficient at the pass for snowshoeing beginning sometime in December and continuing into early May. Routes beginning from lower trailheads will have a correspondingly shorter season. This relatively high elevation also lends itself to the vagaries of winter, particularly since much of the terrain is open and exposed to the prevailing winds and driving snow of severe storms.

PERMITS

Day Use & Overnight Use: Currently the Forest Service does not require permits to enter the Eldorado or Toiyabe National forests for day use. A wilderness permit is necessary for overnight stays in the Mokelumne Wilderness (Trip 70).

Sno-Park: A Sno-Park permit is required for parking at the Meiss Meadow Sno-Park 0.2 mile west of Carson Pass (Trips 67-69).

MAPS

Mokelumne Wilderness	*Eldorado National Forest*	*Toiyabe National Forest*
1:63,360, 2001, plastic	1:31,680, 1997, paper	1:31,680, 1999, paper
Eldorado, Stanislaus and	Eldorado National Forest	Toiyabe National Forest
Toiyabe National Forests		

FOREST SERVICE

Carson Ranger District
1536 S. Carson Street
Carson City, NV 89701
(775) 882-2766

Eldorado National Forest
Supervisor's Office
100 Forni Road
Placerville, CA 95667
(916) 622-5061

Toiyabe National Forest
Supervisor's Office
1200 Franklin Way
Sparks, NV 89431
(775) 331-6444

IMPORTANT PHONE NUMBERS

Avalanche Report   (530) 587-2158
Sno-Park Permit Information   (916) 324-1222
Road Conditions   (800) 427-7623
Weather   (530) 541-1151

WEBSITES

Avalanche Report   www.r5.fs.fed.us/tahoe/avalanche
Sno-Park Information   www.ohv.parks.ca.gov/SVRAs/snopark
Toiyabe National Forest   www.r5.fs.fed.us/htnf
Eldorado National Forest www.r5.fs.fed.us/eldorado/

TRIP 63

High Meadows & Star Lake

see map on page 207

Duration: Half day to Meadows;
      full day to Lake
Distance: 6.5 miles round trip;
      10 miles round trip
Difficulty: Moderate; difficult
Elevation: 6525/7775; 6525/9125
Maps: *Freel Peak* 7.5' quadrangle

Introduction: High Meadows is a picturesque area above the southeast shore of Lake Tahoe in the shadow of Freel Peak and Jobs Sister. Before the recent construction of the Tahoe Rim Trail, the road to High Meadows provided the sole route to isolated and lovely Star Lake. The only problem was that the road crossed private property and was off limits to public access. In 2003 the Giovacchini family of Carson Valley sold the 1790-acre tract of land known as High Meadows to the Forest Service via the American Land Conservancy. Nowadays recreationists can legally travel to High Meadows and then continue to Star Lake.

The road into High Meadows is gently graded and easy to follow, offering snowshoers a straightforward route through dense forest to a series of broad clearings along Cold Creek. The meadows provide an excellent destination for parties desiring a 3.25-mile trip with minimal elevation gain that requires only a modicum of routefinding. More ambitious snowshoers can continue southeast from High Meadows on a stiffer climb upstream along Cold Creek to beautiful Star Lake.

How to get there: From the intersection with US 50 in South Lake Tahoe, drive on Pioneer Trail for 3.2 miles (or 4.5 miles from Highway 50 in Meyers) and turn onto High Meadows, which is just northeast of Sierra House Elementary School. Follow High Meadows for 0.7 mile to the edge of a subdivision and the end of the plowed road. Park as space allows.

Description: Follow the continuation of the closed road on a very mild climb through a mixed forest. At 0.75 mile you cross a wood bridge over a tributary of Cold Creek, pass by an old cabin, and then start climbing a little more steeply just past a small meadow. The road follows some power lines for a while before ascending to the top of a forested flat. From there you make a short drop to two crossings over Cold Creek at 1.6 and 1.75 miles.

Beyond the creek crossings, make a steady climb up the nose of a forested ridge between twin channels of Cold Creek. As you progress up the hillside, the forest thins enough to allow a decent view of the south end of Lake Tahoe and the peaks of Desolation Wilderness above the southwest shore. Beyond the view, veer right where a secondary road follows a power line cut and proceed to a Y-junction, 3 miles from the trailhead.

Bear left at the junction and continue along the road past an old cabin. About 25 yards past the cabin, you reach a T-junction and turn right, soon reaching the fringe of High Meadows. The exact course of the snow-covered road is a bit difficult to ascertain in the open terrain of the meadows, but it continues to a crossing of the aspen-lined creek near the south end of the meadows.

To reach Star Lake, climb the left side of the canyon above Cold Creek. Along the way, good views of Lake Tahoe can be had through the scattered trees of a mixed forest. Continue the steady ascent toward the head of the canyon, reaching the chilly lake at 5 miles from the trailhead. The scenic lake reposes in a picturesque cirque below the rugged northwest ridge of Jobs Peak.

The shore around Star Lake provides excellent basecamps for peakbaggers longing to climb the three major peaks in the area—Jobs Peak, Jobs Sister, and Freel Peak. While all three summits require a stiff climb, the routes are not technically challenging.

FYI: The Giovacchini family retained 490 acres of land near High Meadows, but an easement allows public access across the property via the road. Stick to the course of the road as best as you can while traveling through the area in winter.

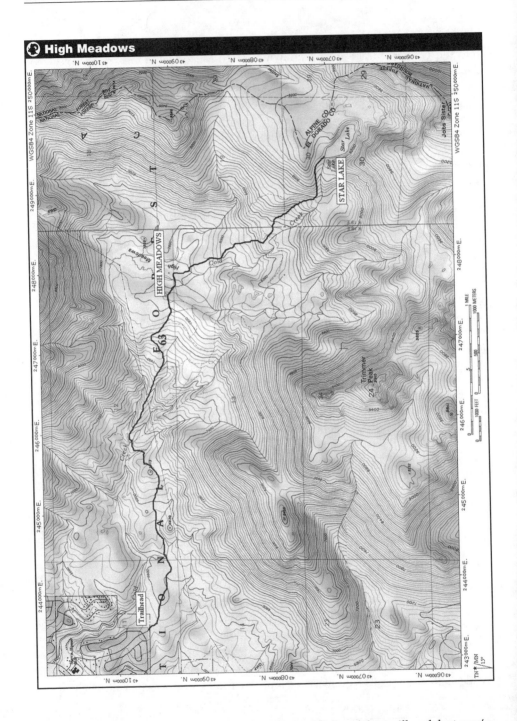

Warm-ups: Nothing is available in the immediate vicinity of the trailhead, but you're not far from myriad dining and drinking choices in South Lake Tahoe.

TRIP 64

Scotts Lake

see map
on page
216

Duration: One-half day
Distance: 3 miles round trip
Difficulty: Easy
Elevation: 7115/8035
Map: *Freel Peak* 7.5' quadrangle

Introduction: The journey to Scotts Lake is a short, easy trip to a high mountain lake with spectacular views of the region east of Carson Pass.

How to get there: Travel on Highway 88 to Hope Valley, east of Carson Pass. Find a small plowed parking area on the west shoulder of the highway, 1.5 miles west of the junction with Highway 89.

Description: You could follow the marked ski trail that corresponds to the path of the winding road to Scotts Lake, but competent snowshoers can take a more direct approach by gaining a bearing on the low saddle in the ridge just south of Waterhouse Peak, as Scotts Lake sits right below this saddle. From the highway, head on a westerly course across a flat and up the forested hillside. After a mile of moderate ascent, the grade eases just before you reach the lake. Scotts Lake provides an ideal setting for admiring the splendid scenery, particularly the rugged north face of Stevens Peak.

FYI: If you're looking for a spot to test your winter camping skills, Scotts Lake provides a pleasant setting not far from the highway.

Warm-ups: A mile east of the Highway 88/89 junction, the restaurant at Sorensen's Resort provides pleasing dishes made from fresh ingredients in a quaint mountain setting. The charming cafe is open each day from 7:30 a.m. to 8:30 p.m. The resort also provides overnight accommodations in comfortable cabins. Phone: (530) 694-2203 or (800) 423-9949.

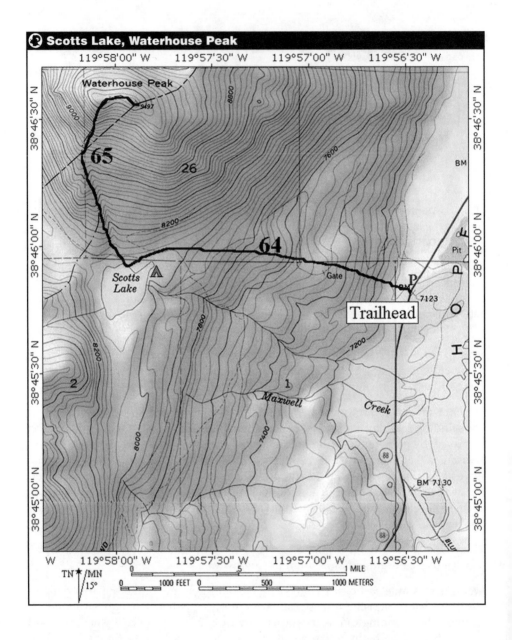

Scotts Lake, Waterhouse Peak

TRIP 65

Waterhouse Peak

Duration: Three-quarter day
Distance: 5 miles round trip
Difficulty: Difficult
Elevation: 7115/9497
Map: *Freel Peak* 7.5′ quadrangle

see map
on page
216

Introduction: Absolutely gorgeous views of the northern Sierra are the chief reward for the steep climb to the summit of Waterhouse Peak. A clear day with little or no wind is the perfect time to attempt the peak. The degree of ascent and the potentially difficult snow conditions on the upper part of the mountain combine to make this trip one for experienced snowshoers only. Due to the high angle of the slopes, the climb should be made when the avalanche danger is minimal.

The Crystal Range southwest of Lake Tahoe as seen from Waterhouse Peak

How to get there: Follow directions in Trip 64.

Description: Follow directions in Trip 64 to Scotts Lake. From the lake, begin the steep climb up the forested south slopes of Waterhouse Peak. About half way up the mountain, the trees begin to thin, and eventually they all but disappear. The grade of the slope also increases a bit as you gain altitude. Above tree line, the snow conditions may become hard-packed, requiring a high degree of skill and much caution. Nearing what appears to be the top of the mountain, you reach a small plateau that must be crossed in order to reach the base of the summit rocks. Beyond the plateau, a short, steep climb completes the ascent.

From the top of Waterhouse Peak, you are blessed with one of the most dramatic views in the Carson Pass area. To the south, a vast array of peaks presents itself—you could while away the hours trying to identify them all. Gazing toward Tahoe, you have a beautiful view of the lake as well as a dramatic presentation of the Crystal Range peaks of Desolation Wilderness. Nearby, the mountains surrounding Carson Pass seem close enough to reach out and touch.

FYI: Waterhouse Peak is a popular climb for advanced skiers in search of the perfect powder run. The snow on the peak's north slopes stays in good shape for long periods, attracting a sizable population of skiers on weekends. However, you should be alone on your side of the mountain, as the ski crowd follows the standard and much easier route from Luther Pass to the summit.

Warm-ups: See Trip 64.

TRIP 66

Crater Lake

see map on page **219**

Duration: One-half day
Distance: 2.75 miles round trip
Difficulty: Moderate
Elevation: 7360/8595
Maps: *Carson Pass* 7.5′ quadrangle

Introduction: A short, but steep ascent leads to a beautiful lake nestled in a dramatic cirque basin. While hundreds of weekend recreationists may be cavorting on the

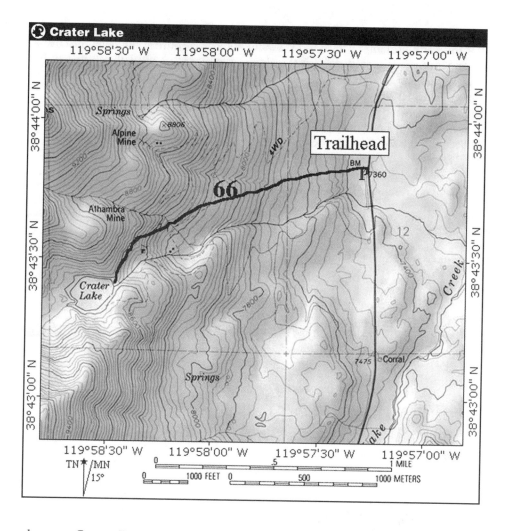

slopes at Carson Pass just a few miles away, chances are that you and your party will remain relatively undiscovered on this trip, in spite of the minimal distance required to reach such a spectacular setting. Excellent views of the Hope Valley and Carson Pass areas occur on the open slopes below the lake.

How to get there: On Highway 88 find a small plowed area on the west side of the highway, 4.4 miles east of Carson Pass and 4.1 miles west of the Highway 88/89 junction.

Description: Begin a moderately steep ascent just above the north bank of the creek which drains Crater Lake. Aiming for the low spot in the ridge above, located 0.85 mile southeast of Stevens Peak, you pass through a light forest composed primarily of lodgepole and ponderosa pine with some white fir and an occasional cedar. Near the damp soils of the creek you will also find some quaking aspen.

As you continue the climb, the forest begins to thin, allowing for nice views of the areas around Hope Valley and Carson Pass. Cross-country skiers tend to utilize a couple of roads that zigzag up the slope on opposite sides of the drainage, but snowshoers can assume a more direct approach up the moderately steep hillside. Near the head of the creek, the terrain becomes steeper, requiring that you make an angling traverse to gentler slopes along the creek just below the rim of the basin. Follow the creek on a mellow grade for 500 feet before climbing steeply again to the rim and then dropping down quickly to Crater Lake.

The lake is set in a spectacular amphitheater rimmed by steep rock walls midway between the summits of Stevens and Red Lake Peaks. From the lip of the basin you have great views of the surrounding peaks and valleys.

FYI: Venturing toward the steep walls at the head of the canyon above Crater Lake should be done only when snow conditions are stable.

Warm-ups: See Trip 64.

TRIP 67

Red Lake Peak

see map
on page
222

Duration: One-half day
Distance: 5 miles round trip
Difficulty: Moderate
Elevation: 8560/10063
Maps: *Carson Pass* & *Caples Lake* 7.5′ quadrangles

Introduction: Without mountaineering equipment and the ability to use it, the actual summit of Red Lake Peak may be beyond your grasp. However, an easily accessible high point is just a few feet below the true apex. Supreme views of Lake Tahoe and the mountainous terrain of Carson Pass are the chief rewards. The trip ascends open slopes for almost the entire route, providing pleasant scenery throughout.

Red Lake Peak holds the distinctive historical honor of being the first Sierra peak ascended by European-Americans, as well as providing the vista point for the first recorded view of Lake Tahoe. On February 14, 1844, John C. Fremont, with his cartographer Charles Pruess, reached the summit and recorded the following statement concerning the ascent and the view, "With Mr. Pruess, I ascended today the highest peak up to the right: from which we had a beautiful view of a mountain lake at our feet, about fifteen miles in length, and so entirely surrounded by mountains that we could not discover an outlet." Although Fremont's estimate fell short by a good 6 miles, his description certainly captured the essence of the lake.

How to get there: The Meiss Meadow Sno-Park is 0.2 mile west of Carson Pass on the north side of Highway 88 (a portable toilet is nearby).

Description: Head west, from the parking lot, generally contouring along the slopes of the lightly forested hillside. As you curve into a minor drainage, head for the obvious saddle to the north. Climb across open slopes, reaching the saddle in little over a mile. The bare terrain allows striking views to the south of Round Top and the surrounding peaks and ridges of the Carson Pass area.

Turning northeast from the saddle, you begin an angling ascent across moderately steep, wide-open slopes below Red Lake Peak. Choose a line of ascent that leads to the upper slopes, curving beneath the first rock outcropping on the ridge above. Once beyond the outcropping, Red Lake Peak comes into view and you can assume a direct line toward the mountain. Head for the high point on the rounded ridge directly south of the rocks which form the true summit. You may encounter difficult snow conditions on the windswept west slopes near the top.

As from most of the high points in the Carson Pass area, the view from the summit of Red Lake Peak is quite dramatic. Lake Tahoe glistens in the winter sun, surrounded by snow-capped peaks, including the Crystal Range in Desolation Wilderness. The immediate array of peaks and canyons around Carson Pass composes one of the most rugged landscapes anywhere in the Tahoe region.

Onward to Red Lake Peak

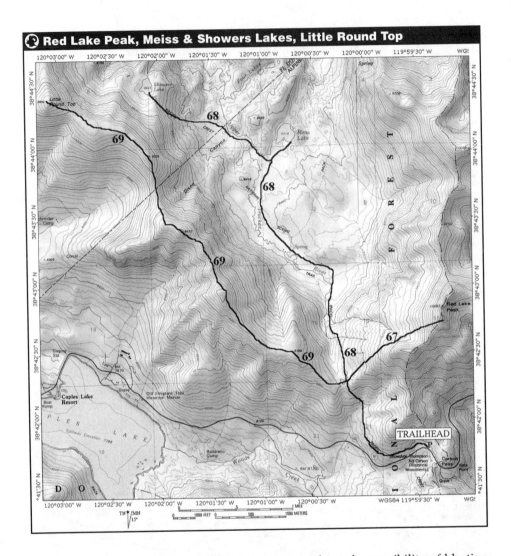

Red Lake Peak, Meiss & Showers Lakes, Little Round Top

FYI: Signs at the Sno-Park warn backcountry users about the possibility of blasting for avalanche control along the Highway 88 corridor. The potential danger occurs on the steep slopes above the highway southeast of the summit of Red Lake Peak. Avoid wandering off the route on the east side of the ridge. Contact the appropriate authorities regarding avalanche conditions.

Warm-ups: Rustic Kirkwood Inn boasts of being one of the first resorts to operate in the northern Sierra. Modern-day travelers can partake of freshly cooked dishes created with a local flair for breakfast, lunch and dinner. The moderately priced establishment also has a full bar and an appetizer menu. Kirkwood Inn is on Highway 88, 0.4 mile west of Caples Lake.

TRIP 68

Meiss & Showers Lakes

see map on page **222**

Duration: Three-quarter day to Meiss Lake
Full day to Showers Lake
Distance: 7 miles round trip to Meiss Lake
10 miles round trip to Showers Lake
Difficulty: Moderate
Elevation: 8560/8795
Map: *Carson Pass* & *Caples Lake* 7.5' quadrangles

Introduction: With a low point of 8300 feet, this hike insures an adequate snowpack throughout a long season. In addition, the trip to Meiss and Showers lakes provides the snowshoer with a variety of impressive scenery. The first mile of travel passes through wide-open slopes toward a saddle, where you have superb views of the high peaks surrounding Carson Pass. Beyond the saddle, travelers encounter the expansive, gentle basin of the Upper Truckee River meadows, a fine location for roaming across level terrain between tall ridges.

The round trip to Meiss Lake is a reasonable task, the mile-long ascent to the saddle being the only part of the journey requiring much of a sustained effort. Even though Showers Lake is just a little over a mile farther, reaching its scenic basin demands more energy in order to surmount the much steeper terrain.

How to get there: The Meiss Meadow Sno-Park is 0.2 mile west of Carson Pass on the north side of Highway 88 (a portable toilet is nearby).

Description: Head west, from the parking lot, generally contouring along the slopes of the lightly forested hillside. As you curve into a minor drainage, head for the obvious saddle to the north. Climb across open slopes, reaching the saddle in little over a mile. The bare terrain provides striking views to the south of Round Top and the surrounding peaks and ridges of the Carson Pass area.

Leaving the saddle, which is the high point of your trip, a short, moderate descent leads north through a narrow valley where large cornices may appear along the ridge crest to the west. If they worry you, pick a descent route up the hillside on the east side of the valley to avoid any possible avalanche run-out. Beyond this potential hazard, you encounter the gentle terrain of the expansive Upper Truckee River valley. The nearly level gradient of the large basin provides easy snowshoeing as you follow the general course of the frozen river through widely scattered evergreens. The ridge to the west, which culminates at the summit of Little Round Top, provides a pleasant backdrop for the wide-open basin.

Even though the distance from the saddle to Meiss Lake is 2.5 miles, the gently descending grade along the Upper Truckee provides the illusion of a much shorter distance. The pleasant scenery seems to help you move quickly as you approach Meiss Lake.

Unless you are paying very close attention, missing the lake is relatively easy, because the frozen body of water blends in perfectly with the flat floor of the basin. The lake is at the northeast end of a large clearing, just south of some low hills with a dense covering of trees. The lake, 3.5 miles from the trailhead, is a worthy goal for most parties, particularly when you remember that the trip back to the saddle is uphill.

Directions to Showers Lake: If you want to push on toward Showers Lake, head west across the open basin and the drainage of the Upper Truckee River into a more moderate forest cover. To reach the lake, you must leave the easy terrain of the basin and begin a healthy climb up a tree-covered hillside, eventually following the route of the Pacific Crest Trail as shown on the *Carson Pass* topo map. Continue the ascent until you crest the low ridge directly above the lake's south shore. After a short drop, you reach picturesque Showers Lake, 1.25 miles from Meiss Lake and 5 miles from the Sno-Park.

FYI: From Showers Lake you can save a little distance on the return trip by heading straight back along the course of the Upper Truckee River, rather than retracing your route back to Meiss Lake as shown on Map 30.

Warm-ups: See Trip 67.

TRIP **69**

Little Round Top

see map
on page
222

Duration: Full day
Distance: 10.25 miles round trip
Difficulty: Moderate
Elevation: 8560/9590
Map: *Carson Pass* & *Caples Lake* 7.5′ quadrangles

Introduction: This little-known route to the summit of Little Round Top provides nearly continuous, awe-inspiring views. Beyond the first mile, the path follows an exposed ridge for another 4 miles, where snowshoers are continuously treated to some of the most fantastic scenery in the greater Tahoe Sierra region. Even if you are short on time and unable to complete the trek, you can turn back at any point, satisfied with the extraordinary scenery.

The ridge route requires only minimal routefinding and the terrain is not particularly steep for any great distance, making this trip suitable for all but beginning snowshoers provided they have the stamina for the 10-mile journey.

How to get there: The Meiss Meadow Sno-Park is 0.2 mile west of Carson Pass on the north side of Highway 88 (a portable toilet is nearby).

The route to Little Round Top Peak

Description: Head west, from the parking lot, generally contouring along the slopes of the lightly forested hillside. As you curve into a minor drainage, head for the obvious saddle to the north. As you approach the saddle, bear left and ascend a moderately steep slope a short distance to the ridge crest. Follow the ridge until you reach the base of the first high point, where the slope becomes more moderate. Climb to the top of the high point, 1.75 miles from the trailhead, where you have excellent views of Round Top Peak south across Highway 88 and of part of Lake Tahoe to the north.

As you descend, the ridge bends slightly west, providing a chilling view of the nasty cornices that frequently appear on the east side of the ridge ahead. Obviously, you should avoid the extreme right-hand edge of the ridge near these cornices. Where the ridge narrows as it curves back north, make a mildly ascending traverse over to the base of a significant peak. Then climb steeper slopes to the summit of the 9450-foot peak, 2.5 miles from the Sno-Park. As expected, the view from here is magnificent, including the meadows surrounding the Upper Truckee River immediately below you to the northeast as well as the snowy peaks around Carson Pass and Lake Tahoe.

Now descend moderate slopes 0.25 mile to a saddle and then follow the ridge north-northwest up mild slopes to the next high point. A short descent leads to another saddle, after which you ascend once again, to Peak 9422 (as shown on the *Caples Lake* topo map), 3.25 miles from the trailhead.

A half-mile descent brings you to the start of the final, lengthy ascent along the ridge to Little Round Top. Initially, the route climbs over moderate slopes to Point 9325, after which the terrain mellows considerably as the ridge curves around to the west. For the next 0.75 mile the grade is easy, and then a short moderate climb leads to the summit of Little Round Top.

Even more spectacular views greet you at the summit. The unobstructed vista covers a vast area of the northern Sierra Nevada, from Lake Tahoe and the surrounding peaks to the north, all the way south to the peaks around Sonora Pass. The more immediate topography is both dramatic and striking, particularly the airy summits of both Desolation and Mokelumne Wilderness areas. The trip back to the Sno-Park promises another 5 miles of great views.

FYI: Almost the entire route is near or above 9000 feet, and along a treeless, exposed ridge where high winds are common. Plan your trip for a day when the winds are forecast to be light. As previously mentioned, avoid the east edge of the ridge where enormous cornices appear.

Warm-ups: See Trip 67.

TRIP 70

Caples Lake to Emigrant Lake

see map on page **228**

Duration: Three-quarter day
Distance: 8.25 miles round trip
Difficulty: Moderate
Elevation: 7685/8600
Maps: *Caples Lake* 7.5′ quadrangles

Introduction: Two lakes, one huge and easily accessible and one much smaller and harder to reach, provide the dramatic contrasts of this trip. For 2 miles near the beginning of the route, you snowshoe the easy terrain along the southwest shore of Caples Lake, enjoying the lovely scenery across the immense body of water. At the end of the journey, alpine Emigrant Lake lacks the size of its larger neighbor but possesses a stark beauty nestled in a cirque basin at the base of steep cliffs.

The first 2.5 miles require little in the way of navigation as the path around Caples Lake is clearly defined. Beginners may elect not to proceed any farther than where Emigrant Creek enters the lake at the south end. Beyond Caples Lake, the route passes through thick forest, and finding the entrance to the cirque basin requires a bit more routefinding skill.

Potentially, the trip to Emigrant Lake, which is almost entirely within Mokelumne Wilderness, should provide a reasonable expectation of solitude. However, some skiers do reach the lake from Kirkwood Meadows via the ski lift in Emigrant Valley.

How to get there: Parking is the chief problem. If you can find a plowed space along Highway 88 close to the Caples Lake dam, grab it. Otherwise, on State Highway 88, drive to the Kirkwood Cross-Country Ski Center parking lot, 0.4 mile west of the dam at Caples Lake. Kirkwood has allowed use of their parking lot for recreationists who are not using their ski trails. The appropriate thing to do would be to politely ask permission to park there, rather than assuming you have a right to do so.

Description: From the Kirkwood Cross-Country Ski Center cross to the south side of Highway 88 and climb steeply up the slope. On a general traverse across the hillside above the highway, head east toward Caples Lake. After nearly 0.5 mile, drop to the

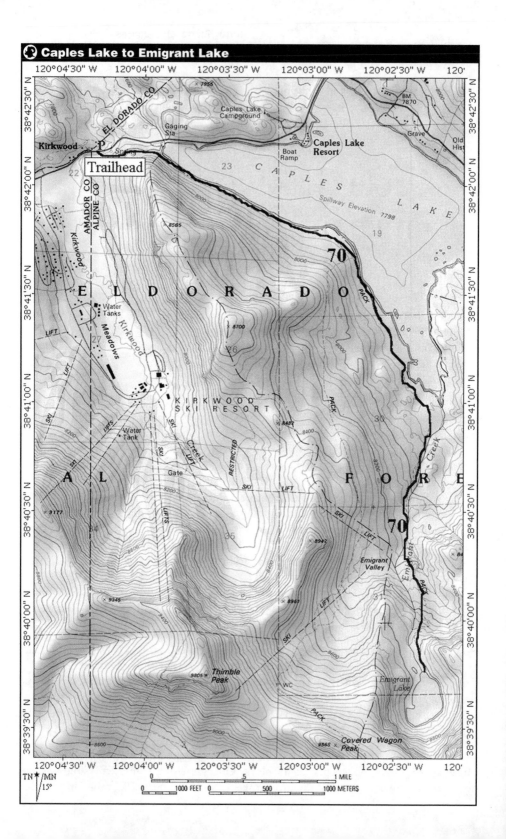

shoreline of Caples Lake and follow the lake's southwest edge, paralleling the Mokelumne Wilderness boundary.

As you follow the easy terrain along the shoreline of expansive Caples Lake, you can admire the beautiful scenery across the lake. To the northeast lies the long ridge culminating in Little Round Top (see Trip 69) and directly east stands the dark rock of Black Butte. On the point across the lake is the rustic architecture of the Caples Lake Resort.

Two miles of easy snowshoeing beside Caples Lake bring you to the inflow of Emigrant Creek, at the south tip of the lake. Open terrain at the inlet allows you to take your bearings before you enter moderate forest cover where the route turns south up the drainage. The lake lies at the base of the rock cliffs below Melissa Coray Peak at the head of the canyon.

Follow the west bank of the creek into a mixed forest of pine and fir. For the next 1.5 miles climb mildly through the trees following Emigrant Creek. Half-way up the canyon stay to the left of a prominent rock hill, continuing on a southerly bearing. Routefinding can be a little tricky as you progress up the forested drainage, for Melissa Coray Peak is out of view. Head for the cirque basin immediately east of Covered Wagon Peak, which remains visible at various points along the ascent. About 0.5 mile from the lake the terrain becomes steeper for a short distance before leveling out and then dropping to the shoreline of Emigrant Lake.

The lake is dramatically located in a classic cirque bowl, rimmed by the sheer cliffs of a rock amphitheater. Covered with snow, the horseshoe basin casts a cold and foreboding presence on the winter visitor. The preponderance of avalanche debris piling up at the base of the rock walls at the head of the canyon should discourage any thoughts of possibly progressing too far beyond the lip of the cirque.

FYI: Ambitious mountaineers can extend their journey by ascending one of the peaks (Melissa Coray, Covered Wagon, or Thimble) along the crest of the ridge for a superb view.

Warm-ups: See Trip 67.

CHAPTER 12

Yosemite National Park

Yosemite is California's premier natural attraction. Images of Yosemite Falls and Half Dome are etched into the nation's psyche, even among those who have never set foot in the park. A more dramatic natural landscape than that of Yosemite Valley is hard to imagine, with vertical rock walls rising 3500 feet to the rim of the valley above, spectacular waterfalls exploding off the rim and plunging to the floor below, myriad granitic domes scattered along the rim painted silver against the backdrop of the azure blue Sierra sky, and the pleasant Merced River sinuously flowing through the valley amid beautiful meadows and mixed forests of oaks and conifers. The lure of Yosemite is strong and many answer its call, as evidenced by the incredible number of tourists who flock there every summer and, to a lesser extent, each spring and fall. What awaits the ardent snowshoer is the grand opportunity to visit the park in winter sans crowds.

The overwhelming number of park visitors common in the summer decreases dramatically during winter, providing the best opportunity for recreationists to experience an uncrowded visit. The winter months are certainly the most peaceful in the valley and the rest of the park is virtually deserted. The summer hordes are a distant memory, traffic jams are unheard of, no one waits in line for anything, and backcountry permits can be obtained at a moment's notice.

Of course, the scenery is no less spectacularly beautiful in winter. In fact, some argue that winter is the prettiest season, when snow clings gracefully to the crevices and ledges of the valley walls and dusts the limbs of the evergreens and the bare branches of the oaks. Although the low elevation of the valley means a notoriously inconsistent snowpack, when snow does carpet the gorge with a fresh coat of white, the valley is transformed into a wonderfully memorable scene.

When snow conditions are not favorable for recreational pursuits in the valley itself, Yosemite has a number of higher-elevation alternatives offering much more consistent conditions in both depth and quality of the snowpack. The park has three other centers of winter activity: the Mariposa Grove, Badger Pass, and Crane Flat areas are winter hubs for a wide variety of experiences. All three of these centers offer marked routes for skiers and snowshoers tailored to a wide range of skill levels. For those who desire an even more challenging outing, the Yosemite backcountry (94% of the park is designated wilderness) is full of opportunities for off-trail travel or multi-day adventures. Arrangements can be made for guided trips as well.

Native Americans were the first inhabitants of Yosemite Valley. By 1851 they were driven out to a reservation near Fresno by the Mariposa Battalion, whose members were the first European-Americans to set foot in the valley. After their "discovery" of Yosemite, the area gathered more and more interest. The year 1857 saw both the construction of the first hotel and the arrival of Galen Clark, who would eventually become the park's first guardian. The age-old debate of development versus protection was born, managed through the years by a number of state and federal agencies until Yosemite officially became a national park in 1906. The debate continues to the present day as the Park Service attempts to control the ever-increasing influx of visitors.

Much to the delight of recreationists, snowmobiles are banned from the nearly 760,000 acres of Yosemite National Park. However, 714,000 of those acres are wilderness, which requires a permit for all overnight stays, and national-park status demands that all visitors pay an entrance fee (see Permits below).

Yosemite National Park has many more routes than the ones presented in this chapter that are worthy of consideration by snowshoers. For additional trips consult *Snowshoe Trails of Yosemite* (see Suggested Reading in Appendix II). Since the recent budget crunch facing the National Park Service may affect winter services, calling ahead to check on the current situation in Yosemite is probably a wise idea.

Location: Yosemite National Park is about 125 miles directly east of San Francisco.

Access:

Big Oak Flat Entrance: The northernmost route leading to Yosemite Valley follows State Highway 120 east from Manteca to the Big Oak Flat entrance. Beyond the entrance the Big Oak Flat Road climbs 7.5 miles to a junction with the Tioga Road at Crane Flat (the Crane Flat winter trailhead is 0.5 mile up the Tioga Road). Continuing on the Big Oak Flat Road another 9 miles brings you to the junction with Highway 140, the El Portal Road, which is the main arterial into Yosemite Valley.

Arch Rock Entrance: Highway 140 heads northeast from Merced to the Arch Rock Entrance near the town of El Portal. From the entrance, the El Portal Road follows the course of the Merced River to junctions with the Big Oak Flat and Wawona roads, then continues on into Yosemite Valley.

South Entrance: Highway 41 leads motorists north from Fresno to the South Entrance (the Mariposa Grove trailhead is nearby). From the entrance, the Wawona Road travels past the Wawona area, climbing 17 miles to the road's high point at the junction with the Glacier Point Road near Chinquapin (the Badger Pass trailhead is 5 miles up the Glacier Point Road). From this junction the Wawona Road continues another 8.5 miles to the junction with the El Portal Road, the main route into Yosemite Valley.

Amenities: Within the park one can find most of the basic necessities, plus a lot of other things that could easily be done without. Lodging and dining are available all week long in the valley and on weekends and holidays at Wawona. Gasoline is not available in the valley but can be purchased at Crane Flat and Wawona. Although these stations operate on limited daylight hours during the winter, credit or ATM cards can be used when the stations are closed. Yosemite Village offers a large general store, mountain shop, art gallery, visitor center, post office, delicatessen, bank and fast food eatery.

In the valley the use of public transportation is strongly encouraged, and one day soon may be mandatory. The free Yosemite Valley shuttle-bus system operates from 9:00 a.m. to 10:00 p.m. and takes winter visitors to 15 different stops around the valley (Trips 73-75).

Twice daily the Badger Pass bus makes round trips from the valley and Wawona to Badger Pass, whenever the ski area is in operation and weather permits (Trips 76-77). Check at the front desk of the lodging facilities for the current schedule.

Additional recreational opportunities are available in the valley during the winter months including ice skating at the rink in Curry Village. If the snow line is well above the valley, a number of hiking trails should be available during winter, although the Fourmile Trail to Glacier Point and parts of the Mist and John Muir trails are typically closed for safety reasons.

Badger Pass offers snowboarding and cross-country, telemark and downhill skiing, ranger-led snowshoe tours, and guided overnight trips into the backcountry. Snowshoes and ski equipment can be rented at Badger Pass as well. For more information contact the Yosemite Cross-Country Ski Center: (209) 372-8444.

Season & Weather: Snowfall in Yosemite Valley, at 3900 feet, is highly unpredictable, making trip planning a long way ahead of time something of a nightmare. Sporadically, snow will fall in the valley, occasionally it will stick, and sometimes it may even hang around for a few days or a week. Unless you have the luxury of leaving home at the drop of a hat to chase the latest storm, a successful snowshoe venture in the valley is more a matter of serendipity than planning. Oftentimes, for trips originating in the valley, hiking up to the snowline before donning your snowshoes is common.

The snow in Yosemite Valley fails to imply an accurate picture of conditions in the higher elevations of the park. Snowfall is substantially greater and temperatures may be as much as 30° colder. With every gain in altitude comes a greater possibility of good snow in both quantity and quality. While snow in the valley may be a dubious proposition at best, Tuolumne Meadows at 8600 feet offers a very high probability of a decent snowpack from sometime in November all the way through June in some years. The three winter-trail areas at Mariposa Grove, Badger Pass and Crane Flat should have adequate snow cover during the average winter season, from December through early April.

On the whole, Yosemite has a high percentage of sunny days. Most storms that come approach from the Pacific, dropping sizable amounts of snowfall before moving east. Typically, a storm lasts a day or two, followed by a period of sunny or partly sunny skies. However, severe storms lasting for more days and dropping incredible amounts of snow are not uncommon. Some days the weather in the backcountry of Yosemite is idyllic; some days it can be life threatening. The wise snowshoer is prepared for all possible weather conditions.

PERMITS

Entrance Fees: The first regulation to be overcome when visiting Yosemite National Park is the entrance fee. A 7-day pass is $20 per vehicle, a yearly Yosemite Pass is $40, and a Golden Eagle Pass is $50, which provides unlimited access to all national parks for one year. Fees are usually collected at the entrance stations. If you happen to enter when no ranger is in the station, you will be expected to pay upon exiting the park.

Day Use & Overnight Use: A permit is not required for day trips in the Park. Any overnight stay in the Yosemite backcountry requires a wilderness permit. They may be obtained at the Visitor Center in Yosemite Village or at Badger Pass Ski Area. Advance reservations are not necessary for winter excursions.

MAPS

Yosemite National Park & Vicinity
1:125,000, 1999, plastic
Wilderness Press
(800) 443-7227

Crane Flat Winter Trails
Glacier Point Road Winter Trails
Mariposa Grove Winter Trails
Various scales, paper
Yosemite National Park

PARK SERVICE

U.S. Department of the Interior
National Park Service
PO Box 577
Yosemite, CA 95389
(209) 372-0200

IMPORTANT PHONE NUMBERS

California National Parks	(415) 556-0560	Yosemite Association	(209) 379-2646
Friends of Yosemite	(415) 434-1782	Yosemite Institute	(209) 379-9511
YNP—Campground Reservations		(800) 436-7275	
YNP—Cross-Country Ski Center		(209) 372-8444	
YNP—Curry Village Ice Skating Rink		(209) 372-8341	
YNP—General Information—live operator		(900) 454-YOSE	
YNP—Lodging Reservations		(559) 252-4848	
YNP—Road Conditions (24 hour)		(209) 372-0200	
YNP—Ski Conditions (Badger Pass)		(209) 372-1000	
YNP—Snow Conditions (24 hour)		(209) 372-1000	
YNP—Wilderness Permit Reservations		(209) 372-0740	

WEBSITES

Ansel Adams Gallery	www.anseladams.com
National Park Service—Yosemite	www.nps.gov/yose/
YNP—Reservations	www.reservations.nps.gov
Yosemite Area Traveler Information	www.yosemite.com
Yosemite Association	www.yosemite.org
Yosemite Concession Services	www.yosemitepark.com
Yosemite Fund	www.yosemitefund.org
Yosemite-Sierra Visitors Bureau	www.yosemite-sierra.org
Yosemite West	www.yosemitelodging.com

Tuolumne Grove of Giant Sequoias

see map
on page
235

Duration: One-half day
Distance: 2.5 miles round trip
Difficulty: Easy
Elevation: 6200/5725
Maps: *Ackerson Mountain 7.5' quadrangle;*
Crane Flat Winter Trails

Introduction: Many would argue that a trip to Yosemite without a visit to at least one of the three groves of giant sequoias is an incomplete experience. In days gone by, park visitors could drive their vehicles down into the Tuolumne Grove to admire the immense trees. As at the other two groves in Yosemite, the Park Service wisely discontinued this practice years ago. Now one must walk, ski or snowshoe the 1.25 miles to see these giant specimens. The journey into the grove is easy, as the closed road leads down the slope at a moderate grade. The return trip will be harder, but is not particularly difficult for anyone in reasonable shape.

Although not as tall as the coastal redwood, *Sequoiadendron giganteum* is certainly the most massive tree in the world, attaining an average girth of 10-20 feet. The giant trees survive only between 5000 and 6000 feet elevation and only in areas of metamorphic bedrock which is nutrient-rich enough. The most notable tree in the Tuolumne Grove is the Tunnel Tree, a massive sequoia that could have been one of the park's tallest specimens before death and the elements toppled the upper part of the tree. In 1878 a tunnel was carved through the 20-foot-wide base, hence the name. The Tuolumne Grove harbors another dozen trees 10 feet in diameter or greater.

Of the three groves in Yosemite, this is the most popular during winter, so don't expect solitude on a weekend of reasonable weather. If this route is too congested for your taste, consider the nearby Merced Grove instead.

How to get there: Drive on the Big Oak Flat Road to the junction at Crane Flat with the Tioga Road. This junction is 7.3 miles east of the Big Oak Flat entrance and 9.1 miles west of the junction with the El Portal Road (Highway 140). Follow the Tioga

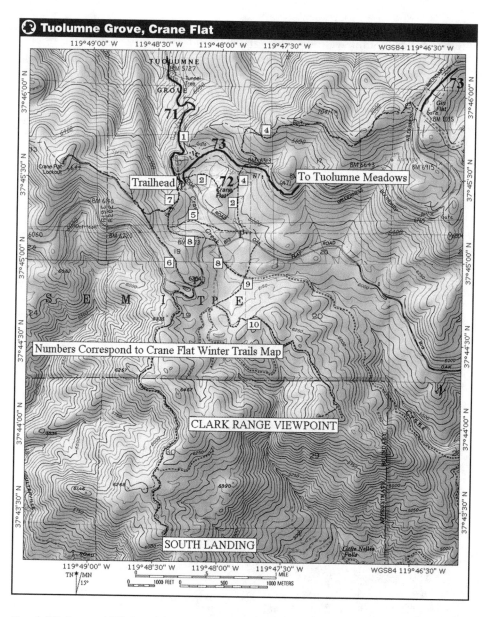

Tuolumne Grove, Crane Flat

Road (Highway 120) 0.6 mile to the Crane Flat winter parking area. Restrooms and a pay phone are nearby.

Description: From the parking area, head south past the restrooms and find the closed gate at the beginning of the road leading down to the Tuolumne Grove, corresponding to Crane Flat Winter Trail #1 and the route of the Old Big Oak Flat Road. Begin your trip with a slight descent through mixed forest of fir and cedar. Quickly the road makes a couple of sharp bends and then develops a more moderate rate of descent. Continue the decline around more curves, eventually reaching the signed entrance to the Tuolumne Grove, where the descent temporarily abates.

You continue down into the grove, encountering the first giant sequoias as you sweep around a hillside. A short lateral trail to the right leads to the Tunnel Tree, a sequoia with not only a hole in its base, but also a top resembling a tuning fork. The lateral trail loops back around to join the main road after a short distance. Wander around at your leisure, enjoying the 25 trees in the grove, then climb back up the road to the trailhead.

FYI: For an interesting extension to your trip, consider continuing down the Old Big Oak Flat Road past Hodgdon Meadow to the Big Oak Flat entrance. The total distance is 6.5 miles and is almost entirely downhill. You will have to arrange a pick-up at the entrance.

Warm-ups: After a chilly day in the backcountry, the Mountain Room Lounge in Yosemite Lodge provides snowshoers with the possibility of a warm spot next to a roaring fire, a fine setting for enjoying a hot drink or a snifter of brandy. During winter, the lounge is open 5–9:30 p.m. during weekdays and noon–10 p.m. on Saturday and Sunday.

Tunnel Tree in the Tuolumne Grove of giant sequoias

TRIP 72

Crane Flat Trails

see map
on page
235

Duration: One-half day
Distance: Varies
Difficulty: Easy
Elevation: 6200
Maps: *Ackerson Mountain 7.5′ quadrangle;*
Crane Flat Winter Trails

Introduction: If you are new to the sport of snowshoeing, or if traveling with young children, Crane Flat has much to offer. Well-marked trails radiate from the winter parking area, providing plenty of opportunities for novices, big or small, to gain their "snow legs." Most of the shorter trails pass through the meadows of Crane Flat, making few demands on technique or routefinding.

Due to the ease of getting around on these trails, Crane Flat is a popular weekend park destination. Most beginners don't mind the reassuring presence of crowds, but when you are ready to seek more of a backcountry experience, other trails in the area will provide a greater challenge. Not only will you find other snowshoers at Crane Flat, but a large percentage of beginning cross-country skiers will most likely be present also, Remember to practice proper winter etiquette and refrain from walking on the ski tracks.

What you won't find at Crane Flat are the extraordinary views typically associated with Yosemite National Park. The lack of waterfalls, granite domes and craggy peaks aside, you will find pleasant surroundings of snow-covered meadows bordered by conifers lightly-dusted by a recent storm and plenty of gentle terrain upon which to tread.

How to get there: Drive on the Big Oak Flat Road to the junction at Crane Flat with the Tioga Road. This junction is 7.3 miles east of the Big Oak Flat entrance and 9.1 miles west of the junction with the El Portal Road (Highway 140). Follow the Tioga Road (Highway 120) 0.6 mile to the Crane Flat winter parking area. Restrooms and a pay phone are nearby.

Description: Armed with a copy of *Crane Flat Winter Trails* a novice can find plenty of short, easy routes that are well-marked to follow around the meadows of Crane Flat. Routes 2 and 5, along with parts of routes 4, 7, 8 and the Tioga Road, can be combined to create brief loop trips requiring no considerable elevation gain or routefinding.

FYI: The service station at Crane Flat is open only from 9:00 a.m. to 5:00 p.m., but you can purchase gas 24 hours a day with a credit or a debit card. You can also obtain a copy of *Crane Flat Winter Trails* for a nominal fee when the station' is open. The station also has a limited supply of snacks and groceries.

Warm-ups: The nearest watering holes to the trailhead are in Yosemite Valley. Generally speaking, the cafeteria at Yosemite Lodge was created for those who eat to live as opposed to those who live to eat. However, the Coffee Corner is an oasis in the midst of this vast culinary wasteland. Open between the essential caffeine intake hours of 6:30 a.m. to 4:30 p.m., congenial coffee purveyors agreeably distribute their wide variety of lattes, mochas and espressos in every form short of an IV. If all you desire is a regular cup of joe, they have that too. While it may not be exactly like the ubiquitous Starbucks to which you've grown accustomed, can any one of their franchises boast a view of Yosemite Falls from outside their front door?

TRIP 73

Tuolumne Meadows

see map
on page
239-240

Duration: Multi-day
Distance: Varies: 39 miles one way from Crane Flat
via Tioga Road eastbound
22 miles one way from Yosemite Valley via John Muir Trail
16 miles one way from gate on Tioga Road westbound
Difficulty: Difficult to extreme
Elevation: 6200/8580 (Tioga Road eastbound)
3980/8580 (John Muir Trail)
7450/9945/8580 (Tioga Road westbound)
Maps: *Ackerson Mountain, Tamarack Flat, Yosemite Falls, Tenaya Lake, Falls Ridge, Merced Peak, Vogelsang Peak,* & *Tioga Pass* 7.5' quadrangles

Introduction: Tuolumne Meadows is the Sierra's largest subalpine meadow, and second only to Yosemite Valley in popularity. Thousands of visitors pass through the meadows each summer, but closed roads and the resulting lengthy approaches put this favorite summer destination out of reach for tourists during the shortened days of winter. However, a growing number of outdoor enthusiasts come here each win-

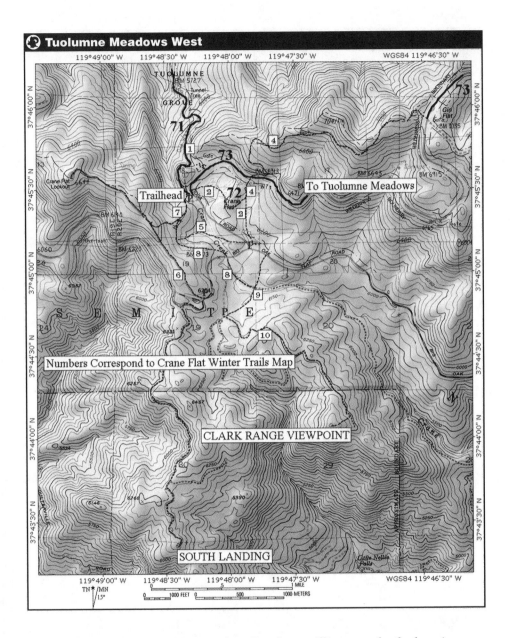

Tuolumne Meadows West

ter to ski, mountain climb, or snowshoe. For those willing to make the long journey, the area sparkles with majestic scenery and unparalleled beauty.

The first choice prospective visitors must consider when contemplating a trip to the meadows is what route to travel. None of the options is easy, each one requiring a considerable investment in time and energy just to reach the meadows. From the west side, the first of the two most logical choices are along the Tioga Road, beginning at Crane Flat. The second option follows the route of the John Muir Trail. Of the

Tuolumne Meadows East

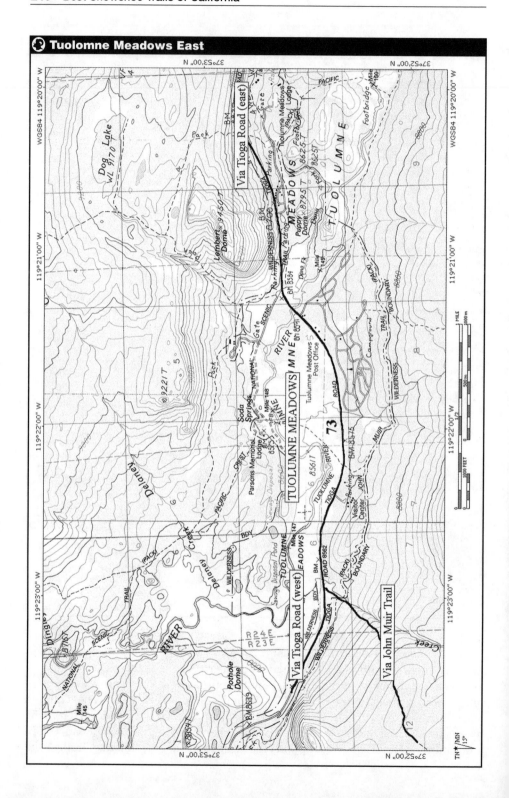

two, the Tioga Road presents fewer routefinding difficulties, although the overall distance to Tuolumne Meadows is approximately 39 miles from Crane Flat. The trip along the John Muir Trail involves considerably more routefinding than the road, but is shorter at approximately 22 miles from Yosemite Valley.

From the east side, only one option exists. From a closed gate on the Tioga Road nearly 4 miles from US 395, travelers can continue up the steep section of Highway 120, over Tioga Pass and then on to Tuolumne Meadows, a total distance of approximately 16 miles. For a fee, the folks at Tioga Pass Resort have been picking up and transporting the gear of skiers to their facility near the Saddlebag Lake junction, lightening the load for the 6-mile ski up the road to their lodge. Unfortunately, the operators of Tioga Pass Resort have expressed a general disdain for snowshoers, so don't expect the same consideration if this option appeals to you.

Once you overcome the major distances just to arrive at Tuolumne Meadows, you can stay at the park's Ski School Hut on a first-come, first-served basis. However, even if you plan on staying there you should carry a tent and suitable overnight gear as there is no guarantee that you will be able to find space there. For guided trips you can contact the Yosemite Cross-Country Ski Center and Ski School (see introduction to Chapter 12).

Any winter trip to Tuolumne Meadows is a serious multi-day undertaking that should be attempted only by those who are experienced in winter travel and in extended snow camping. Keep a close eye on the weather at all times and be prepared for all possibilities.

How to get there:

Tioga Road Eastbound: Follow directions in Trip 71 to the Crane Flat winter parking area.

John Muir Trail: Follow directions in Trip 74 to the day-use parking Area at Curry Village or travel on the shuttle bus to stop #19 (Lower Pines Campground).

Tioga Road Westbound: Follow directions in Trip 88. From the Ranger Station, continue up the Tioga Road to the closed gate, 3.7 miles from US 395.

Description: Tuolumne Meadows provides snowshoers with grand opportunities for wide-ranging explorations. The meadows themselves are quite extensive, granting those willing to go to all the trouble to get there a number of possibilities for exploration. Sprinkled with granite domes and resting in the shadow of high Sierra peaks, the meadows are worthy of as much attention as you can afford to give them. A more scenic winter landscape is hard to imagine.

From a base camp in Tuolumne Meadows, there are numerous creek drainages to trace, frozen lakes to find, and snow-covered peaks to climb. The only limitations to your explorations will be time and agreeable weather. Armed with the *Tioga Pass* and *Vogelsang Peak* quadrangles, outdoor adventurers can roam to their heart's content. The Tuolumne Meadows area has the potential for being the site of a great winter experience.

FYI: As for all overnight stays in the Yosemite backcountry, you need a wilderness permit. And for a journey of such proportions, a detailed description of your plans should be left with a reliable person back in civilization, complete with the phone number of the appropriate agency to contact if you don't return as scheduled.

Warm-ups: You're on your own for this one. Often when I plan a long trip into the backcountry, no matter what the season, I pack along something for a special occasion near the middle or end of the journey. Choose a favorite food or a hot drink that is a bit extravagant—at least by backcountry standards—tuck it in the recesses of your pack and bring it out for a treat when your party could use a lift. Tentbound days are greatly relieved by such pleasures.

TRIP 74

Yosemite Valley — West Loop

see map on page 245

Duration: Full day
Distance: 11 miles loop trip
Difficulty: Easy to moderate
Elevation: 3970/3870/4065
Maps: *Half Dome* & *Yosemite Falls* 7.5′ quadrangles

Introduction: On those infrequent occasions when an adequate layer of snow blankets Yosemite Valley, a more attractive setting in which to snowshoe is hard to imagine. Fresh snow on the valley floor, on the ledges of the vertical granite walls, and atop the valley rim transforms the gorge into a veritable winter wonderland. The hush created by new-fallen snow combines with the greatly reduced number of winter visitors to produce a serene setting totally outside the experience of those who visit the park in other seasons. Common Yosemite landmarks are still here, their stunning beauty accented by a blanket of powder, but gone are the crowds and the congestion.

Due to variations in snowfall, planning a snowshoe trip for Yosemite Valley is a highly speculative proposition. Average winters will definitely see significant accumulations of snow at times, but trying to determine those periods ahead of time is tricky work. Once a cold Pacific storm leaves a sufficient layer of snow in the 3900-foot valley, typically moderate temperatures are not too far behind. Consequently, the snow that does fall in the valley doesn't hang around for extended periods. Snow in Yosemite Valley usually is in good condition for a few days at most, quickly turning into a wet mush and then melting altogether not long afterward. Snowshoers wishing to tramp in the valley will need to pay special attention to the weather when planning their trip.

When adequate snowfall is present, snowshoers can take advantage of the highly developed network of hiking trails that crisscross the valley floor, making any number of short, medium or long trips possible. While the West Loop described here is 11 miles long, a number of options are available for shortening the trip. The west end of the loop provides the best opportunity for solitude, while the east end offers considerably less, especially around the bustling Yosemite Village and Yosemite Lodge areas.

How to get there: Until plans are implemented prohibiting visitors without overnight reservations from driving private vehicles into Yosemite Valley, parking is available at the day-use parking area near Curry Village. Whichever of the three main highways drivers follow to the valley, ultimately they will end up on Southside Drive, the two-lane, one-way road that leads all motorists into the valley. Follow signs to the day-use parking area near Curry Village and park in the lot as space is available.

From stop #14 (Curry Village) next to the parking area, free shuttle buses run every 20 minutes and go to 14 other stops throughout the valley. From stop #14, or other points in the valley, ride the shuttle bus to stop #7 (Yosemite Falls) and follow the description below. During the winter, buses do not run to stops #15-18 (Upper Pines Campground, Happy Isles, Mirror Lake and Stables).

Because of frequent bear problems, do not leave any food, anything that looks like it contains food, or anything that remotely smells like food in the car overnight. Bear-proof lockers are provided in the parking area for any suspect items.

Description: From the Yosemite Falls parking lot (Bus Stop #7), find the Valley Loop Trail behind the restroom building, signed: EL CAPITAN 3.2, TOP OF YOSEMITE FALLS 3.8. You head southwest on a nearly level grade through light forest, paralleling the Northside Road. Pass Swan Slab, which provides a nice practice area for novice climbers, and reach a junction with the Yosemite Falls Trail at 0.5 mile.

The massive granite face of El Capitan

From the junction, you continue through light forest and boulders, passing above Camp 4 Campground. Climbers from bygone days remember this site as the camping haven for rock climbers who flocked to the valley in the 1960's, lured by the prospects of the increasing popular sport of big-wall climbing. Even today, most of the campers at Camp 4 are climbers.

Beyond, Camp 4 you draw closer to the road and eventually cross to the south side of the highway, skirting Leidig Meadow. Nearing the Merced River there are fine views of North Dome, Royal Arches, Clouds Rest and the upper part of Half Dome. Soon you reenter light forest of ponderosa pine, incense cedar and black oak, leaving the views behind. Cross Eagle Creek on a wooden bridge and come to a small clearing with a splendid view of El Capitan. Continue along the easy grade of the trail, reaching a junction with an unsigned lateral trail.

Soon entering another small meadow, you have nice views of El Capitan, Three Brothers and Cathedral Rocks. Continue along the trail as it follows the course of the Merced River, passing the El Capitan Picnic Area and bending around to meet the Northside Road once again. Follow the road for a short distance and then cross to the north side. A sign at the crossing reads: EL CAPITAN 0.4, BRIDALVEIL 4.1.

Paralleling the road, you walk through a tunnel of young cedars, quickly crossing a wide road providing climbers access to El Capitan. Walking beneath the massive wall of El Capitan, thoughts of the effort involved in climbing such a face flood your mind. Cross another climber's access road and then quickly come to a Y-trail junction, 3 miles from your starting point. The left-hand trail heads south to the El Capitan Bridge. If a shorter loop is desired, see FYI below.

For the full loop, take the right-hand branch at the junction, following a sign marked BRIDALVEIL FALL 3.7, POHONO BRIDGE 1.9. Proceed along the trail as it veers away from the highway on a slight climb. Aside from the periodic traffic noise, this stretch of trail is quiet and peaceful. At 4 miles, cross Ribbon Creek. Beyond the creek you reach a road which leads to a wood-cutting area. Follow the trail as it angles back toward and then runs parallel to the highway. As the west end of the valley narrows, the trail, the road, and the river come closer to one another, as they must share a shrinking piece of valley floor. The increased sound of the tumbling water in the Merced River indicates that the nearly level grade of the upper valley has increased here as well. You continue through light forest, eventually sighting the Pohono Bridge ahead. After a short descent, you curve down to the road and cross the Pohono Bridge, 5.25 miles from the Yosemite Falls parking area.

After you cross the Pohono Bridge, find the resumption of the Valley Loop Trail just above the south bank of the river. Go upstream 0.25 mile until the trail veers south away from the river to circumvent Bridalveil Meadow. Near the meadow, there are pleasant views of El Capitan, Cathedral Rocks, Leaning Tower and Dewey, Crocker, Stanford and Old Inspiration points. The trail parallels the Southside Road about 20 feet from the pavement to the far end of the meadow, where it heads back toward the river through light forest. You follow the peaceful river on its winding course with nice views of Half Dome and El Capitan across the waters. Following the river, the trail circles back around to the roadway but quickly veers away again.

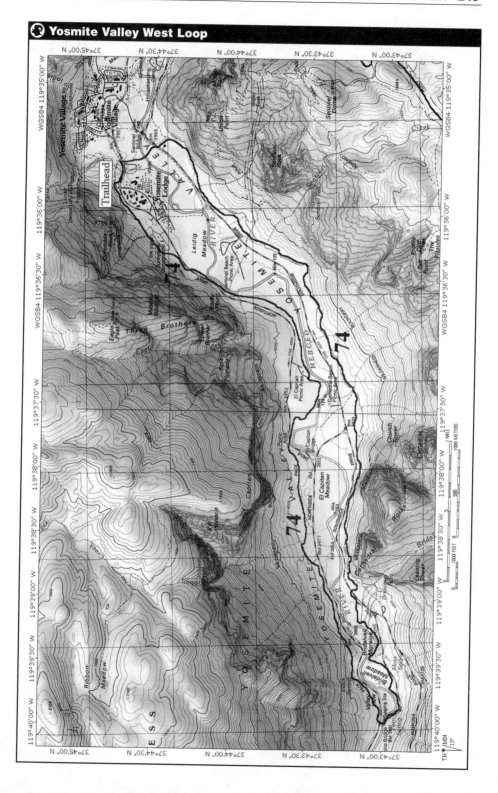

Yosemite Valley West Loop

Trailhead

The next potential obstacle is the crossing of multi-channeled Bridalveil Creek. If the temperatures have been cold and the flow of water is low, ford the channels and proceed up the route of the trail. However, if warmer conditions have increased the amount of water, a better option is to avoid the fords by going alongside the road to the resumption of the trail beyond the last channel of Bridalveil Creek. Whichever way is chosen, past the creek the trail comes back besides the road for 200 yards, eventually crossing the Southside Road near the V14 road marker at the Bridalveil Falls viewpoint, 6.5 miles from the Yosemite Falls parking area.

Just past the road is a T-junction, the right-hand trail leading back to Bridalveil Falls. Bear left and quickly come to a Y-junction. Veer right, following signed directions for CURRY VILLAGE 5.5, STABLES 6.0. From the junction, make a moderate climb above the river and the road across a rocky slope directly below Cathedral Rocks. Traveling through light forest, the climb soon abates; follow the trail on a moderate descent back toward the road. The floor of the valley starts to widen again as you proceed up the canyon on a slight rise. Reach another T-junction at the 8-mile mark. Traditional Yosemite signs of metal with cut-out letters give the following destinations and mileages: EL CAPITAN 1.4, YOSEMITE FALLS 4.0, STABLES 6.7 (left, southwest) and CAMP CURRY 3.9, STABLES 4.4 (straight ahead, east-northeast).

From the junction, proceed straight ahead into a lighter forest cover where there are nice views of El Capitan and the Three Brothers on the north wall and Cathedral Spires on the south. Back in trees, the views diminish as a mild climb is made up the valley. Continue up the mildly graded trail, getting your first glimpse through the trees of Yosemite Falls. After crossing Sentinel Creek, approach a small clearing for a grand view across the valley of Yosemite Falls. A short distance farther, you encounter a junction with the Fourmile Trail at 9.5 miles. Closed in winter, the Fourmile Trail climbs steeply from the valley floor to Glacier Point.

From the junction continue heading northeast on the mildly graded trail, still enjoying some fine views across the valley. The road draws near once more as you approach the Swinging Bridge Picnic Area on the opposite side of the highway. Soon you head back into light forest and then pass behind the Yosemite Chapel, the oldest structure in the valley. At the far end of the chapel grounds, you reach a 3-way trail junction at 10.5 miles.

Turn left (northwest) at the junction and head out toward the road. You cross Southside Road and follow the trail through the meadows and over a footbridge. Continue across the meadows to the path across Northside Road, turn left (west) and proceed down to the Yosemite Falls parking lot.

FYI: For a shorter variation, 3.5 miles of the loop can be shaved off by turning south from the Y-junction 3 miles from Yosemite Falls and following that trail out to the Northside Road. Walk down the road and across the El Capitan Bridge, from where there is an excellent view of Cathedral Rocks, finding the continuation of the trail just beyond the bridge. Then head east and then southeast to a crossing of the Southside Road. Once across the road, proceed up the trail to a junction with the Valley Loop Trail, 0.75 mile from the Y-junction.

Warm-ups: For those dinner patrons tired of the a la carte prices and the mundane food at the cafeteria, the Mountain Room at Yosemite Lodge offers tired snowshoers a pleasant change. Enjoy the splendid views of Yosemite Falls while seated cozily in the newly remodeled restaurant, and sit back and relax while waiters deliver superbly broiled steaks, creative seafood dishes, or pasta specialties to your table. Warm sourdough bread accompanies each meal, and the dinner salads are made with a mixture of fresh greens (I recommend the raspberry vinaigrette dressing). The wine list is more than passable, and even the desserts provide plenty of tantalizing temptations.

The Mountain Room is open daily from 5 to 9 p.m. The prices range from moderate to moderately expensive, and major credit cards are accepted. Reservations and long waits are both unheard of during the winter months. The accepted dress is casual.

T R I P **75**

Yosemite Valley — East Loop

see map
on page
249

Duration: Three-quarter day
Distance: 6.25 miles loop trip
Difficulty: Easy to moderate
Elevation: 3970/4170
Maps: *Half Dome* & *Yosemite Falls* 7.5' quadrangles

Introduction: Compared to the West Loop, this route offers less in the way of solitude, as along the way you pass by a number of bustling centers of activity, including Curry Village, the Ahwahnee Hotel, and Yosemite Village. However, many sections of trail away from these areas are lightly used, particularly when snow carpets the ground. Forested areas beside the Merced River or Tenaya Creek can be quite peaceful, especially in the midst of winter. This trip offers some fine views of some of Yosemite's most famous landmarks, such as Yosemite Falls, Royal Arches and Half Dome.

Following the valley floor for the most part, this loop trip requires little elevation gain and the routefinding is straightforward. Classic Yosemite cut-out metal signs provide travelers with plenty of directions at all major junctions. As on the West Loop, connecting trails and roads offer many shortcuts and variations. If you happen to be in the valley when the snow conditions are ideal, this trip provides a fairly easy and very enjoyable experience.

How to get there: On Southside Drive, follow signs to the day-use parking area near Curry Village. From bust stop #14 (Curry Village) next to the parking area, free shuttle buses run every 20 minutes and go to 14 other stops throughout the valley. Ride the shuttle bus to stop #7 (Yosemite Falls) and follow the description below.

Description: From the parking lot at Yosemite Falls, you proceed east toward Yosemite Village on the bike/pedestrian path that parallels Northside Road. After 0.2 mile, turn south, cross the road, and head out into the meadow. You follow the path across a footbridge over the Merced River and continue to a crossing of Southside Road near Yosemite Chapel, 0.5 mile from your start. Behind the chapel, locate the T-trail junction and turn northeast up the left-hand branch.

You walk through an area of boulders and oaks, following the trail as it winds around, eventually drawing near the road in more of an evergreen forest. Your trail joins the bike path as you walk directly alongside the right edge of the pavement for nearly 0.25 mile, before the hiking path veers away from the road to the right. At this point a sign reads CURRY VILLAGE .9, STABLES 1.4.

Climbing briefly above the road, you pass the ramshackle Housekeeping Camp across the road; this eyesore is slated for closure soon. Near the end of the camp, but on your side of the road, is the LeConte Memorial. Operated by the Sierra Club, the memorial was built in honor of Joseph LeConte, an eminent Berkeley geologist who linked the formation of Yosemite Valley to glaciation. The memorial originally occupied a site in Curry Village and served as the valley's first visitor center, but was relocated to the current site in 1919.

The bike path and the hiking trail coincide again briefly near the memorial. Then you veer off away from the road, following the trail into the forest again. Soon you reach the outskirts of Curry Village and head along the paved sidewalk in front of the main entrance. You continue along the walkway past the hamburger stand, the mountaineering school, and the tent cabins at the far end of the village. Paralleling the fire lane, you follow the trail back into forest, passing the wilderness-permit-holders parking area to your right and Upper Pines Campground to your left. Just past the 2.5-mile mark, you come to Happy Isles Nature Center. The center is closed during winter, but the bathrooms remain open all year.

Leaving Happy Isles, you walk along the road across the Happy Isles Bridge spanning the Merced River and find the continuation of the unmarked Valley Loop Trail just a short distance east from the paved road where it loops around to the north. You follow the trail as it parallels the road, the Merced River within earshot. Pass underneath a large overhanging rock and veer away from the road for nearly 0.5 mile until you come to a trail junction near the Tenaya Bridge, 3.3 miles from your starting point.

At the junction, you turn left and cross the closed road to Mirror Lake, following a sign STABLES 0.5, YOSEMITE FALLS 2.8. Soon you walk beside Tenaya Creek, from where you have fine views of Washington Column and the Royal Arches on the

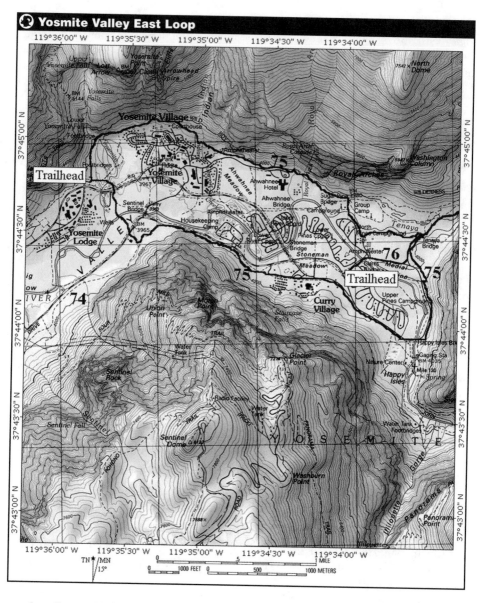

Yosmite Valley East Loop

north valley wall. Quickly, you come to the stables, at 3.75 miles, and as you enter the compound, you must bear sharply to the right (northwest), following a sign reading INDIAN CAVES .9, YOSEMITE FALLS 2.0, EL CAPITAN 5.3.

In light-to-moderate forest cover, you pass North Pines Campground, cross Tenaya Creek on a foot bridge and reach another junction, near the 4-mile mark. Continue straight through the campground and immediately find yet another trail junction just across the paved road. Turn left (west) at the junction, following directions on a sign for YOSEMITE FALLS 2.0, EL CAPITAN 5.3.

As you walk through light forest, more views of Royal Arches await you on the steep wall above. Drop down to the Ahwahnee Hotel, 0.5 mile from the junction, veering to the right just before reaching the edge of the parking lot. As the trail parallels the road into the hotel grounds, you pass through another field of large granite boulders. Proceeding along the route, not far from the road, you have pleasant views across Ahwahnee Meadows to the south wall of the valley. After a brief glimpse of the upper part of Yosemite Falls, your route drops into the Church Bowl area, 5 miles from the beginning.

Leaving Church Bowl, the trail turns away from the road and begins to climb. You cross Indian Canyon Creek on a small wooden bridge and continue the moderate climb as the trail winds across the hillside. After 0.3 mile of climbing, the trail begins a lengthy descent, but not before you have a nice view of the valley. As you descend, the route passes behind the numerous buildings of Yosemite Village. Ignore a lateral trail heading down to some stables on your left and continue the descent to the end of the village, where you find another T-junction at 5.75 miles.

You continue straight ahead at the junction, toward the bridge at the base of Lower Yosemite Falls. An easy stroll leads to the bridge, and then you follow the path as it curves around alongside a branch of Yosemite Creek. Walk along the path to your beginning point at the Yosemite Falls parking lot.

FYI: Adequate snow cover in the valley occurs sporadically throughout the winter—refer to comments in the Introduction of Trip 74.

Warm-ups: The dress code along with the potential amount of your check is quite enough to dissuade the average snowshoer from venturing into the dining room at the Ahwahnee Hotel for dinner. However, casual dress is acceptable for breakfast and lunch, and the prices, while certainly not a bargain, are not nearly as stiff for these meals. Besides, the food is superb and the atmosphere is unmatched. You might be fortunate enough to be seated at a table with a floor-to-ceiling view of Yosemite Falls. For a fantastic carbo-loading, pre-snowshoe warm-up, try the blueberry pancakes. I'm pretty sure the coffee isn't the same stuff you find at the other restaurants in the valley, but if it is, then the classic Ahwahnee cups must be responsible for improving the taste.

The Ahwahnee dining room is open for breakfast from 7 a.m. to 10:30 a.m. and for lunch from 11:30 a.m. to 2:30 p.m. If you're tempted to try the Sunday brunch, my advice is to skip it unless you can eat such great quantities of food as to get your money's worth.

TRIP 76

Mirror Lake & Tenaya Canyon

see map
on page
252

Duration: One-half day
Distance: 6.5 miles loop trip
Difficulty: Easy
Elevation: 4000/4120
Maps: *Half Dome* & *Yosemite Falls* 7.5′ quadrangles

Introduction: Depending on the current conditions, you may find enough snow in Yosemite Valley to call this journey a snowshoe trip. Even if you have to walk the road to Mirror Lake before donning your snowshoes, during most winters you should have many days of adequate snowpack in the canyon above the lake. The nearly level grade, combined with the fact that you couldn't get lost unless you made a steep climb out of the canyon, makes this trip well-suited for snowshoers ready to break away from marked winter trails.

Like most popular valley destinations, Mirror Lake is a tourist magnet during the warmer months. Throngs of visitors walk the road or bicycle part way, drawn at least in part by images of days when Mirror Lake lived up to its name. Almost anyone who has seen any pictures of Yosemite has gazed upon the reflection of Half Dome in the tranquil waters of Mirror Lake. Unfortunately, these glory days are past, as the lake has been reduced to a fraction of its former size. However, the area is still beautiful, the classic face of Half Dome still rises triumphantly over the canyon, and winter images still attract scores of photographers, making Mirror Lake a must-see event for all winter visitors.

Away from Mirror Lake, in the upper reaches of Tenaya Canyon, the number of people diminishes drastically. Unfortunately, the bridge across Tenaya Creek at the far end of the canyon was destroyed during the New Year's flood of '97. Unless repairs are completed, snowshoers will have to retrace their steps, rather than being able to finish the loop. Check with park officials regarding the status of bridge repairs before you begin your journey.

How to get there: Follow directions in Trip 74 to the day-use parking area at Curry Village, or travel on the shuttle bus to stop #19 (Lower Pines Campground).

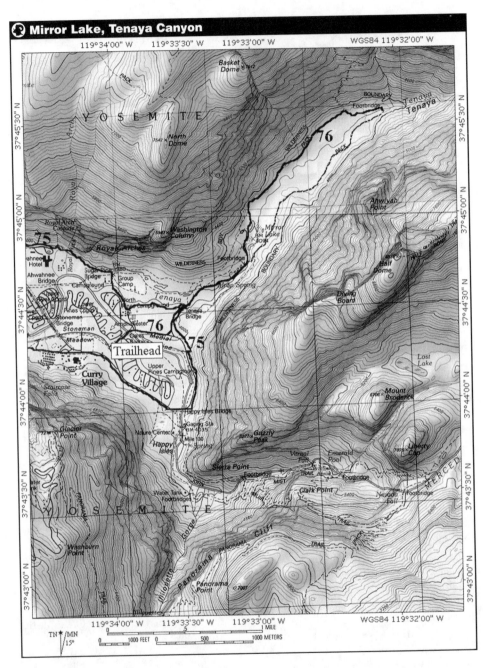

Mirror Lake, Tenaya Canyon

Description: If you parked your vehicle at the day-use parking area, walk northeast down the road a short distance to shuttle bus stop #19. From bus stop #19, travel over Clarks Bridge spanning the Merced River and follow signs for HAPPY ISLES .8, MIRROR LAKE 1.2, which point the way up a closed paved road. Soon you come to a Y and take the left-hand branch signed MIRROR LAKE 1. After a while, reach another Y-junction near a restroom and bear right, following a sign reading MIRROR LAKE .6. As you continue along the road, the looming face of Half Dome comes into view, after which the road draws near to Tenaya Creek. The grade of the road increases as you climb toward Mirror Lake. Where the road ends, 1.25 miles from the bus stop, there is another restroom and a pay phone. Just beyond, the wide path of the Mirror Lake Trail begins.

Nearby is Mirror Lake, or at least what is left of Mirror Lake. There remains a large enough part of a still pond to catch a reflection of Half Dome in the water's surface if you can gain the right angle, but there is no doubt that the fame of Mirror Lake is from former glory. In the recent past, scientists thought that the lake was filling in with sediment, becoming a meadow in a natural progression. Nowadays, they theorize that the "lake" is a pool in a seasonal stream, affected by the speed and the volume of the stream flow, which deposits and scours sand from the pool in cycles. So, who knows? Maybe one day Mirror Lake will regain its grand stature.

Just after the end of the road and the beginning of the trail, a short lateral trail leads over to the shore of Mirror Lake and quickly loops back around to the main trail, providing convenient access for those desiring a closer view. Past the lake, where the main trail passes through a rock slide below steep granite cliffs, you have a nice view across the canyon of Half Dome. Quickly, you head back into light forest and come alongside the creek for a short spell before veering away once again. Proceed through light forest until, a mile from Mirror Lake, you reach a junction with the Tenaya Lake and Tuolumne Meadows Trail. Near the junction one of the classic old iron signs with cut-out letters lists destinations and mileages.

Beyond the junction, storm damage has closed the trail until repairs can be made to the bridge across Tenaya Creek 0.3 mile farther up the trail. The bridge was destroyed during the infamous New Year's flood of 1997, evidence of which is the boulders and debris deposited in the stream channel on your right. Unless the bridge is rebuilt, you can parallel Tenaya Creek up to the bridge site, but without it you may not be able to cross the creek safely.

So far, the Park Service has not shown an inclination to replace the bridge, but if you can find a safe way across Tenaya Creek you could follow the route on the opposite bank back down past the meadows, Mirror Lake, the artificial dam, and a pond to the footbridge which heads back over Tenaya Creek, closing the loop at the junction with the paved road. From there, retrace your steps down the closed road to the bus stop.

FYI: Mirror Lake was called Ahwiyah by the original residents of the valley. The name means "quiet water," which is perhaps a better appellation for the current condition of the lake.

Warm-ups: The pizza at Degnan's Fast Food in Yosemite Village may not be on a par with the styles found at gourmet eateries in New York, Chicago, or San Francisco, but if you're dying for a pizza-fix, you can get one from 11 a.m. to 4 p.m. While the quality of the pizza may be average at best, you can wash it down with some fine beers from the deli next door. You can also find a host of other fast-food items at Degnan's.

TRIP **77**

Dewey Point Ridge Trail—Meadow Trail Loop

Duration: Three-quarter day
Distance: 7-mile loop trip
Difficulty: Moderate
Elevation: 7180/7450/7385
Maps: *El Capitan* 7.5′ quadrangle;
  Glacier Point Road Winter Trails

see map
on page
255

Introduction: At nearly 7200 feet, Badger Pass is a main hub of winter activities within Yosemite, and the trip to Dewey Point may well be the most popular winter journey for outdoor recreationists anywhere in the park. A sunny weekend day will see hundreds of skiers and snowshoers being drawn to the edge of the cliff. However, crowds should not deter you from the experience of gazing across the deep cleft of Yosemite Valley to the imposing sheer granite face of El Capitan. Other Yosemite landmarks visible from the point are almost too numerous to count, including many of the high peaks in the center of and on the east edge of the park.

Two marked routes head toward the vista at Dewey Point—Ridge Trail #14 and Meadow Trail #18. By far the less physically taxing is the Meadow Trail, as the grade is extremely gentle from the Glacier Point Road to the junction where the two trails meet. This is the route most cross-country skiers use. By comparison, the Ridge Trail rolls up and down like a drunken sailor on a stormy sea. Still, by snowshoeing standards the Ridge Trail is a reasonably pleasant route. For variety, this trip follows the Ridge Trail to Dewey Point and returns via the Meadow Trail. Finally, rather than return from the end of the Meadow Trail on the Glacier Point Road, you can climb up to the old Glacier Point Road near Badger Pass and follow it back to the trailhead at the Badger Pass Ski Area.

How to get there: From the junction with Wawona Road at Chinquapin, drive up the Glacier Point Road 5 miles to the parking area at Badger Pass. Follow the blue signs to the upper parking lot, where you will find the Glacier Point Road trailhead.

Description: Begin your adventure by following the snow-covered Glacier Point Road north through light forest, observing the rules of etiquette by avoiding the

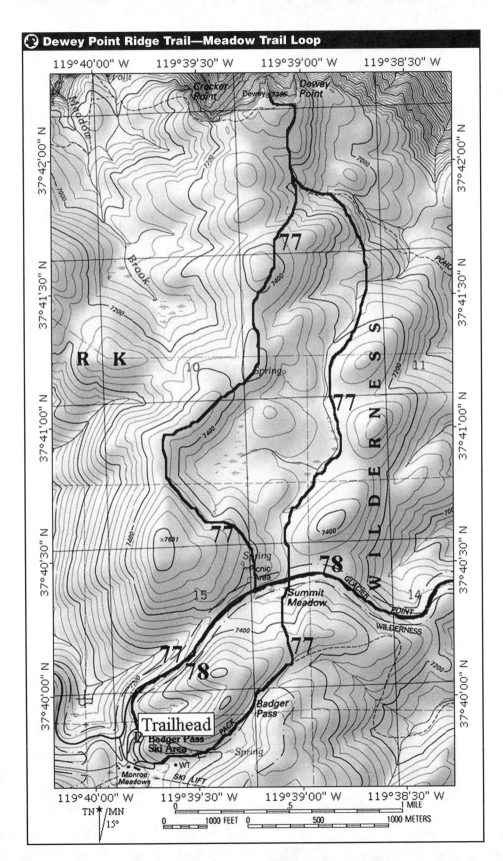

machine-set cross-country ski tracks that run all the way to Glacier Point. Follow the well-traveled road on a mild ascent for 0.75 mile, to the beginning of a slight descent where you will find the signed Dewey Point Ridge Trail #14 to your left.

Leave the road and follow the marked trail into forest on a moderately steep initial climb. The grade eases a bit as you reach the top of a rise and then continue through the trees. Some level stretches of snowshoeing take you through sparse forest with limited views of the surrounding topography. The route undulates, periodically gaining the crest of low hills and rises, affording partial, tantalizing views of the Clark Range and the upper walls of Yosemite Valley. In the midst of a descent, you reach the well-signed junction with the Dewey Point Meadow Trail #18, at 2.5 miles from the parking lot.

Remain on a northerly course as your route continues to climb and drop over and around more hills until a long descending traverse goes around a final hill and over to Dewey Point, 3.5 miles from the trailhead. You stand at the very edge of the gaping cleft of Yosemite Valley, 3500 feet below. The view is incredible from this position directly across from the massive granite wall of El Capitan, with the Three Brothers just to its right. Immediately before you are the back sides of Leaning Tower, Cathedral Rocks and Cathedral Spires. On the northeast and east horizon, you can identify many of Yosemite's tallest mountains, such as Mt. Hoffman, Mt. Conness, and peaks of the Clark Range (make sure you bring a map to help identify the plethora of visible peaks). This awe-inspiring view is the primary reason that a trip to Dewey Point is the quintessential Yosemite winter trip.

Unless preparations have been made to spend a night camped in the snow, you must tear yourself away from the magnificent scenery and begin the return trip to Badger Pass. Retrace your previous steps for a mile back to the junction between Trails #14 and #18. For the loop option, follow #18 on a gentle journey through medium forest. A short but steeper descent across an open hillside leads to a long expanse of meadow. You proceed across the flat meadow, reaching the Glacier Point Road at the far end, 2.5 miles from Dewey Point.

You can elect to simply follow the mundane new Glacier Point Road a little over a mile back to your vehicle, or you can head directly across Summit Meadow, making the short climb over the ridge and intersecting the old Glacier Point Road 0.4 mile from its replacement. Once you reach the old road, turn southwest and follow the marked trail over inauspicious Badger Pass and down to the Badger Pass Ski Area, 1.25 miles from the Glacier Point Road and 7 miles from the starting point.

FYI: The cross-country ski center at Badger Pass rents snowshoes for $11.50 per day. If renting, note that snowshoes must be returned by 4:00 p.m. to avoid additional charges.

The 5-mile section of road from Chinquapin to Badger Pass is open only when the ski area is in operation, usually from the first significant snowfall of winter through Easter weekend. Call ahead to make sure the road is open before arriving at the park.

Weather permitting, each day free buses take skiers and snowshoers from Yosemite Valley to Badger Pass Ski Area whenever the resort is in operation. Buses leave Curry Village, the Ahwahnee Hotel and Yosemite Lodge daily, and the Wawona Hotel on weekends, at two different times during the morning. Buses depart Badger Pass at two different times in the afternoon for the return trip. Check for specific times at the front desks of the aforementioned accommodations.

Stunning scenery from Dewey Point

Warm-ups: Choices are limited, but the lodge at Badger Pass Ski Area does have a run-of-the-mill snack shop. On the second floor, an adult version serves assorted beers, limited hot drinks and nearly passable nachos and pizza. The snack shop is open from breakfast to 4:30 p.m. and the upstairs area is open from 11 to 5. For more refined cuisine, see the options in the valley (Trips 72-76) or at the Wawona Hotel (Trip 79).

View from Dewey Point

Glacier Point

see map
on page
260-261

Duration: 2-4 days
Distance: 21 miles round trip
Difficulty: Difficult
Elevation: 7180/7830/7214
Maps: *El Capitan* & *Half Dome* 7.5′ quadrangles;
Glacier Point Road Winter Trails

Introduction: Thousands of Yosemite tourists make the trek up the Glacier Point Road for the superb views virtually every summer day between Memorial Day and Labor Day. Buses and cars fill the parking lot, and the short trail to the viewpoint is lined with examples from the full gamut of humanity. Listening ears will often detect a number of foreign languages being spoken by passersby along the paved path. After the road is closed by the approaching snows of winter, the once-busy tourist stop is left in solitude for the hearty few willing to travel the 21 miles under their own power. The absolutely incredible views are just as magnificent, nearly 3200 feet above Yosemite Valley, but the added tranquility of a winter visit makes the experience almost too good to be true.

There certainly is a cost to be paid for the extraordinary opportunity to stand on the edge of Glacier Point in the winter, peering into the deep chasm of Yosemite Valley and gazing across the horizon above the lofty peaks that form the Sierra Crest. That price is the long trip required just to reach the view. Skiers have the advantage of a machine-set track thanks to the Park Service, but snowshoers will have to make their own way along the 10.5 mile route. All but the superhuman will need a minimum of two days for the trip out and back, and extra days would possibly make the journey even more enjoyable. A multi-day outing would provide extra time for visiting other points of interest along the way, including stops at Taft Point and Sentinel Dome to name a few.

Any overnight excursion into the Yosemite backcountry during winter necessitates additional planning and equipment, and an accurate weather forecast. Snow camping in the Yosemite backcountry requires a wilderness permit, obtainable at the Badger Pass Ski Area or the valley visitor center. An extended period of fair weather during the longer days of late winter or early spring can provide the basis for a particularly exceptional adventure.

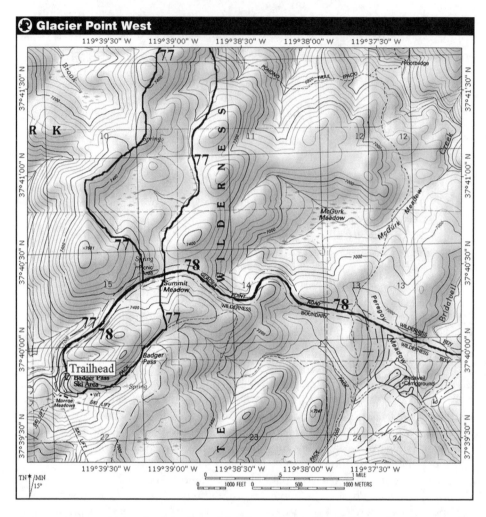

How to get there: From the junction with Wawona Road at Chinquapin, drive up the Glacier Point Road 5 miles to the parking area at Badger Pass. Follow the blue signs to the upper parking lot, where you will find the Glacier Point Road trailhead

Description: From Badger Pass Ski Area, follow the mildly ascending Glacier Point Road through medium forest for 0.75 mile. A subtle descent then leads quickly past the junction with the Dewey Point Ski Trail #14 (see Trip 77) and on to Summit Meadow, 1 mile from the parking lot.

Continue along the road on a very gentle climb for 0.25 mile past Summit Meadow, until the road begins a 1.5-mile long, mild, slightly winding descent. Just beyond the 2-mile mark, catch a glimpse of a part of the Clark Range dead ahead up the road cut. As you continue down the Glacier Point Road, the descent ulti-mately leads to a junction at 2.75 miles for the signed winter trails emanating from Bridalveil Campground.

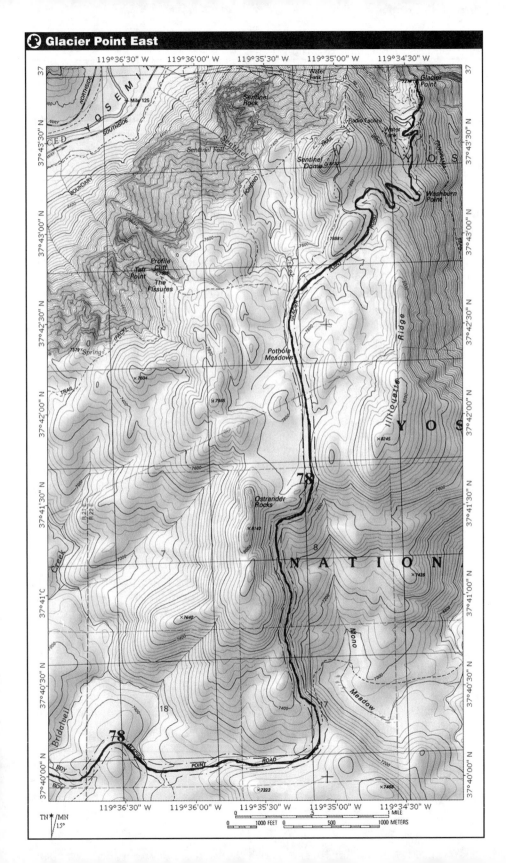

Remain on the Glacier Point Road, making a short climb away from Bridalveil Campground and Peregoy Meadow. Soon you follow the road on a gentle descent to a crossing of Bridalveil Creek. Beyond the creek, climb moderately up the tree-lined road, passing through a section of burned timber from a 1987 fire. You continue the ascent, reaching a signed junction with the Ghost Forest Loop/Bridalveil Creek Snow Trail #21 at 4 miles from the trailhead.

Heading east, stay on the Glacier Point Road, climbing moderately through a light pine forest interspersed with more dead timber from the 1987 fire. A 0.75-mile climb from the junction leads to the Horizon Ridge Ski Trail #15, one of the three marked routes to Ostrander Lake. Continue ascending the path of the winding road as it bends north, passing a sign for MONO MEADOWS at 5 miles from the Badger Pass Ski Area parking lot. One-half mile farther up the road, past the half-way point of your journey, fine views begin to appear through the scattered pines of Mt. Starr King, Mt. Clark and other peaks and domes of the Clark Range.

The moderate climb continues until the 7-mile mark, where easier terrain makes for pleasant snowshoeing over the next couple of miles. Proceeding up the road, you pass Pothole Meadows and begin to see the striking hulk of Sentinel Dome. At 8 miles from the parking lot, you reach the summer trailhead for the 1-mile hike to Sentinel Dome and the 1.25-mile hike to Taft Point. If this is a multi-day adventure and time is available for these side trips, the views are more than rewarding. Although the navigation is straightforward, the route to Taft Point has the advantage of being marked for winter travel.

Beyond the Sentinel Dome and Taft Point trailhead, the Glacier Point Road begins a twisting descent that lasts most of the way to Glacier Point. Passing through a forest primarily of red fir, the narrow, serpentine road closely follows the route of the original Glacier Point wagon road built in 1882. The winding descent through the trees is briefly interrupted at 9.5 miles by a spectacular vista over the precipitous cliffs at Washburn Point. Not only can the sweeping ridge of peaks along the Clark Range be seen directly to the east, but Half Dome is clearly visible to the northeast as well.

Away from Washburn Point, the road continues to snake down toward the Glacier Point parking lot. You have another spectacular view around a big sweeping curve before arriving at the parking area, 10.25 mile from the starting point at Badger Pass. Glacier Point itself is another 0.25 mile north. To call the view from the point spectacular seems entirely inadequate.

FYI: A guided tour to Glacier Point can be arranged with overnight dormitory-style accommodations at the recently constructed Glacier Point Winter Lodge. Call the Yosemite Cross-Country Ski Center & Ski School at (209) 372-8444 for more information.

Warm-ups: See Trip 77. For additional recommendations in Yosemite Valley consult Trips 72-76, or for the Wawona Hotel check out Trip 79.

see map
on page
264

TRIP 79

Mariposa Grove— Lower Loop

Duration: One-half day
Distance: 2.25-mile loop +
4-mile round-trip walk or snowshoe
Difficulty: Easy
Elevation: 5150/5980
Maps: *Mariposa Grove* 7.5′ quadrangle;
Mariposa Grove Winter Trails

Introduction: Any visit to Yosemite National Park is incomplete without a trip through one of the park's three groves of giant sequoias. The Mariposa Grove is the largest of the three, with over 200 big trees that are at least 10 feet in diameter. Moreover, the Mariposa Grove has the oldest giant sequoia in the park, the Grizzly Giant, estimated to be somewhere around 3000 years old. At the height of tourist season, from May through October, Mariposa is also the most visited grove, when trams carry sightseers up the 2-mile access road to the visitor center and beyond. Absent this easy access, winter enthusiasts can enjoy the grove in peace and quiet, when a fresh snowfall carpets the ground and gracefully clings to the branches.

The price of experiencing the sequoias in such seclusion is having to walk or snowshoe those first 2 miles up to the lower grove. Once there, snowshoers can choose from a variety of different routes that weave through the grove. Routes are marked and easy to follow, although they all involve a steady climb. The following trip is the shortest, leading you to many of the grove's most famous landmarks, including the Grizzly Giant, Tunnel Tree, and Fallen Monarch.

While standing amid these huge specimens you begin to appreciate what difficulties must be overcome just in order for these trees to reproduce. Two elements are essential for the propagation of *Sequoiadendron giganteum*: fire and water. First, fire is needed in order to remove the humus from the ground and expose the mineral-rich soil overlying the metamorphic bedrock. Then sufficient moisture must be present to allow the seeds to germinate and survive. Since Sierra summers are traditionally dry, an ample snowpack is necessary to keep the ground moist until fall rains can provide supplemental moisture. These two important factors are somewhat rare during the

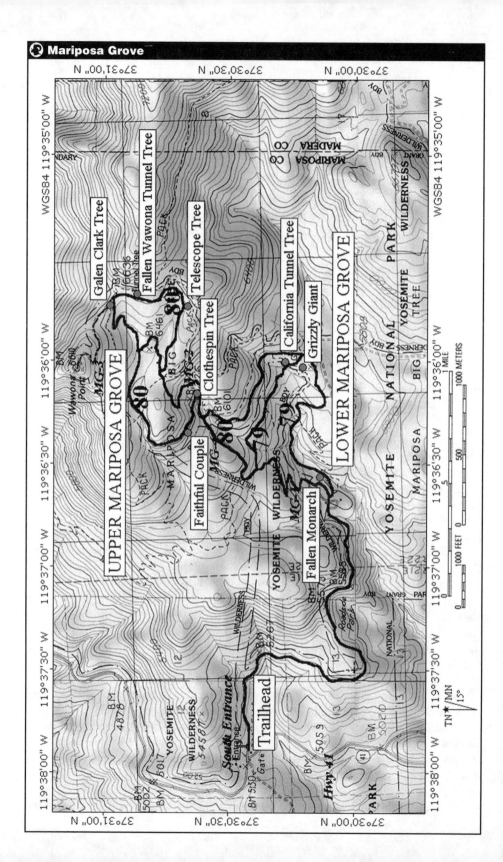

Mariposa Grove

current Sierra epoch, but fortunately the giant sequoia typically has a very long lifespan and needs only one seedling to survive in order to replace itself.

How to get there: The trailhead is near the south entrance of Yosemite, approximately 60 miles north of Fresno. Just past the entrance station, where Highway 41 bends west, find the ample parking area for the Mariposa Grove.

Description: The first part of the trip is either a hike or a snowshoe along the 2-mile road to the Mariposa Grove. The Park Service usually has one side of the road plowed from the parking lot up to the beginning of the lower grove, giving you the option of snowshoeing the snow-covered side or walking on the pavement. Whichever way you choose, follow the road as it climbs and winds through light-to-moderate forest.

A giant sequoia in the Mariposa Grove

Pass a restroom and picnic area at the 1.25-mile mark and continue to climb steadily. Two miles from the parking lot, you begin a short descent near a curve in the road and reach the signed entrance to the Mariposa Grove. The rest of the road remains unplowed during winter.

At the end of the access-road loop is a winter-information area signboard where a *Mariposa Grove Winter Trails* map can be purchased for a nominal fee. Rather than continue up the snow-covered road straight ahead, follow the loop a short distance around to the start of the MG-1 Trail. The wide path is delineated by rectangular yellow markers attached to trees. Climb straight up through moderate forest until the first giant sequoia appears, after which the path makes a winding ascent through the trees. A half mile from the trailhead you reach a signed three-way junction with the MG-4 Trail.

At the junction, bear right (east) remaining on MG-1 and following the signed directions for GRIZZLY GIANT 0.5. Descend briefly before you resume the climb, still through moderate forest. Where the track narrows, you begin a mild descent down to a small creek. Beyond the creek, you make a quick climb up to an area where you will find the California Tunnel Tree.

Because access to the famed Wawona Tunnel Tree in the upper grove was blocked by snowfall during the winter months, the California Tunnel Tree was carved in 1881, allowing visitors year-round passage through the large hole at the base. When the original tree succumbed to the elements during the winter of 1968-69, the California Tunnel Tree became the only "Tunnel Tree" left standing in the park. While hordes of summer tourists flock to this site to have their photographs taken while standing in the "tunnel," chances are very good that you won't have to wait in line for a similar experience in the winter months.

Leaving the California Tunnel Tree behind, climb up the hillside toward the main road, finding the Grizzly Giant down a short path near the top of the hill to your right. As you stand gazing at the sheer enormity of this tree, you realize that this giant of giant sequoias is aptly named.

Now leave MG-1 and turn down the snow-covered main road, heading back toward the visitor center on a moderate descent. Follow the road as it winds around, and 0.5 mile from the junction you encounter the Bachelor Tree and the Three Graces. Continue down the road, passing more sequoias along the way. Just before the end of the route, you encounter the Fallen Monarch reposing alongside the road. The downed tree gives you a more complete perspective of the sheer enormity of these giant sequoias as you walk alongside this tree for a considerable stretch, its girth rising high overhead. The exposed roots also show you that these giant trees have very shallow roots. In a rather odd conundrum, these huge trees can grow only in the mineral-rich but shallow soils layered above metamorphic bedrock. High winds more than likely toppled this gigantic, shallow-rooted behemoth.

A short distance beyond the Fallen Monarch, you reach the visitor center, thereby closing your 2.25-mile snowshoe loop. From here you must still hike or snowshoe the remaining 2 miles back to the parking lot.

FYI: For a more extensive trip through the Mariposa Grove, see Trip 80.

Warm-ups: The Old World Victorian elegance of the dining room at the Wawona Hotel is a pleasant complement to the more stately majesty of the Ahwahnee dining room back in the valley. However, a marked difference is the casual dress code at Wawona, allowing merely semi-respectable snowshoers to enjoy an excellent evening meal. The selection of entrees is somewhat reduced from the regular-season menu, but the presentation and the ambiance more than compensate for the sparse selection. Prices are moderate to moderately expensive. If you're looking for a buffet or a bargain, head back toward Fresno.

The Wawona Hotel has reduced hours in winter. The dining room was open from lunch on Thursday through Sunday brunch in previous winters. Contact Yosemite Reservations at (559) 252-4848 or the Wawona Hotel directly at (209) 375-6556 for more information about the restaurant hours or about lodging.

TRIP 80

Mariposa Grove — Upper Loop

see map on page 264

Duration: Full day
Distance: 6-mile loop +
        4-mile round-trip walk/snowshoe
Difficulty: Moderate
Elevation: 5150/6640
Maps: *Mariposa Grove 7.5' quadrangle;*
    Mariposa Grove Winter Trails

Introduction: A trip through the giant sequoias is one of the musts for any visit to Yosemite. The graceful touch of fresh snow adds a serene ambiance to the awesome grandeur of these immense and ancient trees. The Mariposa Grove is the largest and most popular of the three groves in the park, but much less visited in winter. Snowshoers can experience the majesty of the big trees without the hordes of tourists common to the summer experience. By traveling the extra distance to the upper grove you earn an even greater degree of seclusion.

Even more big trees will be found on this trip than in the lower grove, including curiosities such as the original Wawona Tunnel Tree (although it did topple in 1969), the Telescope and Clothespin trees, and the Faithful Couple. The Galen Clark, Mariposa and Columbia trees are other major sequoias waiting to be seen in the upper grove. Although the lower grove is quite impressive, many more sequoias will be seen in the upper grove. By following this route you won't miss the notable giants of the lower grove, as seen in the previous trip.

For the most part, the description below follows the marked snow trails on the way to the upper grove and then descends via the main road, thereby minimizing the amount of backtracking. Remember, you will have to hike or snowshoe the first 2 miles up to the trailhead at the beginning of the lower grove, as described in Trip 79.

How to get there: The trailhead is near the south entrance of Yosemite, approximately 60 miles north of Fresno. Just past the entrance station, where Highway 41 bends west, find the ample parking area for the Mariposa Grove.

Description: The first part of the trip is either a hike or a snowshoe along the 2-mile road to the Mariposa Grove. Follow the road as it climbs and winds through light-to-moderate forest. Pass a restroom and picnic area at 1.25 miles and continue a steady climb. A short descent leads to the signed entrance to the Mariposa Grove, 2 miles from the parking area.

At the end of the access road loop is a winter information signboard. Rather than continue up the snow-covered road straight ahead, follow the loop a short distance around to the start of the MG-1 trail. Climb through moderate forest on a winding route for a half-mile to a three-way junction with the MG-4 trail.

From the junction, follow the MG-4 Trail as it climbs north-northwest and then winds around until it assumes a north-northeast bearing. After 0.4 mile you connect into the main Mariposa Grove road curving east.

Head up the road for about 0.1 mile, to where the road curves back around to the west. Here you will find the next trail segment, MG-2, beginning near the Clothespin Tree, a giant sequoia with a thin gap at the base.

You climb moderately along MG-2, quickly following a horseshoe bend in the trail. Continue the moderate ascent until the grade eases near the crest of a hill, where the forest momentarily becomes more open, until the route switchbacks and heads back into medium forest cover. You reach the main road once more, completing the 0.5-mile MG-2 Trail.

At this junction, bear left and follow the road as it curves around, passing a restroom building and then the Mariposa Grove Museum. Having reached the upper grove, you can't help but notice the greater number of giant sequoias scattered around the area. After 2.25 mile you reach the loop road junction, where you should bear right (west).

You continue to climb up the road for another 0.75 mile, reaching the Galen Clark Tree and a junction with the MG-3 Trail to Wawona Point (see FYI). Galen Clark, who came to the mountains because of ill health but eventually lived another 53 years, discovered the Mariposa Grove and was the first guardian of Yosemite State Park.

Another 0.1 mile of ascent leads you to the high point of the route near the Fallen Wawona Tunnel Tree, which greeted tourists from 1881 until 1969, when it succumbed to a particularly harsh winter.

The road now begins a gentle descent, and you reach the Telescope Tree in another 0.5 mile. Stand in the base of the tree and look up through its length to the sky. Back on the road, a 0.25-mile journey returns you to the junction with the road and MG-2, 3.25 miles from the trailhead. If the shortest way back is preferred, follow your original route back to the visitor center. But by following the description below, you can vary your return route, taking the road back to the trailhead.

One of the giant sequoias in the Mariposa Grove

Retrace your steps for 0.25 mile past the museum to the road junction. This time head downhill to your left (west) and follow the road on a long arc around a hill. Along the way you will pass a number of sequoias, including the very thick Mariposa Tree. After 0.75 mile the road bends sharply near the Clothespin Tree and you follow your original steps for another 0.1 mile to the junction with MG-4.

From the MG-4 junction, you continue to follow the main road as it descends for 0.75 mile to a junction with MG-1 near the California Tunnel Tree and the Grizzly Giant. Along the way you pass the Faithful Couple, a pair of sequoias joined at the base but separating near the top.

The remaining mile of road makes a winding descent across a number of small creeks, passing through the lower grove. Along the way, you will see the Bachelor and the Three Graces, as well as the Fallen Monarch. When you reach the visitor center you will have completed the 6-mile loop, but still have another 2-mile hike or snowshoe back to the parking lot.

FYI: If you wish to stay overnight in the Mariposa Grove, park regulations mandate that you camp above the Clothespin Tree. Camping in this area is allowed between December 1st and April 15th. Overnight users must secure a wilderness permit from the Badger Pass Ski Area or the valley visitor center.

The 0.5-mile trail to Wawona Point offers a nice extension to your trip. From the junction near the Galen Clark Tree, follow the path of the old road on a continuous moderate ascent through medium forest cover of mostly pine with some fir. One-third mile from the junction, you follow the road around a switchback. Continue to climb until you reach a large flat at the top of the hill. Head to the edge of the flat for some fine views of the Wawona Basin and, on clear days, the coastal hills across the San Joaquin Valley.

Warm-ups: See Trip 79.

CHAPTER 13

South of Yosemite

Highway 168 heads east through the rolling, oak-covered foothills and up into the heart of the west side of the central Sierra to a quartet of lakes: Shaver, Huntington, Thomas A. Edison and Florence, all of which have popular summer resorts. Nearby, a network of trails lead hikers, backpackers and equestrians into the sublime backcountry of the Monarch and John Muir wildernesses and beyond into Kings Canyon National Park. When winter arrives, snowfall closes the road at Huntington Lake, effectively putting the backcountry beyond out of easy reach.

Five Sno-Parks are scattered along the highway between Shaver and Huntington lakes, allowing recreationists access to this popular winter playground. Unfortunately, only two of these Sno-Parks are off-limits to snowmobiles, and one of the two is best suited as a snow play area. This leaves the Coyote Sno-Park as the only site truly worthy of consideration for snowshoers and skiers along the entire stretch of Highway 168. For those adventurers who don't mind the presence of snowmobiles, the choices are obviously greater, but be forewarned that the remaining areas are extremely popular with snowmobilers, and encounters with the mechanized machines are inevitable.

The Coyote Sno-Park offers a set of 4 marked trails across the slopes of Tamarack Mountain. The trails are all well-marked with cross-country ski diamonds and each and every junction has arrowed signs with cumulative mileages. None of the routes lead over particularly difficult terrain, and the lengths are not very taxing either, varying from 2.2 to 6 miles. Vista points on two of the trails grant good views of the surrounding terrain.

Location: The Coyote Sno-Park is approximately 68 miles northeast of Fresno and 11 miles north of Shaver Lake.

Access: Highway 168.

Amenities: The town of Shaver Lake offers dining, lodging, gasoline and other limited services during winter.

Season & Weather: This part of the Sierra is far enough south to experience the infrequent storm patterns found in the central part of California. Snow conditions may be quite variable throughout the course of any winter season. Checking the snow conditions with the Forest Service prior to driving up the highway is a good idea. Ideally, Pacific storms drop an adequate amount of snow by Christmas or New

Year's Day to inaugurate the winter-recreation season, and then hopefully enough storms occur intermittently to sufficiently augment the snowpack at this elevation through mid-March.

PERMITS

Day Use & Overnight Use: Currently permits are not necessary to enter Sierra National Forest.

MAPS

Pineridge Ranger District Winter Recreation Guide
1:63,360, 1995, plastic
Sierra National Forest

FOREST SERVICE

High Sierra Ranger District
29688 Auberry Road
PO Box 559
Prather, CA 93651
(559) 855-5355

Sierra National Forest
Supervisors Office
1600 Tollhouse Road
Clovis, CA 93612
(209) 297-0706

IMPORTANT PHONE NUMBERS

Sno-Park Permit Information   (916) 324-1222

WEBSITES

Sierra National Forest   www.r5.fs.fed.us/sierra
Sno-Park Information   www.ohv.parks.ca.gov/SVRAs/snopark

TRIP 81

Marmot Loop Trail

Duration: One-half day
Distance: 2 miles loop trip
Difficulty: Easy
Elevation: 7465/7550
Maps: *Huntington Lake* 7.5' quadrangle

see map
on page
274

Introduction: The short, easy Marmot Trail is a pleasant trip for beginners and families. For those who don't happen to be in peak condition yet, this trip can be a great way to kick off the season after the first decent snowfall blankets the southern Sierra. Even in fresh powder the trip should take no more than a couple of hours to complete. Like all the trails emanating from the Coyote Nordic Trailhead, the Marmot Trail is very well-marked with blue diamonds, arrows and skier emblems, as well as mileage signs at each junction. Therefore, just a modicum of routefinding is required. There may not be any spectacular vistas along this trail, but the journey through the sparsely forested terrain is quite enjoyable.

How to get there: Travel State Highway 168 eastbound from Fresno to the Coyote Nordic Trailhead Sno-Park, approximately 11 miles past the town of Shaver Lake. Restrooms are available at the Sno-Park.

Description: Leave the Sno-Park and follow the well-marked trail along the course of a snow-covered road. You quickly reach a Y-junction where you should bear right, remaining on the course of the road. After 0.25 mile leave the road at the next signed junction and make a moderate climb as you follow the markers up the hillside. As you approach the crest of the hill, you bear slightly left and continue on a gentler grade just below the top. Soon you come to another signed junction, this time with the Eagle Trail, which heads northwest toward the Shaver Lake Vista. Veer left at this junction, follow the road back toward the first Y-junction you encountered, and then retrace your steps back to the parking area.

FYI: The network of trails in this area provides plenty of opportunities for extending your trip. See Trips 82-83.

Warm-ups: Located in the small community of Shaver Lake, the Village Cafe and Bakery might be just the typical small-town cafe, but you can score a decent breakfast or lunch at a reasonable price. The cafe is open from 6 a.m. to 3 p.m. all winter.

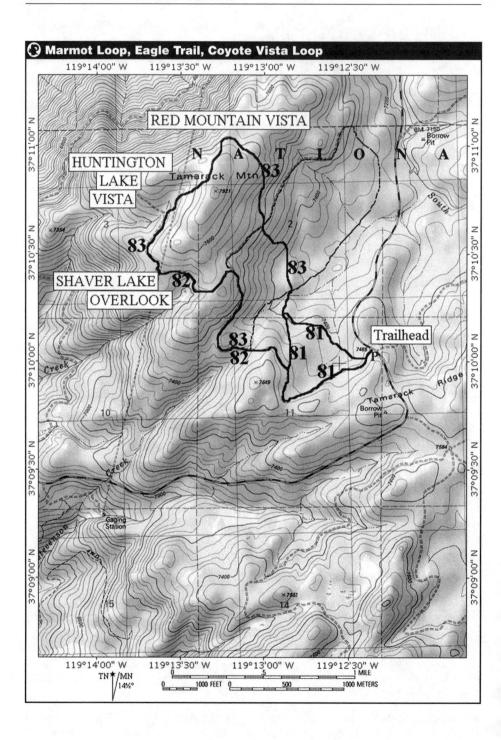

TRIP 82

Eagle Trail to Shaver Lake Overlook

see map on page 274

Duration: One-half day
Distance: 4.25 miles round trip
Difficulty: Moderate
Elevation: 7465/7705
Maps: *Huntington Lake* 7.5′ quadrangle

Introduction: Utilizing one of the well-marked Nordic trails originating at the Coyote Sno-Park, snowshoers can access a fine view of the Shaver Lake basin from the namesake overlook. If the day happens to be clear, views of the Coast Range across the San Joaquin Valley will be an added bonus. The majority of the 2-mile trip to the overlook follows a mildly graded, well-defined road, minimizing the effort and the routefinding. The Eagle Trail provides a pleasant morning or afternoon jaunt for snowshoers of all abilities.

How to get there: Travel State Highway 168 eastbound from Fresno to the Coyote Nordic Trailhead Sno-Park, approximately 11 miles past the town of Shaver Lake. Restrooms are available at the Sno-Park.

Description: Leave the Sno-Park and follow the well-marked trail along the course of the snow-covered road. You quickly reach a signed Y-junction where you continue straight ahead on the left-hand road following directions for EAGLE TRAIL 2.1. Follow the gently graded course of the road as it bends, dips and climbs on the way toward the overlook. Along the way you will pass a couple of well-marked junctions with connections to the Coyote and Grizzly trails.

A sign will herald your arrival at the Shaver Lake Overlook, but you must actually leave the road and snowshoe the short distance over to the viewpoint. As you stand on the edge of the hillside, the lake is revealed in all its glory, a mere 4.25 air miles southwest. Clear days will allow you to gaze all the way across the San Joaquin Valley to the hills of the Coast Range.

Once you have had your fill of the view, retrace your steps to the trailhead.

FYI: Snowfall in the southern Sierra can be quite variable during the course of the winter. Before heading to the mountains you may want to call ahead to the Pineridge Ranger District for an update on current conditions.

Warm-ups: Located at 42136 Tollhouse Road in the town of Shaver Lake, the Sierra House is a five-star restaurant featuring a creative menu and extensive wine list. The Sierra House is usually open for dinner every night and lunch Fridays through Sundays. To confirm winter hours or make reservations, call (559) 841-3576.

Shaver Lake Overlook

TRIP 83

Coyote Vista Loop

see map
on page
274

Duration: Three-quarter day
Distance: 6 miles round trip
Difficulty: Moderate
Elevation: 7465/7860
Maps: *Huntington Lake* 7.5′ quadrangle

Introduction: The Coyote Loop offers snowshoers the best opportunity in this region to sample the beauty of the surrounding countryside away from the presence of snowmobiles. As the route circles Tamarack Mountain, 3 distinct vista points provide views of Red Mountain, Huntington Lake, Kaiser Ridge, Shaver Lake, and on clear days a western panorama extending across the San Joaquin Valley to the Coast Range. The terrain is mostly gentle, with only a few stretches of moderate climbing, and the routefinding along the well-marked trail is relatively easy as well. When fresh snow blankets this section of the Sierra, snowshoers will delight in the pleasures of this trip.

How to get there: Travel State Highway 168 eastbound from Fresno to the Coyote Nordic Trailhead Sno-Park, approximately 11 miles past the town of Shaver Lake. Restrooms are available at the Sno-Park.

Description: Leave the Sno-Park and follow the well-marked trail along the course of a snow-covered road. You quickly reach a signed Y-junction where you bear right, following directions for COYOTE TRAIL 5.7. Stroll through a light pine forest on an easy grade to the next junction, where the Grizzly Trail branches away to the right. Follow the left-hand route, obeying the signed directions for COYOTE TRAIL 5.0. Away from the junction the grade of your ascent intensifies as you climb up the hillside for 0.5 mile to yet another junction, where the Grizzly Trail loops back to cross over your route. You continue up the hill straight ahead following the sign reading COYOTE TRAIL 4.4.

Eventually your ascent becomes more of an ascending traverse as you angle across a moderately steep hillside through light-to-medium forest. The traverse leads you to a clearing at the north end of a ridge at the Red Mountain Vista, 2 miles from the Sno-Park. As promised you do have a fine view of Red Mountain and the surrounding terrain 5 air miles due east.

Away from the first of the 3 designated viewpoints, you continue to climb mildly for another 0.5 mile to the Huntington Lake Vista. You have a fine view not only of the lake but of the high peaks above along Kaiser Ridge within the designated Kaiser Wilderness.

Leaving the Huntington Lake Vista you head over the ridge below the top of Tamarack Mountain and make a brief descent. Eventually the trail levels off and then it climbs gently over a low spot in the ridge. After the grade eases again you reach the sign for SHAVER LAKE VISTA, which is actually off the trail a short distance to your right. From the viewpoint you see the lake below, but are perhaps more impressed with the sweeping vista beyond, which on clear days extends across the San Joaquin Valley to the hills of the Coast Range.

Back on the main trail you have another 2 miles to snowshoe in order to complete your loop. The simplest return route is to follow the Eagle Trail, reversing the description in Trip 82.

FYI: Although the Coyote and Eagle trails share the same path for much of the distance from the Shaver Lake Vista to the Coyote Sno-Park, there are some minor deviations. As previously mentioned, your easiest return is along the Eagle Trail, which follows a snow-covered road all the way back to the parking lot. However, for a slightly more challenging variation, you could follow the Coyote Trail, which veers away from the safety of the road for part of the journey.

If you want to extend your trip, add the Grizzly Loop to your itinerary. From the first junction between the Grizzly and Coyote trails, follow the Grizzly Trail on a 2-mile loop back to the second junction with the Coyote Trail. The first part of the loop follows the course of road, after which you must follow markers through the trees back to the Coyote junction.

Warm-ups: Back before the ubiquitous fast-food chains took over the world, independent burger joints used to make old-fashioned hamburgers, shakes and fries without the aid of processed ingredients with lengthy, unpronounceable names. The Hungry Hut in Shaver Lake is a reminder of those bygone days. As long as you're not watching your cholesterol, you can enjoy such fare on weekdays from 10:30 a.m. to 6:00 p.m. and on weekends from 7 a.m. to 7 p.m.

CHAPTER 14

East Side of the Sierra

As opposed to the west side of the Sierra, which rises gradually from the fertile valleys of California through the foothills and progresses steadily up to the lofty crest, the east side thrusts upward from the Great Basin in urgent drama over an extremely brief span to the climax of the range. Such stark relief produces the impressive eastern escarpment of the Sierra with its precipitous slopes penetrated by deep, narrow stream canyons. This is the side of the range where towering Mt. Whitney, along with a collection of other peaks nearly as tall, reigns majestically over the valleys of the Great Basin thousands of feet below.

The mighty barrier of the Sierra captures most of the moisture from Pacific storms, leaving only a stubborn residue of precipitation for deposit on the successive rows of north-south mountain ranges and valleys of the Great Basin. This rainshadow effect can minimize the snowpack on this eastern fringe of the range. However, average winters will produce plenty of snow farther up the mountains toward the crest.

The awesome scenery on the east side of the Sierra is an impressive sight for travelers on US Highway 395, even if they never get out of their cars. At one time or another most magazines of the West have extolled the virtues of this road for sightseers and tourists. This ribbon of pavement parallels the east side of the entire length of the Sierra, providing many access points

Snowshoers who can overcome the difficulty of the long access from the major population centers of California have most of this region to themselves during winter. Away from the ski areas of Mammoth Mountain and June Lakes, little seems to happen on the east side of the Sierra during the winter months. Consequently, winter recreationists can enjoy the dramatic scenery of high peaks, precipitous canyons and frozen lakes with a reasonable expectation of solitude. For those who want an extended trip, the backcountry abounds with possibilities.

The imposing eastern escarpment of the Sierra has always been a grand obstacle to the activities of man. The oldest settlement in the state of Nevada is Genoa, where Mormon pioneers journeyed to the very base of the range, took one glance at the huge wall of mountains above, and decided that going any further was pointless. Members of the Washoe and Paiute tribes lived on the east side of the Sierra, waiting for summer when Mono Pass snows would melt and they could trade with more prosperous tribes of the western valleys. It wasn't until the mining heyday that any significant routes of travel were built up the steep eastern side of the range, and very few of those ever developed into trans-Sierra roadways. The Tioga Road through Yosemite Park was opened to automobile traffic in 1916. South of the Tioga Road there are over 150 miles without a road crossing the Sierra Nevada. In winter, when highways over Tioga Pass, Sonora Pass and Ebbetts Pass are closed, this number increases to over 200 miles.

Snowmobiles present few problems to snowshoers and skiers on this side of the range. Perhaps the long drive, the steep topography, or the periodic lack of a sufficient snowpack at the start of trips deters them from visiting the east side. Whatever the reasons, encounters will be few.

Location: Trips in this chapter extend along the east side of the Sierra from Pickel Meadows on the Sonora Pass Highway (State Highway 108), in the north to Rock Creek near Tom's Place in the south.

Access: US 395 provides the principal access to all eastside routes. Winter closes all the mountain passes that cross the Sierra between Highway 88 (Carson Pass) in the north and Highway 178 (Walker Pass) in the south. Oftentimes, one of the most difficult challenges will be just getting to the trailhead from the highway, depending on snow and road conditions.

Amenities: Many of the smaller towns that thrive on tourism during the summer offer greatly reduced services in the winter. However, Bishop and Mammoth Lakes will be able to meet most every need.

Season & Weather: Winter on the east side of the Sierra can be either gloriously pleasant when the skies are blue and the temperatures mild, or absolutely abominable when the skies are gray and cold and fierce winds are pelting your body with blowing shards of snow. Conditions at the meeting zone of the eastern Sierra and the western edge of the Great Basin are often extreme, with wide swings from nighttime lows to daytime highs and from stormy days to sunny days. Although snowfall can be minimal at the foot of the mountains, massive amounts of snow can fall just a few miles away near the crest. Be prepared for all possibilities when venturing into the Sierra on the east.

Heading toward the Sierra Crest from near Parker Lake

Estimating the snow season on this side of the range is difficult at best. Recreationists should try to obtain the current conditions before leaving home. In general, an average year will see a decent snowpack from December or January through March or April.

PERMITS

Day Use & Overnight Use: Permits are required for overnight stays in the Ansel Adams Wilderness and John Muir Wilderness.

Sno-Park: A valid Sno-Park permit is necessary for parking at the Rock Creek Sno-Park (Trip 90).

MAPS

Ansel Adams Wilderness
1:63,360, 1987, paper
Inyo & Sierra
National Forests

Hoover Wilderness
1:63,360, 1987, paper
Toiyabe & Inyo
National Forests

Inyo National Forest
1:126,720, 1993, paper
Inyo National Forest

John Muir Wilderness
Sequoia-Kings Canyon Wilderness
1:63,360, 1992, paper
Inyo & Sierra National Forests
Sequoia & Kings Canyon National Parks

Toiyabe National Forest
1:126,720, 1994, paper
Toiyabe National Forest

FOREST SERVICE

Toiyabe National Forest
Carson Ranger District
1536 S. Carson Street
Carson City, NV 89701
(775) 882-2766

Toiyabe National Forest
Supervisor's Office
1200 Franklin Way
Sparks, NV 89431
(775) 331-6444

Inyo National Forest
Lee Vining Ranger District
PO Box 429
Lee Vining, CA 93541
(760) 647-3044

Inyo National Forest
White Mountain Ranger Station
798 North Main
Bishop, CA 93514
(760) 873-2500

Inyo National Forest
Mammoth Ranger District
PO Box 148
Mammoth Lakes, CA 93546
(760) 924-5500

IMPORTANT PHONE NUMBERS

Avalanche Report   (530) 587-2158   Road Conditions   (800) 427-7623
Sno-Park Permit Information (916) 324-1222   Weather   (530) 541-1151

WEBSITES

Avalanche Report   www.r5.fs.fed.us/tahoe/avalanche
Inyo National Forest   www.r5.fs.fed.us/inyo
Sno-Park Information   www.ohv.parks.ca.gov/SVRAs/snowpark
Toiyabe National Forest   www.r5.fs.fed.us/htnf

T R I P **84**

Pickel Meadow

see map
on page
283

Duration: One-half day
Distance: Varies
Difficulty: Easy
Elevation: 6740/6760
Maps: *Pickel Meadow* 7.5′ quadrangle; *Hoover Wilderness*,
    Toiyabe & Inyo National Forests

Introduction: The flat expanse of Pickel Meadow provides beginners with an ideal setting for getting used to a new activity. Tailoring wanderings to suit your desires is quite easy. Reaching the West Walker River requires only a 0.25 mile of travel, while circling the meadows could result in a 4.5-mile loop.

Rimmed by snow-clad ridges, the meadows are quite picturesque when blanketed with a fresh layer of powder. Located in the rainshadow of the Sierra, Pickel Meadow is best visited in years of heavy snowpack

Aside from seeing soldiers from the Mountain Warfare Training Center across the highway, you should have the area pretty much to yourself, as the Sonora Pass Road is closed in the winter, preventing easy access from the valleys and coast of California.

How to get there: Follow US 395 to the junction with Highway 108 and proceed west on 108. At 3.6 miles, you will reach the east edge of the Mountain Warfare Training Center above Pickel Meadow. Technically, this is as far as CalTrans plows the highway in heavy snow years. However, during most years, continuing another 1.3 miles to the locked gate should not be a problem. This gate officially closes the road in winter. Park alongside the road wherever conditions allow.

Description: From your parking spot, proceed onto the meadow and snowshoe wherever you desire. Pickel Meadow is a large open plain providing easy snowshoeing alongside the West Walker River. If you can find a way across the river at the southwest end of the meadows, extending your wanderings a mile or so up Poore Creek is possible before the terrain becomes steeper.

FYI: Continuous activities occur in and around the MWTC—don't be alarmed by their maneuvers.

Warm-ups: Good luck! Unless you stored a thermos of hot coffee or soup in your car, the closest place to acquire hot food or drink is many miles away. Heading south on

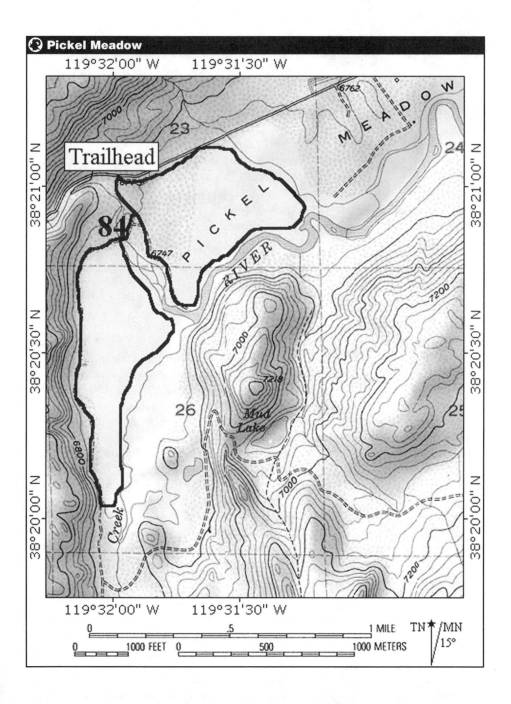

395, your nearest watering holes are in Bridgeport (see Trip 85). Traveling north, you have to journey to Coleville or Walker, where just about everything closes down in the winter, or all the way to Topaz Lake or Gardnerville, Nevada.

TRIP **85**

Twin Lakes

see map
on page
285

Duration: One-half day to three-quarter day
Distance: Varies—up to 9.5 miles round trip
Difficulty: Easy
Elevation: 7085/7200
Maps: *Twin Lakes* 7.5′ quadrangle; *Hoover Wilderness,*
   Toiyabe and Inyo National Forests

Introduction: An easy trip around the shore of a matching pair of beautiful lakes makes your journey around Twin Lakes a wonderful adventure. Most of the route follows the gentle grade of a snow-covered road, creating an ideal situation for beginning snowshoers. The scenery is quite attractive all the way around the lightly forested shoreline. The rugged mountains and the peaks 5000 vertical feet above the lakes create an alpine scene as dramatic as any in the Sierra.

A number of options are available for snowshoers. From any point along the way, you can retrace your steps to the car, satisfied with the delightful scenery en route. An isthmus between Twin Lakes allows the possibility of a shuttle trip of just over 2.5 miles, while a pick-up at the north side of the upper lake at the end of Twin Lakes Road requires a 4.75-mile shuttle. For those without the benefit of a car shuttle, the full round trip necessitates a return of 3.5 miles via the plowed Twin Lakes Road, or of 4.75 miles by following your tracks back to the car.

Whichever alternative you opt for, beneath the steep slopes above the lakes is no place to be when unstable snow conditions prevail. Such situations are not routine for areas in the rainshadow of the Sierra, but are not uncommon either, being most prevalent during and immediately after particularly heavy snowfalls.

How to get there: At the west end of the town of Bridgeport, following signs for Twin Lakes, turn south from US 395 onto Twin Lakes Road. Proceed westbound on two-lane asphalt for 9.5 miles to the left-hand turn onto South Twin Road. Mono County usually plows this road for a short distance, so park at the end of the plowed section of road as conditions allow.

Description: From your car, snowshoe along the extension of the roadway across the bridge over Robinson Creek and through Twin Lakes Campground. As you follow the road around the northeast end of the lake, you have fine views south toward the serrated peaks forming Sawtooth Ridge.

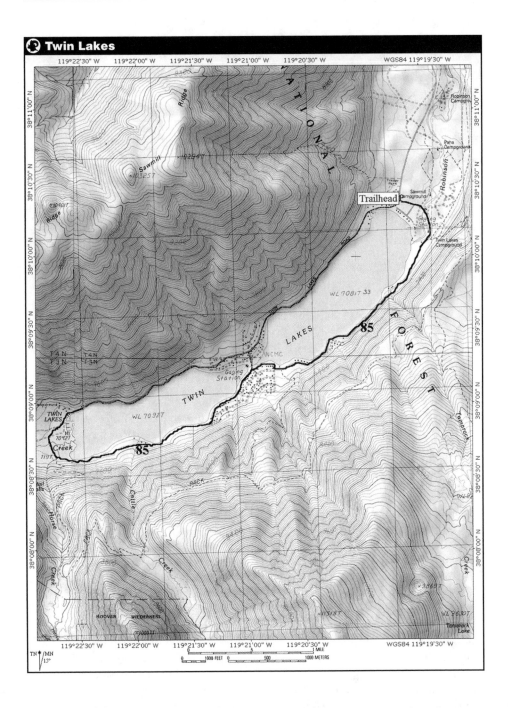

Twin Lakes

Twin Lakes

Continue along the easy path of the roadway on the southeast shore of the first lake. Nearing the end of this lake, follow the road closest to the shoreline through a small subdivision of summer homes. At 2.5 miles from Twin Lakes Road, you reach the narrow isthmus separating the two lakes. If you have arranged a car shuttle, you can end your trip by going across the isthmus another 500 feet to the north-shore road.

To extend your journey, remain on the snow-covered road and proceed along the southeast shore of the upper lake. Just beyond the 3-mile mark, the road ends and you must follow the shoreline without aid of a graded route. At the far end of the lake, turn north and snowshoe through Mono Village to the end of Twin Lakes Road, 4.75 miles from your starting point. Planning a pick-up at the roadend will either save you from retracing your steps or save a 3.5-mile walk along the Twin Lakes Road back to your car.

FYI: As you pass the cabins along the lake and through the Mono Village campground, please respect the rights of property owners.

Warm-ups: For breakfast and lunch, you can't go wrong with Hays Street Cafe, at the corner of US 395 and Hays Street in Bridgeport. Meals are medium-priced and are made from fresh ingredients. Open every day but Monday during winter, the restaurant hours are 7 a.m. to 1 p.m. Call (760) 932-7141 for more information. Like other cafes along this stretch of 395, Hays Street Cafe is subject to periodic closures in winter.

TRIP **86**

Virginia Lakes

see map
on page
288

Duration: Full day
Distance: 11.5 miles round trip
Difficulty: Moderate
Elevation: 8260/9780
Maps: *Lundy* & *Dunderberg Peak* 7.5′ quadrangles;
    Hoover Wilderness, Toiyabe & Inyo National Forests

Introduction: The trip into Virginia Lakes begins at one of the very few plowed parking areas on the east side of the Sierra. The journey takes you on a steady climb along a road to a group of frozen lakes. The scenery along the way is quite pleasant, as the road passes through open terrain with wide-ranging views of the eastern flank of the Sierra. At the lakes, the visual pleasures continue as you experience the picturesque lakes with the dramatic backdrops of Dunberberg Peak and Black Mountain.

Because of the open nature of the terrain and the elevation, the trip into Virginia Lakes should be avoided when foul weather kicks up strong winds. Most of the route is quite exposed, providing little shelter from blustery conditions. Otherwise, if it wasn't for the 5.75-mile distance, the trip would be rated as easy, since the route follows a road for the entire trip, requiring little routefinding.

If you're looking for an area on the east side of the Sierra for an overnight or a multi-day trip, the Virginia Lakes offer plenty of additional possibilities for extending your wanderings (see FYI below).

How to get there: Drive to Conway Summit and turn west onto the Virginia Lakes Road. This junction is 13 miles south of Bridgeport and 12 miles north of Lee Vining. Follow Virginia Lakes Road 0.4 mile to the cleared winter parking area.

Mono County usually begins to plow the road into Virginia Lakes in early spring, allowing late-season snowshoers and skiers the possibility of driving farther up the road to extend their wanderings into the backcountry beyond Virginia Lakes.

Description: You climb away from the parking area, following the snow-covered road on a moderate grade. After 0.25 mile, the grade increases as the road begins a bend around a low hill. For a while you have nice views east across Bridgeport Valley to the Sweetwater Mountains. As you loop around and head southwest, some of the Sierra peaks pop into view, Dunderberg Peak, the most notable summit, being

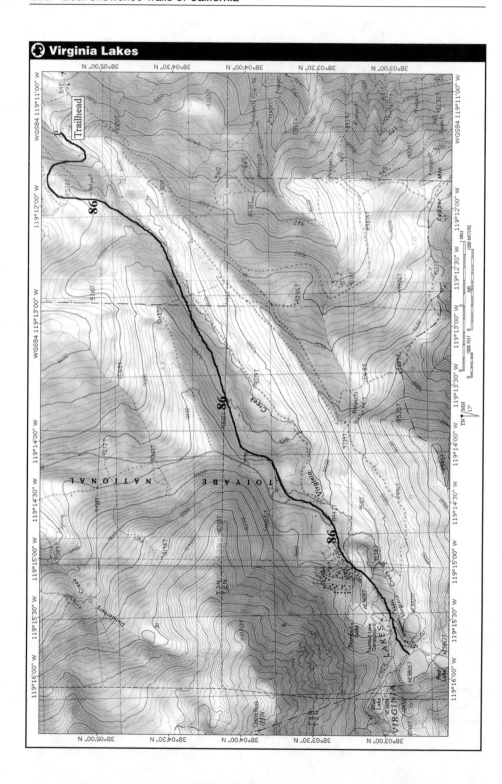

Virginia Lakes

directly west. You continue the steady climb, passing through typical eastside Sierra vegetation—predominantly sagebrush-covered slopes with widely scattered pines and a few isolated groves of aspen.

Views of the Sierra to the south continue to improve as you climb. About 1.5 miles from the trailhead, you draw near Virginia Creek, then continue the ascent quite a way above the north side of the stream. At 1.9 miles, you encounter a junction with a road to your left that descends to Virginia Creek and then follows the stream. If you tire of the walk up the main road, as an option you could follow this road next to the creek for 2.5 miles to its end and then head cross-country for the remaining 1.25 miles to Virginia Lakes.

Remaining on the main road, you cross into Forest Service land, and soon the amounts of pine and aspen increase. As you continue the steady ascent, Dunderberg Peak seems to loom larger with each step. At 4.0 miles you reach a junction with Dunderberg Meadow Road heading north to connections with Green Creek Road and, ultimately, US 395.

Beyond the junction, your rate of ascent eases. As you near a large hump of rock on the left, you begin to see cabins through the trees to your right. Continue along the main road past the cabins and a road to Trumbull Lake, reaching the largest of the Virginia Lakes at 5.75 miles.

The lake enjoys a very pretty setting, nestled beneath the open rugged slopes that rise up to 11,797-foot Black Mountain. A block restroom building is near the lakeshore, but may be locked during winter. For additional picturesque views, Red Lake is just 0.25 mile directly south and Blue Lake is a bit farther northwest. For more options see FYI below.

FYI: Most parties are content with the 5.75 mile one-way journey to Virginia Lake, but for those with more ambitious desires, there are a number of additional lakes situated around the basin and farther up the Virginia Creek drainage. A 1.5-mile trip extension up the route of the hikers' trail will take visitors to Blue, Cooney and Frog lakes. Another 3.25 miles of steep climbing over rugged terrain lead to Summit Lake, perched at the very crest of the Sierra on the northeastern boundary of Yosemite National Park. A journey to Summit Lake is for experienced parties in excellent condition only, but the lake provides an excellent base camp for a multi-day winter trip into this seldom-visited area.

Warm-ups: See Trip 85 & 87.

TRIP **87**

Lundy Canyon

see map
on page
291-292

Duration: Three-quarter day
Distance: 8.5 miles round trip
Difficulty: Moderate
Elevation: 7785/8600
Maps: *Lundy* & *Dunderberg Peak* 7.5′ quadrangles;
        Hoover Wilderness, Toiyabe & Inyo National Forests

Introduction: Lundy Canyon offers snowshoers the opportunity to experience the spectacular scenery of an eastside Sierra canyon with a modicum of effort. The route gains less than 1000 feet in 4.25 miles, and the routefinding on the old road and then the hiking trail is straightforward. From all along the route you have superb views of the steep canyon walls and tall peaks over 11,000 feet. If conditions force you to park at the end of the plowed road rather than at the gate, you will still be blessed with the extraordinary scenery, even if you can't get all the way to the head of the canyon.

   As in most canyons slicing into the steep escarpment of the eastern Sierra, avalanches do occur in Lundy Canyon under the right conditions. Do not enter Lundy Canyon when snow conditions are unstable, as you would be a sitting duck for anything coming off the steep canyon walls.

How to get there: Follow US 395 to the junction with Highway 167, 7 miles north of Lee Vining and 18 miles south of Bridgeport. Instead of turning east onto Highway 167, follow signs for Lundy Lake by turning west up the two-lane paved road. CalTrans plows the first 1.4 miles of roadway, but if conditions allow, continue another 2.2 miles to the closed gate just short of Lundy Lake.

Description: If you had to park at the end of the plowed road, proceed up the road 2.25 miles to the gate. From the gate, you climb up the road 0.25 mile to the east side of Lundy Lake. Follow the road on a level grade above the north shore for the next 1.25 miles to the west end of the lake. While traveling along the road, you have an excellent view of the impressive east face of Mt. Scowden above Lake Canyon.

   At the far end of the lake, pass through Lundy Lake Resort, which offers summer visitors a wide array of amenities but is closed in winter. As you stroll past the general store and cabins, remember to show respect for the property rights of the resort owner by staying on the road. A short climb leads away from the resort until

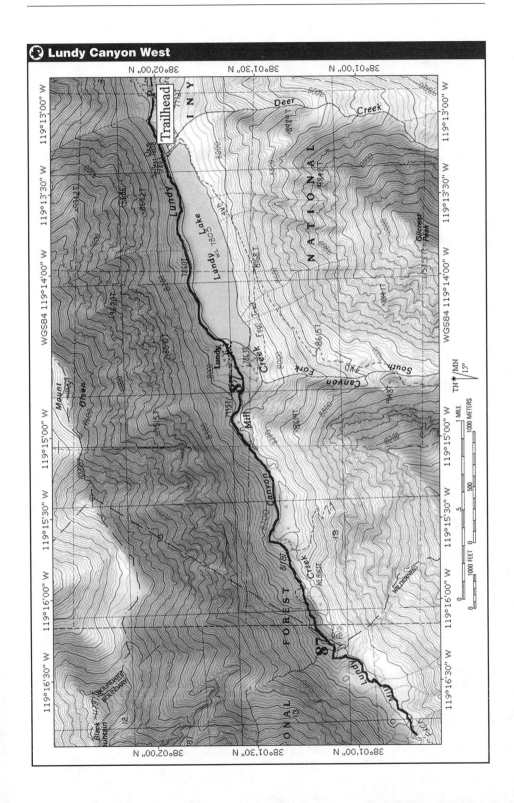

Lundy Canyon West

Trailhead

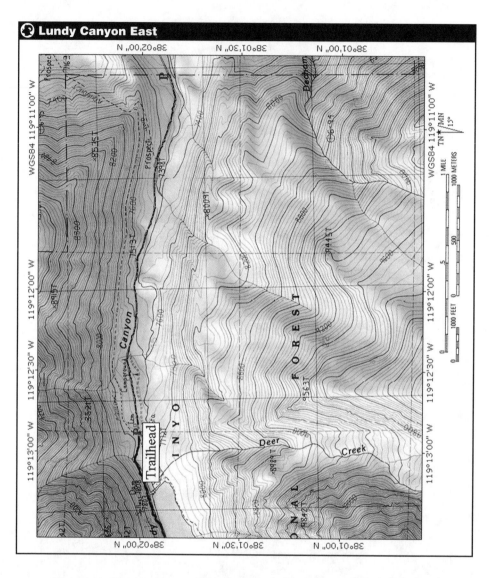

the grade eases as you draw near the creek. You pass some beaver ponds and soon reach the end of the road and the Lundy Canyon trailhead.

From the summer trailhead, continue up the canyon on a mild grade, passing through extensive stands of aspen. As you approach the next beaver pond, you must decide how you will surmount the wall at the far end, where a waterfall spills down a nearly vertical face. The hiking trail makes a winding climb above the cliffs to the right of the pond, and this will be the easiest route for snowshoers if there is not much snow in the canyon and you can discern the path. When ample snow covers the brush, you may be able to snowshoe around the right side of the pond below the fall and ascend the steep wall just to the right of the waterfall.

Whichever way you choose to ascend the wall, your route above it follows alongside the creek before veering away momentarily to cross a pair of side streams coming down from the north. Continue up the canyon past another beaver pond and pass through a light forest of aspen, pine and fir.

Eventually you break out into the open again in the canyon. As you peer at the nearly 2000-foot-high canyon walls, a way up and out of this chasm seems impossible, but a hiking trail does snake up the south side near the creek which drains Lake Helen. The level floor of the basin near the head of the canyon is wide open, sprinkled with dwarfed pines, low-growing aspens, and brush, and is well-suited for exploration. At the conclusion of your wanderings, retrace your tracks to your vehicle.

FYI: For those who are extremely experienced in backcountry travel, zigzagging up the course of the hiking trail out of the canyon and up to the secluded lakes basin above is possible—an incomparable overnight adventure.

Warm-ups: Options for enjoying food or beverage are very limited along the east side of the Sierra during winter. However, 75-year-old Mono Inn, on US 395 just 3 miles south of the junction with the Lundy Canyon Road, may be open for dinner during the winter on Thursday through Sunday evenings. The best bet is to call (760) 647-6581 to check on winter hours and to make reservations if the establishment is open. Owned and operated by a granddaughter of famed photographer Ansel Adams, the recently remodeled inn houses an Ansel Adams Gallery on the main floor and an upscale restaurant below. The restaurant ambiance is elegant, views of Mono Lake through tableside picture windows incredible, and the food superb. Prices for entrees begin at $15. Although the staff was very welcoming to a pair of disheveled snowshoers, we would have felt more at ease in the posh surroundings after a shower and a change of clothes. You can examine the menu and wine list at **www.monoinn.com**, or email your reservation request to Sarah Adams at **sarah@anseladams.com**.

Mono Lake Viewpoint

see map
on page
295

Duration: Three-quarter day
Distance: 7 miles round trip
Difficulty: Moderate
Elevation: 7210/9110
Maps: *Mt. Dana* 7.5′ quadrangle; *Hoover Wilderness,*
Toiyabe & Inyo National Forests

Introduction: Great views of Mono Lake and the central Sierra are the chief attractions of this trip, which follows an old road to the very edge of the eastern Sierra. Standing at the apex of the steep slope that rises 2600 precipitous feet from the shore in little over a mile, a finer vantage point from which to view the lake is hard to imagine. Another half mile from the view of Mono Lake is the climax of a ridge providing equally rewarding views of the eastern front of the Sierra. Thanks to the road, the routefinding is easy, and climbing the steady grade requires just a modicum of conditioning.

Due to the location well east of the crest, you may find little or no snow at the beginning of the trip. You may have to walk up the road a bit to reach the snow.

How to get there: From US 395 just south of the town of Lee Vining, drive 1.2 miles westbound on the Tioga Road, Highway 120, to the right-hand turn onto Log Cabin Road. If conditions permit, you can drive a short distance up it to the snowline and park beside the road. Otherwise, when snow covers the surface, park in the Ranger Station lot across the highway.

Description: From the junction with Highway 120, begin climbing up Log Cabin Road at a moderate grade through sagebrush-covered slopes dotted with pinyon pine. Very quickly you encounter a junction with a road to your right, where you should bear left and continue climbing up the winding course of the main road. As you ascend, alternately you have nice views of a part of Mono Lake, and of the striking east face of rugged Koip Crest, along with 13,057-foot Mt. Dana and 12,773-foot Mt. Gibbs. Two-thirds mile from the Tioga Road, you encounter a junction with a road to your left which heads toward Burger's Animal Sanctuary. Bear right at this junction, pass through an open gate, and proceed up FS Road 1N03.

Just beyond the junction, you bend west and follow a creek for 0.25 mile before turning northwest, 1.0 mile from the highway. The scarcity of trees in this section allows excellent views of the eastern Sierra, including Koip Crest, Mt. Dana, Mt.

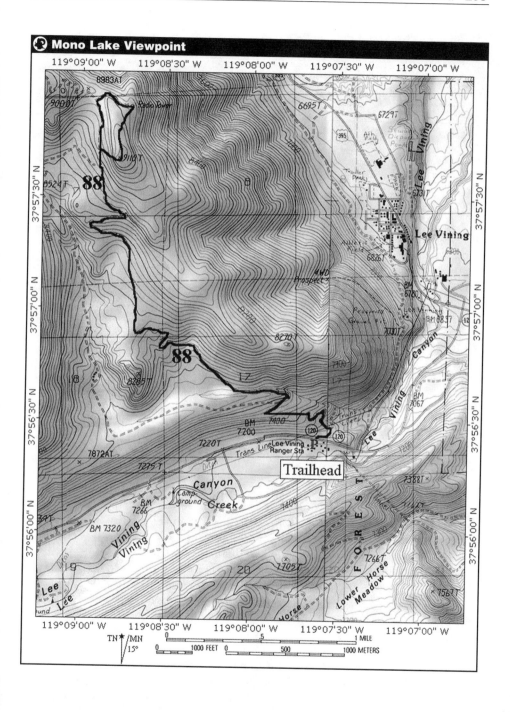

Mono Lake Viewpoint

Mono Lake

Gibbs, Mt. Lewis, June Mountain, and a host of other peaks along with Mono Basin and the Mono Craters to the east. Another 0.5 mile of travel along the road brings you to a series of S curves, where you enter a light forest of mountain mahogany, pinyon pine and ponderosa pine. Follow the winding road, continuing to climb amid a cover of light forest.

Eventually the road straightens and pursues a northerly course for a spell before reaching a trio of long switchbacks, which begin 2.25 miles from the Tioga Road. After the switchbacks, continue north along the road, passing below a rocky hill and heading toward a saddle in the crest ahead. Nearly 3.5 miles from the start, you encounter a Y-junction, where a lesser road curves east. Follow this lesser road to the crest of the ridge, from where you have an incredible, unobstructed view of Mono Lake, 2600 feet directly below. The dramatic plunge in elevation occurs in the span of a mile, creating a veritable nightmare for vertigo sufferers. Watching the subtle interplay of transforming hues on the mysterious lake against the backdrop of the Great Basin sky can be a truly rewarding experience for others.

Once you have sufficiently sampled the views of Mono Lake from the saddle, you should head along the ridge to the high point, 0.3 mile south. From this apex the eastern escarpment of the central Sierra spreads out like the leading wave of a white-capped sea poised to crash upon the eastern valleys. Peaks are almost too numerous to count—be sure to bring a map large enough to help you identify them. Among the more notable mountains visible from this perch are Mt. Lyell, Banner Peak, Mt. Ritter, the Minarets, Mammoth Mountain and Mt. Morrison.

If you don't mind the steep slope and a zigzagging route through mountain mahogany, descending directly from the high point back to the road is possible, rather than returning via the saddle.

FYI: For more variety on your return, connect with the road that passes through Burger's Sanctuary. From the viewpoint, follow your steps back along the road to an area just south of and below the rocky high point. Look for an obscure junction with a road heading west and follow it 0.5 mile to the more obvious road paralleling the creek. Don't worry if you can't make out the path of the road heading west—just head downhill to the west, headed for the creek. Once you find the road, turn southeast and follow it back to the road you came up and then to the trailhead.

Warm-ups: During the height of winter, Nicely's Cafe in Lee Vining is one of the few places for many miles in either direction to get a hot meal. This typical small-town cafe provides reasonable fare for breakfast, lunch and dinner every day but Wednesday.

TRIP 89

Parker Lake

see map on page **299**

Duration: Full day
Distance: 8 miles round trip
Difficulty: Moderate
Elevation: 7135/8320
Map: *Koip Peak* 7.5′ quadrangle

Introduction: A moderate 4-mile climb leads to a pretty subalpine lake occupying a basin carved out at the very foot of the steep eastern face of the Sierra. The rugged terrain above the lake is unreachable since no trail escapes up the precipitous slopes surrounding the shoreline. The first part of the trip passes through typical eastern Sierra sagebrush country, before mountain mahogany and pines begin to appear near the halfway point. Once the trail joins Parker Creek, a series of meadows evidences a damper environment.

By the time you near the lake, a healthy forest of pine and aspen carpets the drainage.

On those rare occasions when snowfall creeps down the mountains and into the eastern valleys, access to this area may be temporarily cut off. However, the Los

Angeles Water Department eventually will plow roads to access their diversion structures, if the snow refuses to melt on its own. At the very worst, you may have to add a mile or so to your journey if you can't get up the roads.

How to get there: From US 395, 2.5 miles north of the junction with Highway 120 East and 2.6 miles south of the junction with Highway 120 West, turn west onto FS Road 1N17, signed OIL PLANT ROAD.

Drive, or snowshoe if necessary, 0.7 mile to the first junction and bear right (southeast). Bear left at 1.3 and again at 1.8 miles, where the other road is signed: BOWLER CANYON. Follow the road around a low hill to a Y-junction at 2.1 miles. Unless you're snowshoeing, ignore the temptation to follow this road up Walker Creek to Walker Lake, as this road is also only periodically plowed and has a locked gate 0.5 mile from the junction. If you left your car at the highway and have made it to this point on snowshoes, follow this road 2.25 miles directly to the east end of the lake, as this will be your most direct route.

For those still behind the wheel, continue along Road 1N17 for another 1.5 miles, 3.5 miles from US 395, to a junction with the road leading up Sawmill Canyon. A sign at this junction should read in part WALKER TRAIL with an arrow pointing up the westbound road. Continue on FS Road 1N17 for another 0.8 mile to a 4-way intersection. Park as near the intersection as conditions allow.

An alternate, if somewhat suspect, approach can be made from the south by heading up the north part of the June Lakes Loop, California Highway 158. In the winter, this road is usually gated 0.3 mile from US 395, but the gate is easily driven around on the wide gravel shoulder. The road is typically plowed for at least the next

Parker Lake near the eastern edge of Yosemite National Park

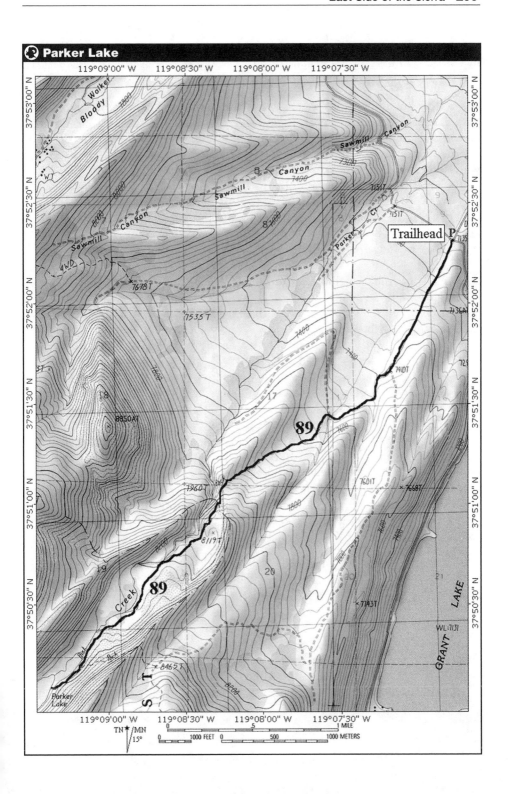

Parker Lake

Trailhead

89

89

Parker
Lake

TN ★ /MN
15°

mile, from where you can turn onto FS Road 1S25 and access the intersection mentioned above, following road signs for PARKER LAKE ROAD and PARKER LAKE, WALKER LAKE. Travel up FS 1S25 for 0.4 mile to the intersection.

Description: Your trip begins as you follow the continuation of FS 1S25 as it climbs through open sagebrush slopes typical of the eastern Sierra. Continue to climb toward the looming east face of the mountains until a short descent interrupts the ascent just past the 0.5-mile mark. Resume the upward journey, passing a junction with FS Road 1S27 heading up the hillside to the south, at 0.75 mile.

A mile from the intersection, the road bends and crosses a tributary of Parker Creek. The process is repeated in another third-mile as the road heads over the western branch of the same stream. On the far side of the creek, you pass a road heading north as you follow the main road around to the east. You continue to climb along the road as it winds up through the sagebrush until it ends at the summer trailhead, 2 miles from the intersection.

Follow the trail as it climbs up through a swale, cresting near the Ansel Adams Wilderness boundary. Directly below you on the right, Parker Creek swings into view as you walk across the hillside high above the aspen-lined creek through scattered mountain mahogany and a few ponderosa pines. An angling traverse takes you across the steep hillside and out into a meadow, where you have an excellent view of the peaks above the head of the canyon.

Beyond the meadow, you continue up the canyon on a mild grade, passing through widely scattered pine and aspen. Above the steep canyon, Parker Creek assumes a gentler, meandering course as the trail draws near the south bank and passes through some more meadows. Approximately a half mile from the lake, the forest thickens, forcing you to weave your way through aspens and pines. Continue to search for the most direct path and eventually you will arrive at the east shore of Parker Lake, 4 miles from the intersection.

Parker is a medium-sized lake, set in a deep canyon surrounded by steep slopes on three sides. The topography up the canyon is even more precipitous, evidenced by the fact that no trail exists beyond the lake. Except for the far shore, the lake is fringed by trees.

FYI: The name "Parker" appears on a handful of geographical features in and around the Mono Basin. Although no one is certain for which Parker they were named, careful inspection of the aspen grove 0.5 mile from Parker Lake reveals at least one tree with an inscription PARKER, 1846.

Warm-ups: See Trip 88.

TRIP **90**

Rock Creek

Duration: Three-quarter to full day
Distance: Varies—up to 15 miles round trip
Difficulty: Moderate
Elevation: 8860/10440
Maps: *Mt. Morgan & Mt. Abbot 7.5'*

see map
on page
302-303

Introduction: Rock Creek and Little Lakes Valley provide spectacular alpine scenery with towering peaks over 13,000 feet and an abundance of stunning mountain lakes. The gentle grade of the Rock Creek Road provides one of the mellowest entrances into the spectacular backcountry along the steep eastern scarp of the Sierra. A plowed road and ample parking area allow winter recreationists to start their trips above 8500 feet. The beautiful scenery and relatively easy access make this area popular with cross-country skiers, especially with groomed trails set by the Rock Creek Winter Lodge. The Lodge charges a fee for the use of their trails, but as long as you avoid their tracks you can follow the roadway into the backcountry.

The mild grade of the Rock Creek Road and the Morgan Pass Trail combined with the high elevation makes this area ideal for skiers. Snowshoers will definitely be in the minority here, as this region is considered one of the most desirable areas in the Sierra for backcountry skiing. Make sure you practice proper trail etiquette. Since there is an abundance of lakes and side canyons situated away from the main route, snowshoers should have no problem finding places of interest off the beaten path.

How to get there: From U.S. Highway 395, approximately 17 miles south of Mammoth Lakes junction and 25 miles north of Bishop, take the Toms Place exit and travel up the Rock Creek Road nearly 6 miles to the Rock Creek Sno-Park.

Description: Begin snowshoeing on the continuation of the Rock Creek Road, climbing steadily toward the eastern Sierra on a mild grade. Nearly 2 miles from the Sno-Park, you pass the left-hand road to the Rock Creek Winter Lodge. Another mile of steady climb takes you near the north shore of Rock Creek Lake before the road bends and passes above the west shore. You continue along the road for another 1.75 miles to Mosquito Flat, site of the summer trailhead.

From Mosquito Flat you can follow the route of the Morgan Pass Trail or chart your own path along Rock Creek through Little Lakes Valley and its succession of

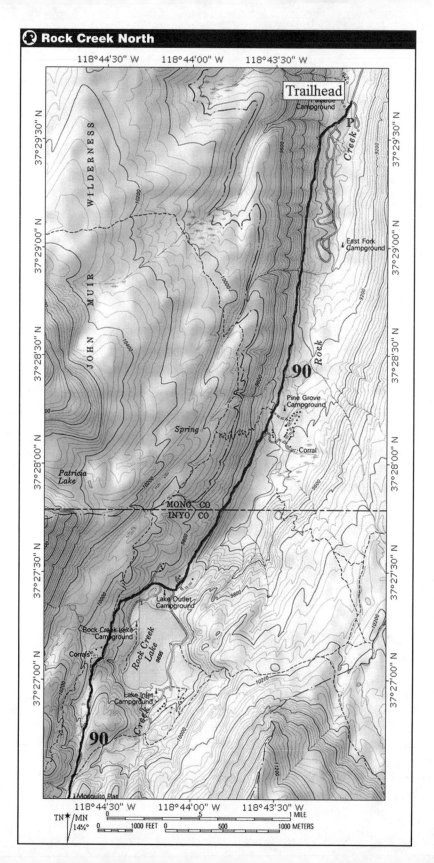

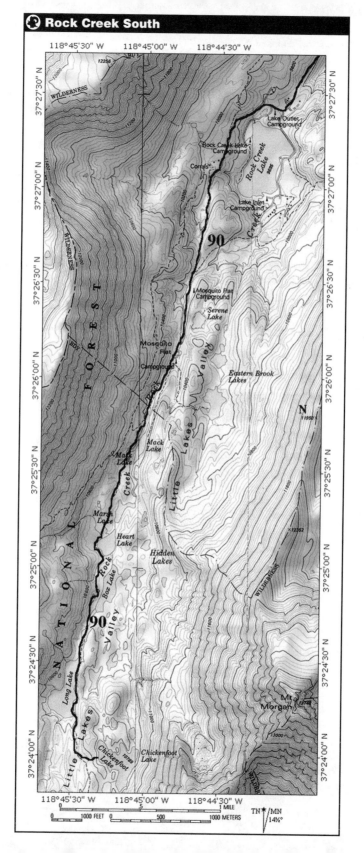

lakes. As you head up the valley, you crest a low ridge just west of Mack Lake, from where you have an excellent view of Little Lakes Valley and the Sierra crest, 5.25 miles from the trailhead. Bear Creek Spire is the dominant peak at the head of the canyon. This area is a good place to turn around if you don't wish to continue farther up the valley.

From the ridge, you can continue on to Marsh, Heart and Box lakes rather easily. Stunning views abound of Mts. Mills, Abbot, Dade, and Julius Caesar along with Bear Creek Spire. For those with plenty of time and energy, farther up the valley are Long Lake and Chickenfoot Lake below Morgan Pass.

FYI: An almost inexhaustible number of scenic destinations are accessible from Little Lakes Valley. For those who are seeking multi-day adventures, this area provides plenty of options for further wanderings.

Warm-ups: There's not much of anything between Mammoth Lakes and Bishop, particularly in the winter. If you're headed back toward Bishop, you can't go wrong at Erick Schatt's Bakery, located on the main drag across from the ranger station. Their sheepherder's bread is famous, but the bakery offers a wide array of other tantalizing treats, including a deli bar offering a nice variety of sandwiches.

In Mammoth Lakes, which tends to be more upscale than Bishop, there is a vast array of eateries all catering to the ski crowd. Perhaps the best place for dinner is Nevados, at the intersection of Main Street and Minaret Road. Call (760) 934-4466 for reservations or more information.

CHAPTER 15

Kings Canyon &
Sequoia National Parks

Although not as famous with tourists as Yosemite, the backcountry of Kings
Canyon and Sequoia national parks is perhaps even more dramatic than the
wilderness found within their more notable neighbor to the north. Deeper canyons
and loftier peaks attract hordes of hikers, backpackers, equestrians, climbers, photographers, and naturalists to the area in summer. However, the problem in winter
is gaining entry to the exquisite wild lands of Kings Canyon and Sequoia national
parks, as access is limited by a lack of all season highways penetrating the parks.
Access to the east side is completely blocked by the virtually impenetrable wall of
high peaks that form the Sierra crest. On the west, only two all-season roads venture
much past the border of the parks. To compound the lack of access, the Generals
Highway, which provides a link between the two parks is oftentimes closed by
snowfall from winter storms.

Nevertheless, winter enthusiasts can find decent snow conditions and beautiful
scenery in Kings Canyon and Sequoia national parks. While the vast majority of backcountry is out of reach to all but those who have the time and stamina required to
reach the hinterlands, there is plenty of pleasant terrain along the western fringe of
both parks to satisfy the weekend warrior in search of giant sequoias, scenic meadows, and fine vistas. Grant Grove in Kings Canyon and the Lodgepole-Giant Forest
area in Sequoia provide decent basecamps from which to venture into the parklands
on several marked ski trails. Away from the marked trails, winter enthusiasts will
need well-developed backcountry skills in order to negotiate the remote terrain. Visitation to the parks is very light in winter, providing snowshoers and cross-country
skiers the chance to experience the beauty in relative seclusion. Fortunately, as in
Yosemite National Park, snowmobile use is banned within the park boundaries.

Comfortable lodges inside and outside the parks provide a pleasant way to
experience the stunning landscape from the trail by day and enjoy the comforts of
civilization at night. The parks also offer two campgrounds for parties who don't
mind camping in the snow. Sequoia has an all-year campground in the foothills
region for those who prefer a one-hour drive to and from the snow country in order
to sleep on terra firma.

Giant Sequoia National Monument borders the two parks on the west side. In 2000 by presidential proclamation, 327,769 acres were set aside primarily to provide additional protection for giant sequoia groves outside the national park boundaries. Although the Forest Service has created three winter recreational areas within the monument, snowmobile use makes them undesirable for most non-motorized users.

Location: Kings Canyon National Park is about 50 miles east of Fresno. Sequoia National Park borders Kings Canyon National Park on the south, and is approximately 40 miles east of Visalia.

Access:

Big Stump Entrance: The northern route into Kings Canyon National Park follows State Highway 180 east from Fresno to the Big Stump entrance. Beyond the entrance, Highway 180 continues 1.75 miles to a Y-junction with the Generals Highway, which heads south toward Sequoia National Park. Continuing north on Highway 180, you reach Grant Grove Village in 1.5 miles and the Hume junction 6 miles farther. The highway into Kings Canyon and Cedar Grove is not plowed very far beyond the Hume junction in winter.

Ash Mountain Entrance: The southern route into Sequoia National Park follows State Highway 198 from Visalia past Lake Kaweah and the resort community of Three Rivers to the Ash Mountain entrance. Inside the park, the road becomes the Generals Highway, which climbs mildly past the Foothills Visitor Center and Potwisha Campground to Hospital Rock Picnic Area. From there, the Generals Highway makes a steep and winding climb to Giant Forest. The road continues past Giant Forest to turnoffs for Wolverton, Lodgepole, and Wuksachi Village.

Generals Highway (Wuksachi Village to Highway 180): During and after winter storms, the Generals Highway may be closed between the Wuksachi turnoff in the south and the entrance to Montecito-Sequoia Lodge in the north. During severe conditions the north section of the road may be closed at the Y-junction with Highway 180. Check with the Park Service for current conditions.

Amenities: Services are limited within the two parks during the winter months. However, lodging and dining are available year round at Grant Grove and Wuksachi Village. Gasoline is not available within the parks at any time of the year. Grant Grove has a visitor center, market (snowshoe and ski rentals), gift shop, post office, restaurant, Azalea Campground, John Muir Lodge, and cabins. On winter holidays and weekends, rangers lead 2-hour snowshoe tours from Grant Grove (snowshoes provided).

The foothills area of Sequoia offers the Foothills Visitor Center, year-round camping at Potwisha Campground, and the Hospital Rock Picnic Area. In the higher elevations, the newly renovated Giant Forest Museum is open to visitors all year. Services at Lodgepole include a visitor center, post office, laundry, and campground. Wuksachi Village has lodge rooms, restaurant, conference facilities, and gift shop (snowshoe and ski rentals).

Near the parks, within Giant Sequoia National Monument, limited services are available during the winter. Hume Lake, 3 miles from the Hume junction on Highway 180, has 24-hour gas (with credit card), laundry, and market. A snack shop is usually open on weekends, when Hume Lake Christian Camps is running camps. Montecito-Sequoia Resort, just off the Generals Highway 8 miles south of the 180 junction, is a full-blown winter resort offering groomed trails, guided backcountry trips, skating, sledding, lodging, and meals.

Outside the parks and the monument, small communities offer basic services. The tiny burg of Squaw Valley on Highway 180 has gas, food, supplies, and a Forest Service Ranger Station. Along Highway 198, near the southwestern border of Sequoia National Park, the town of Three Rivers provides winter tourists with a broad range of services, including gas, auto repairs, motels, restaurants, grocery stores, and a drug store. The closest full-service communities to the parks are Fresno and Visalia.

The frontcountry of Kings Canyon and Sequoia national parks offers nearly unlimited potential for snowshoe and cross-country-ski enthusiasts. Unfortunately, as is the case with most mountainous areas in winter, access to that land is difficult, including finding adequate parking. The Forest Service has developed three winter recreation areas in Giant Sequoia National Monument, at Cherry Gap, Quail Flat, and Big Meadows, with parking and restroom facilities. Unfortunately, even though designated non-motorized routes exist, most of them require that snowshoers and skiers share multiple-use trails with snowmobiles in order to gain access to the non-motorized sections. While this multiple-use approach seems appropriate in the minds of some forest managers, most snowshoers and skiers will find the noise, exhaust, and potential for encounters with the machines unattractive and incompatible with their recreational values.

Seasons & Weather: A location on the west slope of the Sierra Nevada insures that a high percentage of the precipitation from storms passing across the region will fall on the west slopes of the mountains in Kings Canyon and Sequoia national parks during winter. Cold Pacific storms can dump substantial accumulations of snow during the height of winter. However, significant winter snowfall is not guaranteed at this latitude from one year to the next and, even though most trailheads are located near or above 6500 feet, periods of warm temperatures and the Golden State's consistently sunny skies may oftentimes combine with the infrequent snowfall to create less than ideal snow conditions. Checking with the National Park Service about current snow conditions is usually a wise idea before leaving on your trip.

PERMITS

Entrance Fees: As in Yosemite, all visitors to Kings Canyon and Sequoia national parks must pay an entrance fee. A 7-day pass is $10 per vehicle ($5 per person on foot, bicycle, motorcycle, or bus). An annual pass for unlimited entrance into the two parks is $20. A National Parks Pass, Golden Eagle Pass, Golden Age Passport, or Golden Access Pass is accepted for entry into both parks. Fees are collected at the Big Stump and Ash Mountain entrances in winter. If you happen to enter either park when the entrance stations are not staffed, you will have to pay upon leaving the parks.

Day Use & Overnight Use: Permits are not required for day trips in Kings Canyon or Sequoia national parks. Overnight stays do require a wilderness permit, obtainable from the visitor centers at Grant Grove and Lodgepole. Advance reservations are not required. Some camping restrictions exist, so check with the Park Service regarding current regulations.

MAPS

Sequoia and Kings Canyon National Parks
Tom Harrison Maps

Grant Grove Ski Trails
1:24,000, 2000, paper
Sequoia Natural History Association
(559) 565-3759

Cross Country Ski Trails, Sequoia National Park
2003, plastic
Sequoia Natural History Association
(559) 565-3759

PARK SERVICE

Sequoia & Kings Canyon National Parks
47050 Generals Highway
Three Rivers, CA 93271-9651
(559) 565-3341

IMPORTANT PHONE NUMBERS

California Road Conditions — (800) 427-7623
Campground Reservations (National Parks) — (800) 365-2267
Giant Sequoia National Monument-Forest Service — (559) 784-1500
Lodging (KCPS-Grant Grove & John Muir lodges) — (559) 335-5500
Lodging (DNPS-Wuksachi Village) — (888) 252-5757
Montecito-Sequoia Resort — (800) 227-9900
Sequoia Natural History Association — (559) 565-3759

WEBSITES

Campground Reservations (National Parks) — www.reservations.nps.gov
Delaware North Parks Services — www.visitsequoia.com
Kings Canyon Park Services (KCPS) — www.sequoia-kingscanyon.com
National Park Service-Sequoia Kings Canyon — www.nps/seki
Sequoia National Forest — www.r5.fs.fed.us/sequoia
Sequoia Natural History Association — www.sequoiahistory.org

TRIP 91

North Grove Loop

Duration: One-half day
Distance: 1.9 miles loop trip
Difficulty: Easy
Elevation: 6350/6050
Map: *General Grant Grove* 7.5′ quadrangle

see map on page **310**

Introduction: During winter, the North Grove Loop provides a relatively easy trip through a serene forest for snowshoers and skiers in search of a 2-3-hour journey. Beginning in a mixed forest, the route descends into a magnificent grove of giant sequoias, where you will most likely be able to admire the big trees in seclusion. Most of the physical effort is expended on the last half of the loop, as 300 feet of lost elevation must be regained on the way back to the trailhead.

How to get there: Follow State Highway 180 east from Fresno to the Big Stump entrance into Kings Canyon National Park and proceed to the Y-junction with the Generals Highway. Veer left at the junction and continue on Highway 180 past the Grant Grove Visitor Center to a left-hand turn onto the General Grant Tree access road. Go 0.7 mile to the General Grant Tree parking area (restrooms).

Description: From the end of the parking area, begin snowshoeing through the snow-covered tour-bus parking lot to the beginning of the North Grove Loop Trail, which is designated by red markers. Follow the course of an old road to a junction. Turn right (west) at the junction and begin a moderate descent that winds through a mixed forest of incense cedars, sugar pines, and white firs. After a while you encounter some of the North Grove's giant sequoias sprinkled along the drainage of a small creek. The descent ends near the halfway point.

Now you'll have to gain back the 300 feet of elevation lost on the descent, as the route climbs back toward the trailhead. Eventually the sequoias are left behind on the way to the junction. From there, retrace your steps back to the parking lot.

FYI: Backcountry camping is not allowed in the Grant Grove area. However, free overnight camping is available in the winter at nearby Azalea Campground.

Warm-ups: The restaurant at Grant Grove Village offers decent fare at national-park prices for breakfast, lunch, and dinner every day of the week. Hours are 7 a.m. to 7

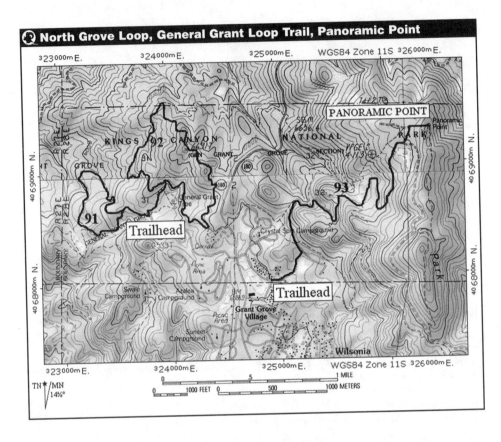

North Grove Loop, General Grant Loop Trail, Panoramic Point

p.m. Sunday through Thursday and 7 a.m. to 8 p.m. Friday and Saturday, although the restaurant is closed every afternoon from 2 to 4:30 p.m.

TRIP **92**

General Grant Loop Trail

Duration: One-half day
Distance: 3.0 miles loop trip
Difficulty: Easy
Elevation: 6350/6675
Map: *General Grant Grove 7.5′ quadrangle;*
Grant Grove Ski Trails

see map
on page
310

Introduction: At 46,608 cubic feet, General Grant is the third largest giant sequoia in the world. Unfortunately, an uncrowded visit to the notable tree in summer may necessitate seeing the giant monarch at night. However, winter presents a much different picture, as the number of visitors paying homage to the big tree declines dramatically. On this loop trip, not only can you experience the awesome grandeur of General Grant in relative peace and quiet, but a venture farther into the forest of Grant Grove is an almost sure-fire guarantee of solitude and serenity.

How to get there: Follow State Highway 180 east from Fresno to the Big Stump Entrance into Kings Canyon National Park and proceed to the Y-junction with the Generals Highway. Veer left at the junction and continue on Highway 180 past the Grant Grove Visitor Center to a left-hand turn onto the General Grant Tree access road. Drive 0.7 mile to the General Grant Tree parking area (restrooms).

Description: From the parking lot, walk up the left side of the plowed path of the General Grant nature trail approximately 250 yards to the

Sign along the Grant Grove Ski Trail

Gamlin Cabin. On the far side of the cabin is the beginning of the General Grant Loop Ski Trail, marked by a brown and white cross-country skier emblem and a green trail marker. Head up the ski trail a short distance to a T-junction. Turn left at the junction and, following additional green ski trail markers, proceed through a dense forest of mixed conifers. Soon you drop into a stream drainage, where the marked route makes a couple of short switchbacks. Heading north-northeast, follow a mild-to-moderate climb up the drainage.

At 1.25 miles from the parking lot, bend southwest and follow a winding climb for a half-mile to the trip's high point. From there, veer south and begin the protracted descent back toward the trailhead. Reach a junction at 2.25 miles and turn right (west), continuing the forested descent. After a while, you make a pair of crossings over a narrow rivulet and then follow its course downstream. Soon the railings around the General Grant area come into view and you reach the ski-trail junction, followed shortly by the nature trail. From there, you could retrace your steps, but a left-hand turn on the nature trail leads to the base of the General Grant Tree and a view of the big giant farther along the trail, before returning you to the parking lot.

FYI: If your party is the first one here after a recent snowfall, pay close attention to the green route markers, especially at switchbacks. Ending up off route in the dense forest may be all too easy without a previous group's tracks to follow.

Warm-ups: If you've got some money to burn, an overnight stay in the John Muir Lodge provides an upscale treat following a vigorous snowshoe outing. Cabins at Grant Grove provide a less expensive alternative to the lodge, but with fewer amenities. Call (559) 335-5500 for reservations, or visit the website at **www.sequoia-kingscanyon.com**.

TRIP 93

Panoramic Point

Duration: One-half day
Distance: 5.0 miles round trip
Difficulty: Moderate
Elevation: 6600/7525
Map: *General Grant Grove* 7.5′ quadrangle;
Grant Grove Ski Trails

see map on page **310**

Introduction: One of the best winter views available in Kings Canyon National Park makes this excursion to Panoramic Point very popular with both snowshoers and skiers. The route is very straightforward, following the course of an unplowed road for most of the distance through a light forest. Upon breaking out of the trees at Panoramic Point, recreationists will experience a dramatic, wideranging vista of the peaks, ridges, and canyons of the Park's backcountry—don't forget the camera!

How to get there: Follow State Highway 180 east from Fresno to the Big Stump Entrance into Kings Canyon National Park and proceed to the Y-junction with the Generals Highway. Veer left at the junction and continue on Highway 180 to Grant Grove Village. Drive past the Visitor Center (restrooms) and follow the road toward John Muir Lodge. Park in the parking area a few hundred feet before the lodge.

Description: From the parking area, walk up the road a short distance to the start of the marked Park Ridge Ski Trail, which begins immediately south of John Muir Lodge. Make a steady climb along the course of the snow-covered roadbed through a light forest of firs, cedars, and pines. The route is marked with yellow trail markers, even though the course of the road cut through the forest is quite obvious. You wind your way uphill for 2 miles to the end of the road at the summer parking area. From there, a slightly steeper climb soon leads to the crest of an open hillside at Panoramic Point.

The view from Panoramic Point is quite stunning, with a parade of alpine summits spanning the horizon from north to south. To the northeast is the deep cleft of Kings Canyon towered over by the Monarch Divide. The snowy summits of the Great Western Divide lie to the east, and in the distance is the Sierra Crest.

FYI: Snowshoers with extra energy to burn can accept the challenge of continuing along the marked ski trail to the lookout at the south end of Park Ridge. This extension will add another 5 miles round trip to your journey. Consult the *Grant Grove Ski Trails* map for more information.

Warm-ups: See Trips 91-92.

View from Panoramic Point

TRIP **94**

Big Baldy Ridge

see map on page **316**

Duration: One-half day
Distance: 4.4 miles round trip
Difficulty: Moderate
Elevation: 7630/8200
Map: *General Grant Grove* 7.5′ quadrangle

Introduction: A 2.2-mile trip along a forested ridge leads to a far-ranging, 360-degree view of the Sierra and the San Joaquin Valley from atop Big Baldy's granite dome. The route is marked, but once you gain the ridge the routefinding is extremely straightforward—just follow the ridge to the summit.

How to get there: Follow State Highway 180 east from Fresno to the Big Stump entrance into Kings Canyon National Park and proceed to the Y-junction with the Generals Highway. Turn right at the junction and continue on the Generals Highway for 6.3 miles to the Big Baldy saddle. Park along the side of the road as space allows.

Description: Head away from the highway, following red trail markers through the forest on a stiff climb of the west flank of Big Baldy ridge. The grade eases where you finally gain the crest and continue south along the ridge. Infrequent gaps in the forest allow sporadic views of the San Joaquin Valley to the west and Jennie Lakes Wilderness to the east. You follow the undulating ridge to a final climb of the slope below Big Baldy's summit. The view from the top is superb. To the east are the snow-capped peaks of the Kings-Kaweah and Great Western divides. To the west are Redwood Canyon and Mountain, the foothills, and the broad plain of the San Joaquin Valley. On days when rains or winds have cleared the air in the valley, the coastal hills are visible in the distance.

FYI: You may see several ski or snowshoe tracks on the west side of Big Baldy Ridge. Avoid the temptation to follow any tracks that don't lead to the ridge, as they were more than likely set by recreationists coming up from Montecito Sequoia Lodge below.

Warm-ups: Montecito-Sequoia Resort is a year-round resort offering guests a wide variety of activities and amenities. During winter, 50 kilometers of groomed trails are

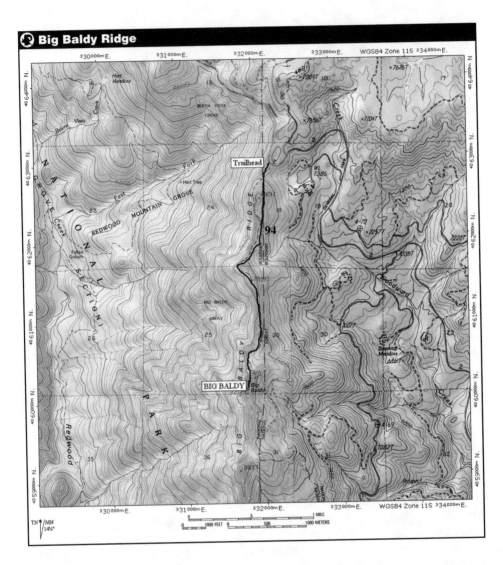

available for cross-country skiing and snowshoeing, along with such other activities as guided backcountry trips, snowboarding, ice skating, sledding and tubing. The resort offers comfortable lodging and delicious meals. Call (559) 565-4251 for reservations or more information.

TRIP 95

Clover Creek Ski Trail

see map
on page
318

Duration: One-half day
Distance: 4.0 miles round trip
Difficulty: Moderate
Elevation: 7630/8200
Map: *Lodgepole* 7.5' quadrangle

Introduction: The 2-mile marked route from Wuksachi Village to a junction with the Twin Lakes hiking trail won't bowl you over with grand views or giant sequoias, but the Clover Creek Ski Trail does offer a serene stroll into the forested frontcountry of Sequoia National Park. The marked route is a fine morning or afternoon trip coupled with a stay at Wuksachi Lodge.

How to get there: From the Ash Mountain entrance, drive on the Generals Highway to the Giant Forest. Proceed on the Generals Highway to Lodgepole and continue another 1.5 miles to the signed right-hand turn toward Wuksachi Village. Follow the access road to the far end of the plowed parking lot and park as space allows.

Description: Follow the marked trail from Wuksachi Village over a pair of short bridges through mixed forest. Soon a set of switchbacks leads you down to a substantial bridge over Clover Creek. Past the bridge, you switchback out of the Clover Creek drainage and follow an arcing traverse around the nose of a ridge, where Jeffrey pine forest parts just enough in spots to allow momentary views across Lodgepole to Wolverton Ridge. Eventually the route veers into the canyon of Silliman Creek and drops to another stout bridge over the creek. A mellow stroll from the bridge along the drainage from Willow Meadow brings you to the summer trail junction with the Twin Lakes Trail. From there, retrace your steps to Wuksachi Village.

FYI: You could create a fine shuttle trip by continuing from the junction along the course of the Twin Lakes Trail 1.5 more miles to Lodgepole. However, bear in mind that the route is not marked and the last half-mile is across an open south-facing slope that sheds its snow relatively early in the season.

Warm-ups: Managed by Delaware North Park Services, Wuksachi Village offers outstanding lodging and fine dining throughout the year. Except for holiday periods,

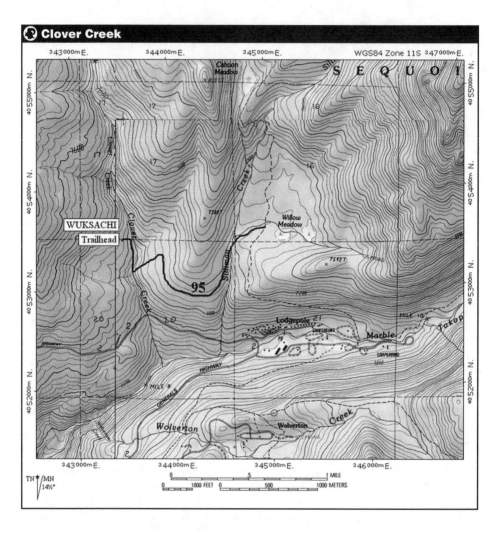

low winter rates will entice overnighters to stay in one of the 102 well-appointed guest rooms. Delicious California fare is found in the dining room for breakfast, lunch, and dinner (reservations required for dinner). In addition to lodge rooms and restaurant, Wuksachi Village has a small gift shop, bar, and conference facilities. Snowshoes and cross-country skis are available for rent. Call (888) 252-5757 for reservations or visit the web at **www.visitsequoia.com**.

T R I P 96

Tokopah Valley

see map
on page
320

Duration: One-half day
Distance: 4.0 miles round trip
Difficulty: Moderate
Elevation: 6825/7250
Map: *Lodgepole* 7.5′ quadrangle

Introduction: A gradual ascent through mixed forest leads to impressive winter views of Tokopah Valley's headwall, where the Marble Fork Kaweah River plummets down Tokopah Falls, and of the massive cliff known as The Watchtower on the south side of the gorge. The nearby Lodgepole Campground is open all year, providing a fine basecamp for recreationists who don't mind snow camping.

How to get there: From the Ash Mountain entrance, drive on the Generals Highway to Giant Forest. Proceed on the Generals Highway to the Lodgepole turnoff. On it, drive past the Visitor Center to the winter campground area and park as space allows.

Description: From the winter campground, head up the canyon to the bridge over Marble Fork Kaweah River. Once across the bridge, head upstream along the north bank on a mild ascent through a mixed forest of red and white firs, incense cedars, and Jeffrey pines. Proceed up the canyon to the edge of the forest. From there, you have grand views of Tokopah Falls (when its flowing) and, across the canyon, of The Watchtower, a rock cliff that soars 2000 feet above the valley floor.

FYI: Since the open areas of upper Tokopah Valley are prone to avalanches, travel beyond the safety of the forest is not advised.

Warm-ups: Services at Lodgepole during the winter are limited to the Visitor Center, laundry, post office, and campground. You can obtain lodging, meals, snowshoe rentals, and convenience items 2 miles away at Wuksachi Village (see Trip 95).

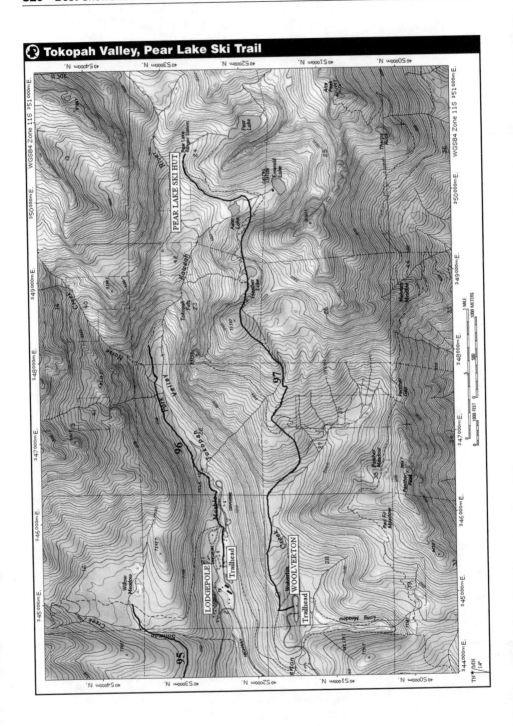

TRIP 97

Pear Lake Ski Trail

Duration: 2-3 days
Distance: 12.0 miles round trip
Difficulty: Strenuous
Elevation: 7270/9530
Map: *Lodgepole* 7.5' quadrangle

see map
on page
320

Introduction: A journey to the exquisite backcountry around Heather, Aster, Emerald, and Pear lakes is perhaps Sequoia National Park's quintessential winter snowshoe or ski experience. With reservations, you can overnight in relative comfort at the Pear Lake Ski Hut (see FYI below), where a multi-day stay would allow for additional forays into more remote backcountry areas. However, this trip is not for everyone. The strenuous 6-mile journey across potentially difficult terrain is for experienced winter travelers in excellent physical condition only. Plan on an early start to take advantage of whatever daylight is available.

The first half of the marked route is primarily through forest cover, where most of the trip's 2500-foot elevation gain occurs on the way to the Hump, a nearly 9500-foot saddle offering stunning views of the surrounding terrain. Beyond the Hump, the open, view-packed terrain making up the remainder of the journey to Pear Lake is prone to avalanches and whiteouts. Travelers must be avalanche-savvy and equipped to meet any challenges that may occur along the way, especially on the second half of the trip, where, in addition to these potential maladies, the route is infrequently marked.

Whether or not your party has reservations to stay overnight at Pear Lake Ski Hut, all groups should pack survival gear, as many fail to make the full 6-mile journey on the first day, due to deep snow, poor weather conditions, or other factors. On the flip side, good weather and excellent snow conditions may allow you to experience the peak of Sequoia's winter grandeur. The four lakes accessible by trail and the trailless backcountry beyond are premier destinations in the summer, resulting in typically full quotas and designated campsites. Hardy winter travelers can experience the majesty of this area with usually very little company.

How to get there: From the Ash Mountain entrance, drive on the Generals Highway to the Giant Forest. Proceed on Generals Highway to the Wolverton turnoff, 1.75

miles southeast of Lodgepole. Drive the access road for 1.5 miles to the Wolverton parking area and park as space allows.

Description: Find the beginning of the marked Wolverton Ski Trail on the north side of the parking area. Climb up the hillside to the crest of a ridge and a T junction with the continuation of the Wolverton Ski Trail to the left and your route along the Pear Lake Ski Trail to the right. The grade eases a bit following an initial steep climb, as the route ascends the drainage of Wolverton Creek. At 1.5 miles, you reach a junction with the route to Panther Gap.

Veer left at the junction and make a long, steady climb up the hillside through red-fir forest to the crest of a ridge, 3 miles from the parking area. Standing atop the Hump, you gaze eastward to fine views of the Silliman Crest and the Tableland.

From the excellent vista, you drop into the basin holding frozen Heather Lake, surrounded by a smattering of pines. The next obstacle to overcome is the ridge separating Heather Lake's basin from the cirque containing Aster and Emerald lakes. From Heather Lake, make a short climb of a sparsely forested hillside and then traverse around the nose of an open ridge with excellent views across the canyon and up to Alta Peak. Wrap around the hillside and then make a slight drop into the next basin.

Pass south of Aster Lake and follow a mildly rising traverse around a spur ridge, where you'll enjoy good views into the deep cleft of Marble Fork Kaweah River and Tokopah Valley, toward the next canyon. Near the 5-mile mark, the route to the hut and the lake diverge. To reach the hut, continue the traverse across the open hillside toward the outlet from Pear Lake. To visit the lake, follow an arcing ascent around the west side of the canyon toward the rock-bound lake at the head of the cirque.

FYI: The Sequoia Natural History Association maintains the Pear Lake Ski Hut, which is available for overnight stays between mid-December and the end of April. The cost is $20 per person per night ($16 for SNHA members) with required reservations awarded through a lottery process (forms must be submitted by November 1st). The hut is equipped with a pellet stove for heating, bunks with mattresses for up to 10 people, gas cooking stove, cooking utensils, and composting toilet. Along with an appropriate assortment of backcountry gear, guests must bring sleeping bags, propane canisters, water filter, and food. All garbage must be packed out upon departure. Visit **www.sequoiahistory.org** to download a reservation form and check out the "semi-current snow conditions," or obtain more information at (559) 565-3759.

Warm-ups: When the day is warm and there's a desire for something refreshing, try concocting a backcountry replica of the frozen margarita. You'll have to stash a packet of lemonade mix and some tequila (in a plastic bottle) into your friend's pack. Once in camp, mix up the lemonade, add a splash of tequila, and pour over a scoop of fresh snow to gain a slushy consistency. To go all out, rub the lip of a cup with a slice of lime and add salt to the rim before adding the liquid. Any of your friend's displeasure for carrying the extra weight of the ingredients should be assuaged after the first sip.

TRIP 98

Sunset Rock

see map on page 324

Duration: One-half day
Distance: 2.5 miles round trip
Difficulty: Easy
Elevation: 6370/6475
Map: *Giant Forest* 7.5′ quadrangle

Introduction: A short, mildly rising ski trail takes you from the Giant Forest Museum to Sunset Rock. The exposed granite dome was so named for the beautiful sunsets one could observe from the top before the ubiquitous San Joaquin Valley smog marred the present-day atmosphere. All is not lost, though, as winter winds and rains often clear the usually hazy valley skies, allowing snowshoers and skiers a rare opportunity to observe the fine vistas and stunning sunsets. However, in order to enjoy the twilight display you'll have to then walk the 1.25 miles back to Giant Forest in the diminishing light—bring your flashlight.

How to get there: From the Ash Mountain entrance, drive on the Generals Highway to Giant Forest. Park near the museum as space allows.

Description: Find the start of the marked Alta Ski Trail on the east side of the Giant Forest Museum and parallel the highway east 0.25 mile to a junction. From the junction, follow the Sunset Trail across the highway toward the south end of Round Meadow and then veer west above the drainage of Deer Creek. Proceed above the drainage for a while through mixed forest until the route veers away from the creek on a mildly rising grade. At 1.2 miles from the museum, you reach a saddle, followed by a very slight descent onto the exposed dome of Sunset Rock.

FYI: Although not as dramatic as views from nearby Moro Rock, from Sunset Rock you'll see such notable landmarks as Ash Peaks Ridge, the deep cleft of Marble Fork Kaweah River, Colony Mill, and Little Baldy.

Warm-ups: The recently restored market is now the home of the Giant Forest Museum, open daily from 8 a.m. to 4:30 p.m. Although the museum provides interesting exhibits relating to the Big Trees, food and drink are not available. You'll have to travel either to Wuksachi Village within the park or Three Rivers outside the park to fill your belly or wet your whistle.

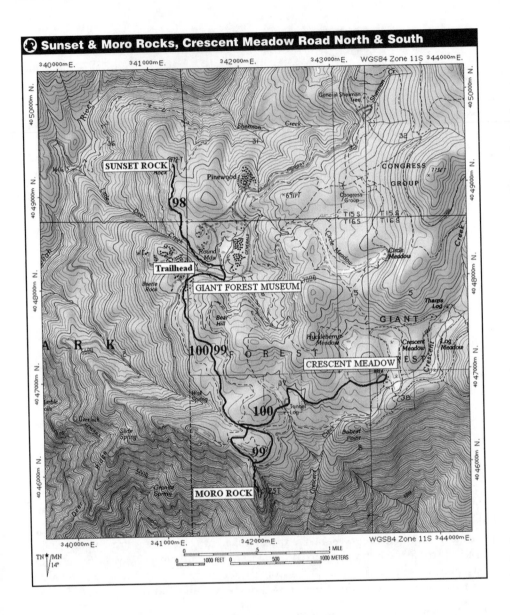

TRIP **99**

Moro Rock

Duration: One-half day

Distance: 4.0 miles round trip

Difficulty: Moderate

Elevation: 6450/6725

Map: *Giant Forest* 7.5′ quadrangle;
Cross Country Ski Trails Sequoia National Park

see map
on page
324

Introduction: The extraordinary view from Sequoia National Park's most famous granite dome is on the checklist for virtually every visitor to the park, filling the road, parking lot, and trail to the top with a steady stream of vehicles and pedestrians every summer day. But in the winter a vastly diminished number of visitors venture along the snow-covered road to the base of the dome. The final 300 feet of elevation along the staircase to the top of Moro Dome may be unsafe due to snow and icy conditions. If not, you may have the dramatic view all to yourself.

How to get there: From the Ash Mountain entrance, drive on the Generals Highway to Giant Forest. Park near the museum as space allows.

Description: Find the start of the Crescent Meadow Road south of the Giant Forest Museum and follow the mildly rising roadbed as its cuts a path through the mixed forest of mostly white firs, with smaller amounts of sugar pines and giant sequoias. The grade eases after the initial ascent, providing easy snowshoeing along the wide swath of the road. At 1.5 miles, you encounter a junction between the road to Moro Rock on your right and the continuation of the Crescent Meadow Road ahead (see Trip 100).

Turning right onto the Moro Rock Road, head south initially and then curve around near the lip of the canyon above Middle Fork Kaweah River. After a half-mile from the junction, you reach the summer parking lot below the massive granite hump of Moro Rock.

When the multiple steps leading to the top of Moro Rock are covered with snow or ice, the parking lot is where you should turn around, as the trail can be extremely dangerous under those conditions. Fortunately, because of the southern exposure the dome is often free of snow and ice in the winter, allowing brave travelers the opportunity to scale the impressive staircase to the incredible view from the top. To the east are multiple snow-capped peaks of the Great Western Divide. Alta Peak (11,204 feet) is the closest prominent peak to the east, a fine potential destination of winter mountaineers. Below is the deep ravine carved by Middle Fork Kaweah River. The Generals Highway is clearly visible as well, with tiny cars snaking down the hillside toward Three Rivers and the San Joaquin Valley beyond. On particularly clear days you may be able to see all the way to the Coast Range in the west. Directly across the canyon are Castle Rocks.

FYI: The nearly 350 steps constructed in 1931 that lead to the top of Moro Rock were subsequently placed in the National Registry of Historic Places.

Warm-ups: The recently restored market is now the home of the Giant Forest Museum, open daily from 8 a.m. to 4:30 p.m. Although the museum provides interesting exhibits relating to the Big Trees, food and drink are not available. You'll have to travel either to Wuksachi Village within the park or Three Rivers outside the park to fill your belly or wet your whistle.

TRIP 100

Crescent Meadow Road

see map on page 324

Duration: One-half day
Distance: 8.0 miles round trip
Difficulty: Moderate
Elevation: 6450/6700
Map: *Giant Forest 7.5' quadrangle;*
Cross Country Ski Trails Sequoia National Park

Introduction: The Crescent Meadow Road cuts a discernible swath through the trees of Giant Forest that is very easy to follow. Couple this easily distinguishable route with a minimal elevation gain, and you have the makings for a very enjoyable winter snowshoe or cross-country ski trip. The entire route travels through serene forest, passing some notable giant sequoias on the way, before reaching skinny Crescent Meadow. Once at the meadow, you can extend your journey in a variety of directions. While the road transports hundreds of auto-bound tourists every summer day, you're apt to see only a handful of fellow voyagers on a winter excursion.

How to get there: From the Ash Mountain entrance, drive on the Generals Highway to Giant Forest. Park near the museum as space allows.

Description: Find the start of the Crescent Meadow Road south of the Giant Forest Museum and follow the mildly rising roadbed as its cuts a path through the mixed forest of mostly white firs, with smaller numbers of sugar pines and giant sequoias. The grade eases after the initial ascent, providing easy snowshoeing along the wide swath of the road. At 1.5 miles, you encounter a junction between the continuation of the Crescent Meadow Road ahead and the road to Moro Rock on your right (see Trip 99).

Remaining on the Crescent Meadow Road, you continue the gentle stroll through the forest. Just 0.2 mile from the junction is the Parker Group, a cluster of nearly a dozen giant sequoias, named after James Parker, a U.S. Army Captain who was Superintendent of Sequoia National Park in the summer of 1893. A short distance past the Parker Group, 2.7 miles from the trailhead, is the Tunnel Log, a sequoia that fell across the road in the winter of 1937. A Civilian Conservation Corp crew subsequently cut a passage through the downed tree to provide vehicle access.

The road climbs more noticeably beyond the Tunnel Log, still beneath the canopy of a mixed forest. At 3.6 miles, you inauspiciously pass the start of a summer trail to Huckleberry Meadow and continue toward Crescent Meadow, reaching the west edge of the long, narrow clearing 0.3 mile farther.

FYI: If time and energy permit, trip extensions are fairly numerous from Crescent Meadow. A short circuit around Crescent Meadow adds less than a mile to your journey. Nearby Log Meadow is just a half-mile to the east. More extensive loops utilizing the marked routes of the Trail of the Sequoias, and the Alta, Crescent, and Bear Hill ski trails provide a fuller experience in Giant Forest.

Warm-ups: The recently restored market is now the home of the Giant Forest Museum, open daily from 8 a.m. to 4:30 p.m. Although the museum provides interesting exhibits relating to the Big Trees, food and drink are not available. You'll have to travel either to Wuksachi Village within the park or Three Rivers outside the park to fill your belly or wet your whistle.

Snowshoe Manufacturers

Atlas Snowshoe Co.
115 Tenth Street
San Francisco, CA 94103
(888) 48-ATLAS
fax: (415) 252-0354
email: questions@atlassnowshoe.com
www.atlassnowshoe.com

C3-Design Innovation
Verts
6146 So. 350 West
Salt Lake City, UT 84107
(801) 281-1331
fax: (801) 281-1333
email: sales@verts.com
www.verts.com

Crescent Moon
1199 Crestmoor
Boulder, CO 80303
(800) 587-7655
fax: (303) 499-2645
email: jakeroll@crescentmoon
    snowshoes.com
www.crescentmoonsnowshoes.com

MSR--Mountain Safety Research
4000 First Ave.
Seattle, WA 98134
(800) 531-9531
fax: (800) 583-7583
email: info@msrgear.com
www.msrcorp.com

Northern Lites
300 S. 86th Ave.
Wausau, WI 54401
(800) 360-LITE
fax: (715) 848-0386
email: snowshoe@northernlites.com
www.northernlites.com

Redfeather
4705-A Oakland St.
Denver, CO 80239
(800) 525-0081
fax: (303) 375-0357
email: rfsnowshoes@earthlink.net
www.redfeather.com

Sherpa Snowshoes
9460 So. 60th St.
Franklin, WI 53132
(800) 621-2277 (Christy)
fax: (414) 423-9806
email: kmarkiewicz@idealmfg
    solutions.com
www.sherpasnowshoes.com

Tubbs Snowshoe Company
52 River Road
Stowe, VT 05672
(800) 882-2748 or (802) 253-7398
fax: (802) 253-9982
email: info@tubbssnowshoes.com
www.tubbssnowshoes.com

Suggested Reading

Browning, Peter. 1991. *Place Names of the Sierra Nevada*. Berkeley: Wilderness Press.

Browning, Peter. 1988. *Yosemite Place Names*. Lafayette, CA: Great West Books.

Bunnell, M.D., Lafayette Houghton. 1990. *Discovery of the Yosemite*. Yosemite National Park: Yosemite Association.

Castle, Ken. 1977. *Tahoe*. San Francisco: Foghorn Press.

Darvill, M.D., Fred. 1998. *Mountaineering Medicine*. 14th Edition. Berkeley: Wilderness Press.

Farquhar, Francis. 1965. *History of the Sierra Nevada*. Berkeley: University of California Press.

Foree, Rebecca Poole. 1998. *Best Places Northern California*. Seattle: Sasquatch Books.

Graydon, Don & Curt Hanson, editors. 1997. *Mountaineering: The Freedom of the Hills*. 6th Edition. Seattle: The Mountaineers.

LaChapelle, Ed. 1985. *ABC of Avalanche Safety*, 2nd Edition. Seattle: The Mountaineers.

Lekisch, Barbara. 1988. *Tahoe Place Names*. Lafayette, CA: Great West Books.

Libkind, Marcus. 1989. Ski Tours in Lassen Volcanic National Park. Livermore, CA: Bittersweet Publishing Company.

Libkind, Marcus. 1995. *Ski Tours in the Sierra Nevada, Volume 1, Lake Tahoe*. 2nd Edition. Livermore, CA: Bittersweet Publishing Company.

Libkind, Marcus. 1985. *Ski Tours in the Sierra Nevada, Volume 2, Carson Pass, Bear Valley*, Pinecrest. Livermore, CA: Bittersweet Publishing Company.

Libkind, Marcus. 1985. *Ski Tours in the Sierra Nevada, Volume 3, Yosemite, Huntington & Shaver Lakes, Kings Canyon, Sequoia*. Livermore, CA: Bittersweet Publishing Company.

Libkind, Marcus. 1986. *Ski Tours in the Sierra Nevada, Volume 4, East of the Sierra Crest*. Livermore, CA: Bittersweet Publishing Company.

Martin, Don W. and Betty Woo Martin. 1999. *California-Nevada Roads Less Traveled.* Henderson, Nevada: Pine Cone Press.

Morey, Kathy. 2002. *Hot Showers, Soft Beds, and Dayhikes in the Sierra: Walks and Strolls Near Lodgings.* 2nd Edition. Berkeley: Wilderness Press.

Muir, John. 1988. *The Yosemite.* San Francisco: Sierra Club.

O'Bannon, Allen & Mike Clelland. 1996. *Allen & Mike's Really Cool Backcountry Ski Book.* Evergreen, CO: Chockstone Press.

Prater, Gene. Ed. Dave Felkey. 1997. *Snowshoeing.* 4th Edition. Seattle: The Mountaineers.

Roper, Steve. 1976. *The Climber's Guide to the High Sierra.* San Francisco: Sierra Club.

Russell, Carl Parcher. 1992. *One Hundred Years in Yosemite. Omnibus Edition.* Yosemite National Park: Yosemite Association.

Sanborn, Margaret. 1989. *Yosemite. Its Discovery, Its Wonders and Its People.* Yosemite National Park: Yosemite Association.

Schaffer, Jeffrey P. 1992. *Carson-Iceberg Wilderness.* 2nd Edition. Berkeley: Wilderness Press.

Schaffer, Jeffrey P. 2003. *Lassen Volcanic National Park and Vicinity.* 3rd Edition. Berkeley: Wilderness Press.

Schaffer, Jeffrey P. 1998. *The Tahoe Sierra.* 4th Edition. Berkeley: Wilderness Press.

Schaffer, Jeffrey P. 1999. *Yosemite National Park.* 4th Edition. Berkeley: Wilderness Press.

Schifrin, Ben. 2004. *Emigrant Wilderness and Northwestern Yosemite.* 2nd Edition. Berkeley: Wilderness Press.

Secor, R. J. 1992. *The High Sierra. Peaks, Passes, and Trails.* Seattle: The Mountaineers.

Selters, Andy & Michael Zanger. 2001. 2nd Edition. *The Mt. Shasta Book.* Berkeley: Wilderness Press.

White, Michael C. 1997. *Nevada Wilderness Areas and Great Basin National Park.* Berkeley: Wilderness Press.

White, Michael C. 1998. *Snowshoe Trails of Tahoe.* Berkeley: Wilderness Press.

White, Michael C. 1999. *Snowshoe Trails of Yosemite.* Berkeley: Wilderness Press.

Wilkerson, M.D., James A. 1983. *Medicine for Mountaineering.* 2nd Edition. Seattle: The Mountaineers.

Index

W

waste disposal, 14-15, 37

Waterhouse Peak, 217-218

Wawona Hotel, 267

Wawona Point, 270

weather, 6--9

Wheeler Loop, 192

Wong's Garden, 189

Woodchuck Flat, 140, 141

Wuksachi Village, 317-318

Y

Yosemite , 3, 9, 230-231

Yosemite National Park, 230-270

Young American Quartz Mine, 98

Yuba Gap, 127, 128, 129, 131, 132, 133, 134, 135, 139

Yuba Pass, 97, 98, 116, 119, 120, 121, 123, 124, 125

Z

Za's, 198

About the Author

Mike White was born and raised in Portland, Oregon. He learned to hike and snowshoe in the Cascades, and honed these outdoor skills while attending Seattle Pacific University. After college, Mike relocated to the high desert of Nevada, where he was drawn to the beauty of the Sierra in both summer and winter.

In the early 1990s, Mike began writing about the outdoors full time. He expanded Wilderness Press's *The Trinity Alps*. He then authored *Nevada Wilderness Areas and Great Basin National Park*, followed by the *Snowshoe Trails* series, *Sequoia National Park, Kings Canyon National Park, Backpacking Nevada, Top Trails Lake Tahoe*, and *Afoot & Afield Reno/Lake Tahoe*. Mike also contributed to *Backpacking California*, and has written for *Sunset* and *Backpacker* magazines and the *Reno Gazette-Journal*. He teaches backpacking and snowshoeing at Truckee Meadows Community College. Mike lives in Reno with his wife, Robin, and their two boys, David and Stephen, along with their yellow lab, Barkley.

Other Snowshoeing Titles
Available from Wilderness Press

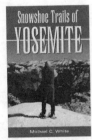

Snowshoe Trails of Yosemite

The easiest way to see El Capitan, Half Dome, and Glacier Point in all their winter glory is on these 41 trips in greater Yosemite, selected for their great scenery and ease of accessibility. Includes maps, directions, difficulty ratings, and "warm up" suggestions.

ISBN: 0-89997-253-5

Snowshoe Trails of Tahoe

The wilderness surrounding Lake Tahoe is California's ultimate winter playground. Choose from 45 of the best snowshoeing trips, ranging from short, easy jaunts, to multi-day treks. Includes maps, directions, difficulty ratings, and "warm up" suggestions.

ISBN 0-89997-234-9

For ordering information, call your local bookseller or visit Wilderness Press at www.wildernesspress.com.